UNDERSTANDING ETHICS

Second Edition

Noel Preston

THE FEDERATION PRESS
2001

Published in Sydney by:
The Federation Press
PO Box 45, Annandale, NSW, 2038
71 John St, Leichhardt, NSW, 2040
Ph (02) 9552 2200 Fax (02) 9552 1681
E-mail: info@federationpress.com.au
Website: http://www.federationpress.com.au

First edition 1996

National Library of Australia Cataloguing-in-Publication

Preston, Noel
Understanding ethics.

2nd ed
Includes index.
ISBN 1 86287 396 8

1. Ethics – Australia. 2. Social ethics – Case studies. I. Title.

170.994

Typeset by The Federation Press, Leichhardt, NSW.
Printed by Ligare Pty Ltd, Riverwood, NSW.

Contents

CHAPTER 1
THE ETHICAL CHALLENGE 1

The Inevitability of Ethics 2
Ethics: An Instrument of Social Transformation 8
How To Use This Book 11
Taking a stance 12
Features of the book 12
The book's structure 13
Short cuts 14
The benefits of ethics study 14
Further reading 15
Notes 15

CHAPTER 2
ENCOUNTERING ETHICS 17

About Ethics 18
Ethics as Part of Philosophy 21
Law and Ethics 23
Ethics and Religion 25
Three Key Issues 28
1 Egoism and altruism 28
2 Freedom and determinism 31
3 Relativism and absolutism 34
Why be Moral? 37
Chapter review 39
Further reading 39
Questions for discussion 39
Notes 40

CHAPTER 3
ETHICAL THEORY: AN OVERVIEW 41

Consequentialism 43
Non-Consequentialism 47
Contractarianism, Justice and Rights 51
An Ethic of Care 55

Virtue Theory 58
Universalism and Communitarianism 62
A Preferred Theory? 63
Chapter review 64
Further reading 64
Questions for discussion 64
Case studies 65
Notes 66

CHAPTER 4
RESPONSIBLE ETHICAL DECISIONS 69

The Idea of Responsibility 70
An Ethic of Response 72
A Decision-making Model 76
Deciding Responsibly: Two Cases 81
Chapter review 86
Further reading 86
Questions for discussion 87
Notes 87

CHAPTER 5
TRUTHTELLING AND HONESTY 89

Preliminary Considerations 90
What is Truthfulness? 92
Self-deception 94
The Case Against Lying 96
Situational (or Selective) Truth? 97
Truth and Response 100
Chapter review 101
Further reading 101
Questions for discussion 101
Case study 102
Notes 103

CHAPTER 6
SEX, LOVE AND MORALITY 105

Setting the Scene 106
What is the Meaning of "Love"? 108

The Purpose of Sex 111
(a) Procreation 111
(b) Power 112
(c) Pleasure 113
(d) Love or affection 114
Are Honesty and Consent Enough? 115
Responsible Sex 116
Sexuality and Public Policy 118
(a) Prostitution 120
(b) Pornography and censorship 121
Chapter review 123
Further reading 123
Questions for discussion 124
Case study 125
Notes 127

CHAPTER 7
MATTERS OF LIFE AND DEATH 129

To Be or Not to Be 130
Persons, Quality of Life and Social Values 131
Euthanasia 138
Life, Death and the State 143
Liberalism, the law and bioethics 143
Capital punishment 145
War 147
A Final Note: On Biotechnology 149
Chapter review 151
An exercise 152
Further reading 153
Case studies 153
Notes 156

CHAPTER 8
PUBLIC RESPONSIBILITY, POLITICS AND THE PROFESSIONS 161

Defining the Public Good 162
Political Ethics 164
Conflict of Interest 169
Public Sector Ethics and an Ethic of Role 170
Professional Ethics 173

Business Ethics 174
Chapter review 175
Further reading 177
Questions for discussion 179
Case studies 180
Notes 182

CHAPTER 9
GLOBAL RESPONSIBILITY AND THE ENVIRONMENT 186
The Challenge 187
Environmental Ethics: Various Approaches 188
1 Anthropocentric 191
2 Extensionist 192
3 Biocentric or ecocentric 192
Animal Rights 196
Overpopulation and Global Poverty 196
Global Ethic for A Global Society 198
Conclusion 200
Chapter review 201
Further reading 201
Questions for discussion 201
Case studies 204
Notes 205

CHAPTER 10
CULTIVATING AN ETHICAL LIFE 208
A Perspective 209
The Life of Integrity 209
Ethics Education 212
Institutionalising Workplace Ethics 216
Epilogue: A letter to my grandchildren 220
An exercise 223
Notes 224

GLOSSARY 226

A NOTE ON THE HISTORY OF ETHICS AND MORAL TRADITIONS 230

INDEX 232

Acknowledgements

I am grateful for the support of the Queensland University of Technology, Centre for the Study of Ethics in providing assistance toward the revision of this new edition. In particular, I acknowledge Douglas Magendanz whose research assistance is reflected throughout the text, though he should not be held responsible for any of the revisions. Thanks also to Chris Holt and Margaret Farmer of *The Federation Press* who suggested that this successful publication be given a further lease of life. Lastly, I am grateful to my family and especially Coralie who not only sought to understand ethics better through this text, but who understands the ethical limitations of its author.

This new edition of *Understanding Ethics* retains the original style and character which was well received by hundreds of undergraduate students and people from all walks of life who had never studied ethics before; however, references have been updated, other case studies have been added and there are several new sections particularly in chapters seven, eight, nine and ten.

It is not easy to be precise about what sources, experiences and influences have produced this book. To a significant degree it is the product of my lifetime inasmuch as it dares to engage the basic question "How are we to live?" The themes of this text had developed in lectures over several years; so I am in debt to my students and to numerous scholars (and their publications) who have contributed to what I have taught. Many of the additions in this edition reflect my life experiences and career opportunities as an applied ethicist over the five years since *Understanding Ethics* was first published. This revised version is dedicated to meeting the same challenge, as was the earlier edition: *to contribute towards a better world in a global society in which the ethical pressures are multiplying.*

Noel Preston, Brisbane, June 2001

CHAPTER ONE

THE ETHICAL CHALLENGE

From *Trainspotting*

RENTON

(voice-over)

Choose life. Choose a job. Choose a career. Choose a family. Choose a ... big television, choose washing machines, cars, compact disc players and electrical tin openers.

Choose good health, low cholesterol and dental insurance. Choose fixed-interest mortgage repayments. Choose a starter home. Choose your friends.

Choose leisurewear and matching luggage. Choose a three-piece suite on hire purchase in a range of ... fabrics. Choose DIY and wonder who the ... you are on a Sunday morning. Choose sitting on that couch watching mind-numbing, spirit-crushing game shows, stuffing ... junk food into your mouth. Choose rotting away at the end of it all, pishing your last in a miserable home, nothing more than an embarrassment to the selfish, ... brats you have spawned to replace yourself. Choose your future. Choose life.

But why would I want to do a thing like that?

Hodge, J, *Trainspotting*, in *Trainspotting & Shallow Grave*
Faber & Faber, London 1996, pp 3-4 [directions and expletives omitted]

Then the serpent said to the woman, "No! You will not die! God knows that on the day you eat it your eyes will be opened and you will be like gods, knowing good and evil."

The Fall according to the Biblical myth

The story is told[1] of a Sydney taxi driver who picked up an overseas journalist during an Australian federal election campaign. The journalist, ever ready to test the local wisdom on the political story he was pursuing, asked the cabbie how he was going to vote in the forthcoming election. The cabbie was forthright: "I'm a conservative voter and my father before me was conservative and his father before him was conservative, but I have decided the time has come when a man must *put aside his principles and do what is right!*"

It is easy to be confused like the cabbie when we attempt to explain and interpret our choices and decisions, particularly if we try to couch that explanation in ethical terms. I have some sympathy with that cabbie who, despite his confusion about ethical terms, had the courage to rethink his moral point of view. Furthermore, this book is dedicated to addressing some of the confusions which exist in the community not merely about what ethics is, but also about the nature of ethical discourse.

This chapter outlines the background and perspective of this text. The task of defining and describing ethics is taken up in the next chapter. However, in a preliminary way we may regard ethics as the study which arises from the human capacity to choose among values. *But what makes that study important or necessary?*

The Inevitability of Ethics

Socrates reportedly declared: "The unexamined life is not worth living". In that declaration he affirmed the importance of self-knowledge and self-reflection if we are to live a good life. Nonetheless, it is unlikely that self-scrutiny alone leads to a life worth living; indeed such introspection may lead to misery. So what does make life worthwhile?

The life and death of Socrates is instructive for answering that question. Socrates himself chose to drink the poisonous hemlock when his fellow Athenians condemned him to death for disturbing the city's good order by disseminating his beliefs and ethical teachings. He turned down an offer to escape the penalty and leave Athens for sanctuary because he judged that his life would not be worthwhile if he did not do what he believed to be the right thing, and stand by his moral principles publicly. Along with many others throughout history, Socrates demonstrated that that which is most worth living for may also be worth dying for.

The examples of Socrates and other great moral leaders such as Jesus Christ, Mahatma Gandhi, Martin Luther King, Nelson Mandela and Aung San Suu Kyi suggest that the life worth living is one that is lived for a worthwhile reason, one which goes beyond self-interest and ultimately, if necessary, beyond self-preservation. The ethical life then is part of what Peter Singer describes as the "great tradition of those who have responded to the amount of pain and suffering in the universe by trying to make it a better place".[2]

However, the message of popular culture contrasts with this. Self-gratification, acquisitiveness, social status and power are repeatedly presented as the dominant and most worthwhile values. Of course those who live by this creed do not always get away with it: they may gain the whole world but lose their soul, their ethical integrity, or the nourishment of human love (to paraphrase a Christian Scripture). Some of Hollywood's greatest movies, like Orson Welles' classic, *Citizen Kane,* the story of a multimillionaire whose life ends in ruin, or more recently Gordon Gecko in *Wall Street,* spell out the judgment that wealth, fame and power can turn very sour indeed. Yet the dominant culture, characterised by an all pervasive consumer lifestyle promoted by the popular media, continues to advance the message that the life worth living is based on self-indulgence and personal aggrandisement.

We live with mixed messages and confusion about what ethics is and what constitutes an ethical life. The point remains that human beings inevitably engage in ethical choices, as we make our lives meaningful. Indeed, there is no human life at all, let alone a worthwhile one, without ethics!

We encounter ethical questions all the time in the ordinary affairs of life. Consider these everyday realities:

- consuming products that have been produced in exploitative labour conditions;
- ending a relationship;
- receiving too much change at the check-out counter;
- borrowing your flat-mate's bicycle without permission;
- setting an example to young children in the use of alcohol;
- owning shares in an industry which produces weapons for warfare; and,
- plagiarising in a university assignment.

We sometimes fail to recognise the ethical character of these somewhat ordinary situations, or, if we do, we dismiss them as matters of personal choice, not requiring justification, accountability or any further reflection.

Of course, extraordinary and devastating situations occur which clearly present ethical dilemmas to those affected. For instance, how are parents to respond when a child is born seriously disabled and deformed? Or how are we to interpret apparently senseless acts of violence? Indeed, how are we to explain the barbarisms which accompanied human rights progress in recent times?[3]

The day I sat down to commence this book, the *Weekend Australian* newspaper[4] gave prominence to two contrasting human interest stories underlining the ambiguity of the human condition in which ethical and moral questions arise. One account described the grisly discovery in a suburban house of a murdered mother and three children. A fourth child remained alive, though badly injured, for several days before the horrific massacre was uncovered. Police were finally notified by neighbours concerned about the family pet not being fed. Without background knowledge one cannot make simplistic judgments about such a dreadful event and its perpetrator. However, it is clear that because of these murders, young lives were snuffed out senselessly and brutally.

The other account, in the same newspaper edition, featured the marriage of a young man who had been born with horribly misshapen facial features and deformed legs. A large tumour in the middle of his face had stopped the midline forming, pushing his nostrils wide apart and his eyes to the side of his head. Yet, there was no brain damage. The newspaper story went on to recount how his family painfully accepted the monstrously ugly infant; and then how, before he was to attend school, a team of surgeons implemented highly skilled and complex procedures to remake the boy's appearance giving him the life chances which have blossomed now into marriage and a career as a journalist.

The contrast is poignant: life-shattering and life-giving. The mutilating actions of human beings can serve such different ends: destructive and re-constructive. The possibility for goodness and hope, and the possibility for evil and despair were writ large in those news stories. They epitomise the tragedy and glory of the human story. This is the paradoxical and ambiguous human condition so graphically captured by Ernest Becker's phrase which describes each member of our species as a "god who shits".[5]

The perverted passion and the dedicated compassion illustrated in these episodes has everything to do with ethics because it has everything to do with the central concerns of ethics: how are we to live together? what is the good, the bad, the evil, the just, the unjust, the unfair? how are we to differentiate and choose between them? In effect, that edition of the *Weekend Australian* showed that we are both children of light and children of darkness, and that it is our capacity for goodness which makes ethics possible while it is our propensity for evil that makes it necessary.

Furthermore, both stories demonstrate another fundamental fact which shapes and necessitates the ethical life: our *interconnectedness*. We depend on others for life and death. We are our brother's/sister's keeper; we are members one of another; we share a common home in this global village. In other words, the good is a *common* good. Our individuality and privacy is never free of social responsibility because we are fundamentally social beings who live in association with others.

Of course we need to recognise that this web of life, and therefore the moral community, extend beyond human interrelatedness. All animals, including human beings, breathe the same air, we exchange common viruses, we all come from stardust, we need each other in the life chain and the biodiversity of species is more important to the survival of life on this planet than is the survival of any particular member of any species including *Homo sapiens*. However to say this, is not to deny the role humans have in caring for life in all its forms – a role which makes us unique moral agents.

Both newspaper stories demonstrate that ethical agency is inherent in the exercise of our humanity, that we experience an ongoing need to choose and act with good or evil purposes. As human beings, consciously or unconsciously, we live our lives purposefully. The issue is whether or not our purposes are good and sufficient for human beings. We make choices which lead to certain actions which have ethical outcomes. The biblical myth of the Garden of Eden is helpful for understanding our condition as ethical beings. It suggests that, because our ancestors ate of the fruit of the tree of the knowledge of good and evil, henceforth we make our way outside the idyllic state of the Garden where God took all responsibility. We do not live in the innocence of the pre-historical Garden of Eden where there is no need to adjudicate on matters of right or wrong. In human history we each make our lives by choices with ethical consequences; as a result, shame and glory accompany this inevitable ethical responsibility. In terms of the newspaper stories both murderer and surgeons as ethical agents must come to terms with the ethical nature of their action.

So, for good or ill, ethical choices arise in this web of interconnectedness. It has always been so, though arguably, as we move into a new millennium, ethical questions are sharper and the importance of ethics is emphasised in a qualitatively new way. One reason for this is the impact of that animal with heightened ethical powers and responsibilities, *Homo sapiens*, on planet Earth and its whole environment. The technological developments of the past 25 years (especially in bio-medical technology) have so expanded human options that the ethical demands of living are escalating:

- we can give a terminally ill AIDS patient a quick, easy death, but ought we?
- we can bring a foetus to full term in a host womb not of the biological mother, but ought we?
- we can improve the Gross Domestic Product by exploiting the resources of our forests, but ought we?
- we can enhance our military defence capacity through spending billions of dollars on space research, but ought we?

And so on. Altogether the situation confronting us is that the human capacity to determine what we can do, has outstripped our ability to decide what we ought to do.

The same proposition holds true in other arenas of human activity which will be discussed in this book. The popular attitude prevails that if you *can* do something (or "if you can get away with it") then there's nothing to stop you. Such a philosophy influences the sexual mores of our society and in many cases the practical code of behaviour in professions and the workplace. Certainly the evidence of the "greed is good" decade of the 1980s suggests that in business and professions such as law and accountancy this attitude was all too common; in public life, the findings of Commissions of Inquiry in most Australian States reveal that not only police but other public officials, elected and unelected, lost their way in terms of public ethical standards. Particularly worrying are surveys amongst higher education students which suggest that cheating and plagiarism are rife. Some might say that even in the human relations industry a corrosive tendency among counsellors and psychologists has been to redefine a sense of moral obligation and foster the view that "if it feels good, then do it".

At a deeper cultural level these trends have been accompanied by shifts in ideology and worldview to accommodate the breakdown in centralised authority systems, such as the church or even some versions of the family, which have traditionally informed our ethical attitudes. From the so-called modernist view of the enlightenment in which there was some consensus about human aspirations, we have moved into a post-modern pluralistic ethical environment. I am not prepared to write off the agenda of the enlightenment vision for human progress, nor to accept a simplistic post-modern or post-structural analysis of our times.[6] Indeed, though we may need to redirect the ethical search and the discourse of ethics, if anything, the moral ambivalence of this epoch and our realisation of the oppression of particular groups (such as women) represent strong reasons to recover the importance of ethical understanding for human living, at both the personal and communal level. Paradoxically, the privatisation of ethical choice which technology often promotes, contrasts with an increased sensitivity to our common fate and interdependence, often expressed through ecological awareness. The experience of globalisation, which may promote long-term and collective considerations, is arguably shaping the ethical agenda as much as the privatisation of morals which can create a false sense of freedom and autonomy. The point is, however, that a variety of social indicators and cultural movements have brought society to a point where the importance and inevitability of ethics is increasingly recognised as a matter to be addressed in a community wide conversation.

Certainly ethics is on the agenda of our social institutions and communities in a qualitatively new way. This trend is most evident in the United States where a strong sense of social decay has broadened the focus beyond a narrow right-wing obsession with family values to a more general concern about the fragmentation of society and the need for character-building programs which revive a sense of community. Australia has seen echoes of this trend. Politicians are starting to tap into a mood diagnosed by social researchers who emphasise the need to rebuild community around a clearer set of values and rules to live by. The constitutional debate about Australia becoming a republic has been accompanied by a push for an

Australian set of values as a preamble to a revised constitution alongside an enhanced civics education program. The responses to the legitimate concern for community-building are not without their ambiguities. Consider, for example, the discourse of "mutual obligation" promoted by some policy planners which is sometimes adopted by government to opt out of the responsibility to protect the rights of individuals.

The widespread development of professional codes, the establishment of ethics education programs in schools and universities, ethics research and consultancy centres, and the formation of professional ethics associations are all testimony to the growing community interest in ethics. For some time in the field of health care an institutionalised approach to ethics has been developing, through ethics committees, codes, education programs, bioethical debate and a national infrastructure via the National Health and Medical Research Council. In other fields a similar start is being made to the enculturation of ethics in professional practice and the workplace.

However, this interest is not without its problems. A strange mixture of companions tend to gather under the banner of ethics; prominent voices such as Pope John Paul II and philosopher Peter Singer both call for a rediscovery of the ethical life but their calls are based on totally different philosophical presuppositions and they arrive at opposing conclusions on many questions. At a less prominent level, letters to the editor or community-based dialogues reveal vast chasms of opinion all in the name of recovering community values, personal responsibility and ethical vision.

Of particular concern in this cacophony is the voice of moral authoritarianism which seizes on punitive solutions like corporal punishment in schools, longer prison sentences or the reinstatement of capital punishment, to enforce moral behaviour. Fundamentalism, in a variety of guises, is promoting a dubious resurgence of self-righteous and judgmental morality.[7] Though there is a growing sense that ethics needs higher priority, well may we ask, whose ethics, and particularly, how are we to avoid moral authoritarianism?

Ethics: An Instrument of Social Transformation

The possibility of ethics being used for reactionary, coercive and authoritarian social purposes is real. Allied to hierarchical, centralised political systems, programs of social engineering have historically been paraded as ethically justified instruments, most notably in fascist

Germany of the 1930s or more recently with South Africa's apartheid policy. Partly as a consequence of this tendency, some in the Marxist tradition are suspicious of the study of ethics. Mindful of the thesis on Feuerbach which serves as an epitaph to Karl Marx ("Philosophers have analysed the world, it is time for us to change the world"), they believe that moral "ideas" are invariably instruments of the ruling class, a form of false consciousness, designed to prevent change in social and economic conditions.[8]

The central point of this concern cannot be denied. I reject any ethical approach which fails to take seriously commitment to a reflective, critical and transformative engagement with changing social and technological conditions by aiming to benefit those most disadvantaged in those contexts. In a nutshell, this means a commitment to reflect ethically about economic issues from the standpoint of the poor, not the rich; or race relations from the standpoint of the least powerful; or environmental questions from the standpoint of the most vulnerable species, and so on.

Such an approach recognises that ethical behaviour takes place within a complex interaction of social forces and vested interests, and that improvement in social conditions or cultural practices requires more than a change of heart or ideas. It aims for a realignment of those forces and interests generally brought about through social struggle and conflict. Clearly then, ethical deliberation and character formation must be complemented by social analysis. Ethics as philosophical reflection is never enough but must interact with a realistic and accurate interpretation of social conditions and the prospects for their transformation.

Ethics as an instrument of social transformation explores the interface between pragmatic tendencies and idealistic impulses. As a counter-hegemonic exercise built around a rhythm of action and reflection, such ethics need to challenge injustice and unethical practices by engaging them, not by distancing from them or being detached. At the personal or social level, ethics must take seriously the question of practical effectiveness, striking a balance between what is feasible and what is desirable. At the same time, the exercise of that responsibility requires vision as well as realistic judgment. Put simply, the perspective underpinning discussions of this book is that the ultimate test for public justification of any social policy or practice is whether or not the most disadvantaged benefit from it and whether it promotes democratic, participatory processes.[9] At the personal level, this ethic exhibits a caring commitment in relationships which gives priority to the vulnerable and the vulnerability in us all.

It follows that the decisive backdrop to all discussions throughout this book is a tapestry which features the following:

- concern to support and sustain the *ecological* environment and its life forms, at a time when millions of hectares of rainforest are extinguished each year;
- concern to challenge and diminish *global injustice* in the human community, at a time when it is reported by the World Health Organisation that millions of children under five die needlessly every year; and
- concern to identify and reverse the causes of *increasing socio-economic inequality in Australia,* at a time when research shows that, as a group, Aboriginal peoples in Australia experience deprivations which are comparable to the worst poverty in the so-called Third World.

These, I suggest, are the touchstone issues in a contemporary Australian understanding of social ethics for they focus on those who are most vulnerable and disadvantaged and to whom response is required if we are to achieve "the common good". These issues are fundamental to many current Australian political debates, for instance about reconciliation, republicanism or protection of native vegetation.

At the same time it does not follow that they are the only ethical issues which matter. We may classify ethical issues as matters of *personal, professional* and *social* responsibility. The touchstone issues outlined above are social or macro questions. In professional ethics, where for instance the matter of informed consent may be critical, or at a personal level, where the matter of familial duty may be important, the macro picture itemised above may not be so obvious or immediately relevant. This does not diminish the ethical importance of those professional or personal concerns. Indeed many of the items discussed in this book will be of that order. However, the links between the personal, the professional and the larger, macro or social dimensions should not be overlooked. Our ability to "act locally" should be informed by how we "think globally". The public sphere and the private sphere are linked in the web of interconnectedness we discussed earlier. Our professional role can never be divorced from its social responsibility and wider impact on family life, the environment, and social justice. Indeed, as the final chapter will argue, moral integrity demands consistency in motivation and action across the various spheres of one's life.

How To Use This Book

Understanding Ethics is a basic text, designed to communicate with those who have never studied philosophy or ethics formally. The book aims to speak to that growing number of interested persons who want to understand more about the study of ethics, ethical issues and the ways ethicists approach them. It is therefore presented as an introductory undergraduate text but it may also speak to members of professions in which discussion about ethics is becoming more evident. In addition, it will be of interest to school teachers who have the opportunity either to teach short ethics courses or to be more explicit about ethical questions in their general teaching; and, it should be useful to higher education teachers who come from disciplines outside the humanities but who recognise the need to incorporate an ethical focus into their teaching. It will also be helpful to community opinion-makers (such as journalists, clergy, politicians, and even parents) whose work is saturated with ethical implications for small and large communities, but who may never have been exposed to a systematic ethics course. Finally, it aims to appeal to general readers of any age who are interested simply because they recognise that ethical decision-making is an important and unavoidable part of human living.

As an introductory and general volume, *Understanding Ethics* is certainly not exhaustive in its treatment of themes. It attempts no systematic review of the history of ethics or of the range of moral traditions present in a contemporary multicultural society like Australia. The approaches this text draws on, and the key figures alluded to throughout, are from the Western Judaeo-Christian cultural heritage, a cultural heritage which in recent decades has been undergoing critical scrutiny in the name of post-modernist, post-structuralist, and feminist revision. It is desirable, though it is not essential for an appreciation of the topics in *Understanding Ethics,* that students of ethics can locate the development of ideas historically and culturally and thereby become familiar with the competing and complementary traditions which inform the approaches taken in this book. A short survey note on the history of ethics and other moral traditions is included at the conclusion of the book to assist in this task.

Taking a stance

If this book lacks definitive positions on moral matters, that is a result of my attempt to be faithful to the fact that ethical discussion respects the autonomy of each participant in the conversation: this is not a dogmatic exercise. If on the other hand this book sometimes betrays a particular point of view and an apparent bias when it comes to certain matters, then that is a result of the author's value commitments which we all bring to such conversations. However, readers should expect such views to be supported by sound argument which can withstand critical scrutiny.

Features of the book

This text is designed not only to assist students of ethics but also to contribute to the community discourse about ethical concerns. In other words and in a word, the best way to use this book is to talk about it. Readers will not be surprised that it has certain features of a textbook:

- an *index* which can help readers cross-check concepts and themes;
- a short *glossary* which gives succinct explanations of technical terms to assist readers unfamiliar with the language of ethics;
- a note on *the history of ethics and moral traditions* appears after the glossary at the conclusion of the book; it could be consulted before reading the next chapters;
- a *summary* at the conclusion of most chapters to assist students identify key understandings;
- *questions* at the conclusion of most chapters to facilitate discussion, because ethical understanding requires dialogue and is enhanced by articulating views with others who in turn may challenge them;
- *case studies* are provided to assist the application of the discussions to possible or actual situations (though the keen student will begin to identify in literature, film, history or lived experience a raft of other examples);
- *endnotes* are an important collection of additional information especially about further source material; and,
- not least of all, a brief *list of further reading items* is provided with each chapter; this is very important because the

discussion in most chapters is so preliminary that further research is needed by students to elaborate their understanding of matters referred to within particular chapters; if these readings are sometimes difficult that should not be a surprise or disappointment; dialogue, re-reading and scanning for key ideas is encouraged and perseverance with difficult readings is called for, as it eventually brings its reward.

The book's structure

Understanding Ethics is constructed in what amounts to three sections.

- The first few chapters introduce the nature, language and frameworks of ethics. They draw on traditions of philosophical ethics developed in the Western Judaeo-Christian derived cultures. Chapter Four presents a procedure for ethical decision-making based on the use of various ethical approaches. I term this *an ethic of response.* The ethic of response is allied to three substantive principles which are used in subsequent chapters: the principle of *respect for life,* the principle of *justice and fairness,* and the principle of *covenantal integrity*.
- The second section, Chapters Five to Nine, explores topical applied ethics issues of interpersonal and social significance ranging through bioethics, sexual ethics, environmental ethics, business ethics, political ethics and questions of social justice. The analysis of these topics is subject to the perspective of the ethic of response.
- The final chapter, "Cultivating an Ethical Life" considers the life of integrity. It offers some analysis of moral education and considerations for ethics educators; in addition, there is a rudimentary discussion about embedding ethics in organisational and institutional life; the book concludes with an epilogue, presented as a letter to my grandchildren, a device in which my more personal views about living an ethical life are given expression.

Short cuts

Some readers - especially those not doing formal courses - may find certain chapters of more interest than others. Not all chapters need to be read or fully understood to find the book worthwhile. In particular, readers so inclined could by-pass the next two chapters which introduce the formal terminology and approaches of ethics in a philosophical mode; they could rely on the glossary to explain technical references in the other chapters.

The benefits of ethics study

Readers of *Understanding Ethics* are entitled to ask, "what will I gain from the study of ethics?". The question can be answered in various ways. At the very least one would expect that reading this book is an introduction to many stimulating and interesting ideas, relevant to life decisions. Furthermore, as well as being an important aspect of a general education, the study of ethics can enhance the capacity for critical judgment and practical decision-making in a variety of personal, workplace and applied contexts. For any whose vocational role involves the formulation of policy for instance, the ability to reflect on ethical issues will be an important asset.

We can identify many characteristics or capacities which are *outcomes of the study of ethics* (even if they are not solely the result of that study), represented diagramatically:

Outcomes of Ethics Study

self-awareness

envisioning alternative

reflective powers

sensitivity to rights and responsibilities

•

sensitivity to ethical dimensions

empathy

recognising consequences

justificatory reasoning

Despite these claims, we must be careful not to suggest that the study of ethics will necessarily or inevitably lead us to become better (more ethical) persons. The items listed above are capacities which can also be appropriated for malevolent, unjust and unethical purposes. However, I argue that the study and exploration of ethical issues can improve behaviours. Of course, embedded within this discussion is the prior issue as to whether (or at least how) ethics can be taught (and learnt). This is a major study in itself and is addressed in Chapter Ten. Through the study of ethics we learn to think more reflectively and systematically about the ethical impact of life-decisions as well as about everyday practice. We can indeed learn to be more consistent and accurate in rehearsing and embracing modes of self and collective evaluation which are based on autonomously chosen values, purposes and justifications.

Those who get most out of this book will be those who argue with it and who begin to transfer ethical perception and reflection to the relationships and tasks of their life, by cultivating a respect for the whole moral community of this planet as they seek the good life.

FURTHER READING

Hinman, L (1998) "The Moral Point of View" in *Ethics: A Pluralistic Approach To Moral Theory* (2nd ed), London: Harcourt Brace, pp 1–31. Discusses the importance of the ethical perspective and provides an interesting test to "discovering your own moral beliefs" (pp 7–10). The book itself is an excellent introduction to ethics and can be read in tandem with lectures via the world wide web.

CHAPTER ONE NOTES

1 This is an adapted version of an anecdote used by my friend, Howard Whitton, but in the course of preparing this book I discovered that this story was first used by Joseph Fletcher in his book *Situation Ethics*, SCM Press, 1966, and refers to the 1960 United States election campaign.

2 Singer, P (1993) *How are We to Live? Ethics in an Age of Self-Interest*, Melbourne: The Text Publishing Company, p 235.

3 For an excellent discussion of this issue by an eminent moral philosopher, see Glover, J (2000) *Humanity: A Moral History of the 20th Century*, Jonathon Cape Publishers.

4 *The Weekend Australian*, December 2–5, 1995.

5 Becker, E (1975) *The Denial of Death*, New York: The Free Press.

6 This is not the place to expand on what is a critical debate among social theorists. However, a few observations are offered for those who want to follow this up. While there is much to be learnt from the key thinkers of post-modernism and post-structuralism (like Lyotard, Foucault and Derrida), I do not accept the implication of their work and that of many of their disciples, inasmuch as it invites an abandonment of normative thinking and the moral imperative to envision a better world. I prefer to situate myself in terms of social theory with critical theorist, Jurgen Habermas. For a considered critique of post-modernism and a reconstruction of ethics in the light of this contemporary debate I commend Zygmunt Baumann, author of *Postmodern Ethics,* Oxford: Blackwell, 1993.

7 For a brief excellent discussion of fundamentalism, see Karen Armstrong, "In the Name of God", a Spectrum article in the *Sydney Morning Herald,* Saturday, 4 November 2000.

8 Indeed Karl Marx was openly hostile to morality and forecast no place for it in his communist state. For a readable analysis of the Marxist critique of morality see Allan Wood "Marx against Morality" in Singer, P (ed) (1991) *A Companion to Ethics,* Oxford: Blackwell. For an attempt to discuss ethics within a framework sympathetic to Marx, the writings of Kai Nielsen are important.

9 These views are shaped from various sources. In part they are influenced by the actions and proclamations of biblical prophets such as Amos, Micah and Jeremiah. They also coincide in part with the influential work of American philosopher, John Rawls, which is discussed briefly in Chapter 3. Echoes of these views are found in scholarly discussions like O'Neill, O (1986) *Faces of Hunger: An Essay on Poverty, Justice and Development,* London: Allen and Unwin.

CHAPTER TWO

ENCOUNTERING ETHICS

From *My Dinner with André*

ANDRÉ: Well, here's a view of life – I mean, he talks about the belief of the Hasidic Jews that there are spirits chained in everything – there are spirits chained in you, there are spirits chained in me, there are spirits chained in this table – and that prayer is the action of liberating these enchained embryo-like spirits, and that every action of ours in life – whether it's doing business or making love or having dinner together or whatever – that every action should be a prayer, a sacrament, in the world. Now do you think we're living in a world like that?

WALLY: No –

Quoted from Shawn, W, & Gregory, A, *My Dinner with André*,
Grove Press, New York, 1981, p 80.

Two things fill the mind with ever new and increasing admiration and awe, the oftener and more steadily they are reflected on: the starry heavens above me and the moral law within me.

Immanuel Kant
The Critique of Practical Reason (1788)

About Ethics

In Chapter One we noted that ethics has both a personal and social aspect. Ethics is essential to our life with others in society, as well as to how we live with ourselves, in our "conscience" if you like. However, in practice or even in theory, it may be difficult to distinguish these dimensions.

In general, ethics is concerned about what is *right, fair, just* or *good;* about what we *ought* to do, not just about what *is* the case or what is most acceptable or expedient. This distinction between "ought" and "is" signals the need to distinguish ethical claims from factual ones. It might be a fact that people lie, but that does not falsify the moral principle of honesty. Facts describe. Facts can usually be tested as to their falsity or truth. Ethical claims *prescribe,* rather than describe. They are concerned with how people *ought* to behave and suggest how social and individual behaviour can be improved. As such, ethical claims are debatable and contestable. In ethical discourse we encounter conflicts of value, interest or sentiment, and choices between principles, decisions and actions.

The word "ethics", like many in our language, has its origins in ancient Greece. The Greek word *ethos* meaning "character" or "custom" is the source of the English, "ethics". The term "morality" has a Latin connection and is related to our word "mores" which refers to the habits or customary traditions of a people. Already we have been using a number of overlapping terms which need clarification - not only "ethics", and "morality", but also "values". What are "values"? Values may be defined as those principles or attitudes to which we attribute worth (that is, we cherish or prize them). They become for us guidelines for action with moral significance (such as, "respect for life" or "diligence in work practices").

The terms "morality" and "ethics" are often interchanged. "Ethics" has a double meaning. It may refer to the study of our values and their justification. In this sense it is often called "moral philosophy". On the other hand, ethics may also mean the actual values and rules of conduct by which we live, or our "morality". So, we may say that the study of ethics includes the study of morality which generally refers to "a particular ethic" or "the moral tradition of a given religion or society". Nonetheless, the adjectives "moral" and "ethical" may be accurately interchanged.

Another important distinction to note is that between *meta-ethics* and *normative* (or *prescriptive) ethics*. Normative ethics provides theories which aim to guide our conduct, to help us decide what we ought to do and how we ought to live. Normative ethics provides frameworks by which we may consider the particular issues discussed in later chapters. Chapter Three introduces a range of normative ethical theories.

However, moral philosophy has raised questions about why we should be concerned with morality at all and about what we are doing when we are doing ethics. For instance, in what sense can moral judgments be true or false? Are they merely the expression of feelings? These considerations involve looking at the meaning of ethical terms, the nature of ethics and the grounds for pursuing it. They are referred to as *meta-ethics*. While some moral philosophers devote considerable attention to these important questions, in this text we concentrate on normative ethics.

Normative ethical theories provide frameworks for the application of ethical decisions. In a sense, all ethics should be practical, *applied ethics* if you like, though, as we have said, many moral philosophers concentrate on *meta-ethics* which, they argue, supports a more accurate application of ethics. Applied ethics, the disciplinary basis of this book, draws on philosophical ethics but emerges more from an interdisciplinary field sometimes including the life sciences, the social sciences, the humanities as well as the speculative sciences like philosophy and theology and the hermeneutic (or interpretive) skills associated with them.

As Chapter One indicated, applied ethics seeks to have an effective impact at the level of social and personal practice. In a sense, it recalls the tradition of casuistry[1] which attempted to provide guidance for applying ethics in hard cases. Within this broad understanding of applied ethics there is a significant place for an ethic of role or professional ethics, but this is only part of the picture, even though the popular use of the term ethics is often confused with "professional ethics", as when you hear "that accountant has forgotten her ethics".

There are some further observations to make which sharpen our view of what is distinctive about the ethical perspective. We have briefly noted that ethics involves a justificatory discourse about what we ought to do and what is good. However, we may use the concepts of *ought* and *good* in contexts not specifically moral. For instance, in the appreciation of art (aesthetics) we might say that if a work of art has a harmonic, coherent form it is good. But it is not primarily good in an ethical sense. Similarly, we might say that a carpenter ought to use his tools in a way that demonstrates technical skill and accuracy. That "oughtness" is not necessarily moral. Furthermore, take the case of manners or etiquette. A child might be exhorted to chew with her mouth shut. That is good behaviour and what one ought to do. But if this child eats with an open mouth that is hardly unethical though it may be considered bad manners in certain households. This is not to say however, that there is no connection between manners and morals, only that there is no necessary connection.

In many aspects of life we might be constrained by certain understandings of what is good or what ought to be done without entering into a conscious or rigorous ethical justification. On the other hand, there are some situations in life which require ethical judgment and reasoning where we fail to employ an adequate justification and undervalue the ethical dimension involved. Consider how the pragmatic view prevalent in our culture often takes over from ethical reflection: "if you can accomplish your goal, no matter what it takes, that is good". As a result, a politician may deceive her electorate to win at the polls or a citizen may fiddle his tax return to feather his nest. Pragmatic reasoning is inadequate for capturing many morally salient features of everyday life.

Ethical reflection requires the consideration of sound moral reasons. There may be dispute about what constitute sound moral reasons; but, it is generally acknowledged that ethics requires the use of our powers of reason or rationality. Others might add that we need to go beyond our autonomous reason and appeal to an external authority - the Bible for example. The reliance on rationality and a sense of a moral authority enables ethical reflection to cultivate *disinterestedness*. That is, it involves stepping back from a situation and considering obligations or consequences and not simply responding to one's own personal interests or feelings in a particular case. This approach involves what has been referred to as "taking the viewpoint of the universe".

Let me apply this approach to a hypothetical case where my daughter is raped and brutally murdered. Should I clamour for the death penalty for her torturer? Were I to take a narrow view of the events, influenced by the torment and heartache I feel at what happened to her and my unceasing loathing for her murderer, I might wish him to die, in as cruel a way as possible. From the ethical point of view however, while I would be profoundly affected by empathy for my daughter, I try to adopt a certain disinterestedness and weigh the case on its merits and reflect on the wider ethical implications of capital punishment and of the state adopting the code of revenge or deterrence. As a father I might prefer one course, as an ethical citizen who is also a father, notwithstanding my overwhelming emotions, I might conclude for sound moral reasons (including "the necessity to value all life in society") that, in no case (and therefore in this case) is capital punishment ethically justified.

In the next chapter we will see a range of normative approaches which promote various pathways to ethical decision-making. They all generally affirm the use of reason, moral authority and the need to provide justification which goes beyond mere preference to a level of accountability to some commitment affirmed by the moral agent. Doing ethics then involves evaluation, not simply the sort of evaluation the ethics lecturer employs in marking a student essay, but an evaluation of the moral reasons (fairness, harm, duty and so on) supporting a certain stance on an ethical question.

Ethics as Part of Philosophy

Though we have claimed that applied ethics is not tied exclusively to philosophical ethics, the necessary link between one's ethical approach and one's philosophical beliefs is important and needs examination. Consequently, it is within the wider study of philosophy that the study of ethics has been nurtured.

Philosophy is another term with Greek linguistic origins: *philia* meaning love between friends, and *sophia* meaning wisdom. So philosophy is the pursuit (or love) of wisdom, and we might add, between friends. The latter phrase is important especially in the context of the study of ethics. That study is enhanced in an environment of friendly, social discourse for we develop an ethical view primarily from those we love or who are persons of significance in our lives.

There are many fields within the study of philosophy. Political philosophy or social philosophy is an important companion of applied ethics for instance. Logic (the science of reasoning) and aesthetics (the study of values in art or beauty) are other dimensions of philosophy. But besides ethics, the core business of philosophy is metaphysics (the study of reality) and epistemology (the study of knowledge). Ethics, metaphysics and epistemology overlap and relate, so that, consciously or unconsciously, metaphysical views or one's epistemological assumptions will have a bearing on ethical attitudes.

Philosophising is arguably a distinctive characteristic of the human animal because it involves the art of wondering or the capacity to think about our thinking. Combined with the cultivated skill of language, the human propensity to philosophise is a powerful aspect of how we make meaning of our lives. In our busy lives dominated by materialistic pursuits and at times an environment divorced from nature, we may lose our sense of "the philosophical" but occasionally, as we rejoice at the birth of a child, or as we learn that we are dying, or perhaps when a beautiful sunset appears on the horizon, our capacity to wonder, to ask ultimate questions, may be evoked.

The age-old questions of metaphysics persist: What exists in reality? Is there really cause and effect in reality? Is there a god? What is human nature? These are not unimportant questions for ethics. For instance, if the universe, and life on Earth as part of it, are without moral sense, merely chance events with no purposeful direction, then that assumption would presumably influence how we approach questions of moral authority. Likewise our view on whether human beings are intrinsically evil or good, trustworthy or untrustworthy or a combination of all that, would condition our expectations of what is desirable and feasible ethically. The affirmation in the previous chapter regarding the interdependence of all life is a metaphysical assertion, one that also has empirical verification. As that chapter claimed, that assertion shapes a basic orientation to how we do ethics.

Similarly we might ask time-honoured questions of epistemology: What is knowledge? What are truth and falsity? How do we know? These also are not unimportant questions for ethics. Debates about the merits of universalist or absolutist approaches to ethics swing on certain epistemological assumptions. In particular, what is the source of moral knowledge? Is it socially and culturally constructed or is there some divine blueprint in the universe to be revealed? For instance, were the Ten Commandments a socio-cultural product of 40 years of Israelite nomadism or were they a bolt from heaven, literally a word from God, or is there some other way of explaining the moral knowledge of the law of Moses?

The point is that our ethics rest on metaphysical and epistemological assumptions, consciously acknowledged or unconsciously held. Beliefs, whether religious or not, matter in ethics. Our ethical experience influences what we come to believe just as our beliefs, whether consciously or unconsciously held, shape our ethics. So philosophy helps us clarify some of the assumptions which form our ethical judgment. One such assumption might be the question of the value of life or the sanctity of human life. What we believe in a philosophical or religious sense, about that question, could be crucial to how we approach the topics of the chapters which follow, just as our practical engagement with issues like euthanasia or the environment might reshape our beliefs.

Philosophy as a skill or practice has a lot to contribute to this study in other ways. The study of philosophy may equip us to reason, argue, analyse and question assumptions more effectively and consistently. Philosophers love to ask, "Why?" and "What is your reason?" Authentic ethical deliberation and exploration require an openness which profits from the scepticism of philosophy. But there is a downside, and there are limitations. Philosophy has often become too removed from social reality, an exercise of mind games, which might distort the concern to make ethics practical. To many contemporary critics, philosophy, and with it the study of ethics in the Western tradition, has been too dominated by a rationalistic and cognitive approach hell-bent on discerning universal principles rather than addressing the multi-faceted dynamics of right relationships.

Law and Ethics

Some of the great moral exemplars of human history have defied the law of their societies. In the twentieth century there have been outstanding examples. For instance, Martin Luther King Jr's campaign of civil disobedience against segregation in the United States in the 1950s and 1960s was based on the premise which he reiterated in many forums that there is a moral duty not to cooperate with unjust laws because that is to cooperate with evil. Inspired by the civil rights movement, thousands of young people in the Vietnam War period defied the laws of conscription on moral grounds. Perhaps the most outstanding case of morality versus law in recent political history is the movement against the laws of apartheid led by Nelson Mandela in South Africa. Appealing to a higher moral law, the African National Congress refused to submit to the law of the state. Both Mandela and King were directly influenced by Mahatma Gandhi's philosophy and practice of moral resistance to unjust laws in India. In contemporary Burma, the mantle of civil disobedience is now being taken up by Aung San Suu Kyi in the struggle for that country's people for democratic rights. These exemplars make the claim that the law deserves no respect if it fails to uphold "respect for persons and the environment". In other words the law must serve the common good. They demonstrate the view that not everything that is legal is ethical, or indeed that not everything ethical is legal.

Yet clearly there is a close relationship between the law and ethics. Former United States Supreme Court Chief Justice Earl Warren expressed the relationship thus: "the law floats on a sea of ethics". We may try to summarise this relationship in a few simple propositions:

- the development of the law has been influenced by ethics, but ethics is not necessarily based on law;
- the reasons for significant laws governing human beings and their institutions (criminal laws, laws about the incorporation of business or protecting the environment) are overwhelmingly ethical reasons;
- law is commonly a public expression of, and sanction for, the morality of a given society;
- the law should be continually subject to the scrutiny of ethical critique.

This final point suggests that there is an ongoing tension for the institution of law in society between law as the expression of "positive morality", which is the morality actually accepted and shared by a given social group, and "critical morality", the morality which transcends the current standards adopted by a society. This is the tension at work in the confrontations promoted by Martin Luther King and Nelson Mandela. It is also evident in the social struggle to change laws which discriminate against homosexuals for instance. On this view the expression of positive morality through the law should be subject to critique. In this sense, law floats uneasily at times on a turbulent sea of ethics.

Throughout this book we will touch on questions where law and ethics interface. One might regard abortion as immoral, but in a liberal democratic society should it be a criminal offence? One might regard the consumption of certain drugs as harmful and a social evil, but is that problem best handled in society by making the sale of drugs like heroin illegal? Here, we encounter the question as to whether the law is a moral teacher or guide in society, a question which leads in turn to major matters of civil liberties including the ethics of censorship: when should the state restrict the freedom and rights of the individual?

Issues of ethics in the law and the practice of law are becoming more prominent in the study of law and preparation of the legal profession. Of course, the ethical practice of law has always been concerned with proper procedures. The new interest in legal ethics should not be a surprise as the attempt to codify society's requirements for all sorts of social interactions, not least of all in the area of information technology, is becoming more and more complex. Along with this trend is the need for those who are considered to be the administrators of justice in our society to understand the subtleties of the meaning of "justice". Ethics education of lawyers and ethical reform for the institution of law remain ongoing priorities for any society aspiring to be a just society.

Finally however, it must be conceded that a lawless society will be an unethical one, and defiance of the law on ethical grounds remains a grave act of conscientious objection requiring a full public justification. The implicit contract to live together in society requires the sanctions of the law, for certainly there is always a fair proportion of society's members who will not be persuaded by ethical argument or consensus alone and who will act against the interests of others. Though the rule of law keeps under control the fear that without the constraint of law, immoral behaviour might become the order of the day, we are a sad, uncivil, and unethical society if the only reason people do not rape, pillage and murder is because there is a law against these deeds. "Respect for the law" is ultimately only a moral obligation because of a commitment to an ethical vision of a just society or an ethical principle like "respect for persons".

Ethics and Religion

There can be no doubt that, historically, religion has served as a most powerful sanction and motivation for people to behave morally. If we asked orthodox Jews why their society had a very strong taboo against suicide, we would discover that these values and ethical practices derive from their religious history and a view about the valuing of human life. If we asked Native Americans about their patterns of hunting buffalo, we would discover that the taboos and rituals associated with this practice are supported by religious beliefs and a worldview about the interconnectedness of all beings.

Religion has often been one vehicle for articulating views about the nature of persons. For example, the view that human beings are made in the image of God has been a powerful influence on moral judgment. Also, religion has provided rewards (hope of heaven) and punishments (fear of hell) which have underlined the moral imperative. On the contrary, many of religious faith interpret the moral imperative governing their lives not in terms of reward and punishment but much more positively, depending on intrinsic rather than extrinsic factors like the fate of one's immortal soul. Consequently their moral action is based on a sense of love and unity with all creation because they are thereby linked with their God who is the source of love and the creator of all.

Certainly in the Judaeo-Christian heritage there is a strong strand linking faith and ethics. Prophets like Amos and Jeremiah denounce religious practice which fails to produce ethical behaviour declaring: "to know God is to do justice". A central precept of practical theology in this tradition as in most religions, is that one's relationship to God is reflected in one's relationship to all others.

Nonetheless, while we can find many examples of outstanding religious leaders who were also moral exemplars, history abounds with numerous cases where the perpetration of injustice, oppression and war has received religious backing. This is the sad reality of recent history in that cradle of religious traditions, the Middle East. The fact is that not all religious people are good and not all good people are religious. What is more, it is difficult to identify good outcomes of religious ethics that are unique to people of religious persuasion. If this is so, what connection is there between religion and morality?

This question finds its way into works as diverse as a Dostoyevsky novel, a Woody Allen film or the Socratic question in Plato's *Euthyphro*: "Is what is holy, holy because the gods approve it or do they approve it because it is holy?" Pursuing this inquiry is neither esoteric nor provocative, for it opens up intensely practical questions which implicitly and necessarily impinge on our daily lives: "why be moral anyway?"; "what enables us to live morally?"; or "how is an ethical society to be cultivated?" (questions we look at later in this chapter and in the final chapter).

This inquiry also impacts on matters of public policy. For instance:

- can democratic values and institutions be sustained without presupposing a supreme being?
- should moral education be linked to religious education or will that result in indoctrination?
- what beliefs should society allow as a basis for conscientious objection?

The arguments that link religion or belief in God with ethics are sometimes summarised as the Divine Command theory, and in the general community can be recognised in certain biblical precepts (such as the Ten Commandments) or official church teachings (such as a papal encyclical on moral matters). Broadly speaking, these arguments rest on three assertions which are problematic in a philosophical and rational sense: (1) God is the source of all moral goodness, (2) God guides us to an understanding of the moral good and, (3) God provides the motivation for being good.

Immediately, we can see problems: what do we mean by "God"? For some that term refers to an all-powerful being; for others it refers to a cosmic, transcendent force operating in and through all of existence; and for yet others, non-theists, the term has no referent at all. It is apparent that these themes go beyond the scope of this book and reside in the realm of theology and the philosophy of religion, although, as pointed out earlier in this chapter, matters of metaphysics and epistemology may well influence our approach to ethics.

If we want to sustain the view that belief in a god is a prerequisite for an ethical world view, we conflict with very influential ethical systems such as that developed by Immanuel Kant who, though a believer, insisted that moral knowledge is a product of human reason.

The proposition connecting theistic[2] belief and morality is bedevilled by debatable issues such as:

- how can an all-powerful god allow evil?
- why does the coincidence of moral zeal and dogmatic belief often lead to authoritarian self-righteousness?
- does the claim that we need an external moral authority undermine the autonomy of choice which ethics requires?

Nonetheless, as noted earlier, though we do not need to be theists or adherents of an institutional religion to be moral, all systems of ethics draw on metaphysical and epistemological assumptions. In that sense ethical views always rest on belief systems. (The phrase "belief systems" is used advisedly to reflect the form of "faith" rather than "religion" in a cultural, institutional or doctrinal sense.) Faith then may cultivate an ethical disposition in which the self invests confidence in a centre or centres of value and power giving direction to one's life, within communities of shared interpretation, loyalty and trust. For some, faith not only informs ethics but may take them beyond ethics, when either the failure to live according to one's ethic or the uncertainty of what is ethical, requires other resources sometimes referred to as "divine grace".

In summary, my argument is that though an ethical worldview rests implicitly on a belief system, sometimes an atheistic or non-religious belief system, there is no necessary connection between religion or faith (in the traditional sense of belief in a god, the supernatural and an afterlife) and ethics. Indeed, the human era at the conclusion of the twentieth century, is probably the first in which a significant proportion of humanity confronts ethical choices without the reference points traditional religion has provided. For some, the diminishing influence of religion explains what they regard as a breakdown in community ethics; for others, this trend is a liberating one enabling a truly humanistic ethic to emerge; for yet others, the issue becomes one of discovering an appropriate spirituality to support an ethic responsive to this era's challenges.

Three Key Issues [3]

1 *Egoism and altruism*

The question of motivation in ethical matters is a vexed and enduring one. Is it self-interest and perceptions of our own well-being which fundamentally guide our behaviour? Or are we motivated, on occasions at least, by consideration of others, even without regard to our own self-interest, and by a sense of duty or obligation to others? We use the terms *egoism* and *altruism* to identify this distinction. Egoism is acting out of self-interest while altruism involves acting for the benefit of others. Bear in mind that we are talking primarily here of motivations rather than consequences. Paradoxically, it is sometimes the case that egoistic intentions produce good outcomes for others while the reverse is also true. If I intend to help others, but in failing to do this benefit myself, it is not accurate to describe my approach as egoistic. Having said this, our brief discussion here might lead us to query whether the focus on motivation rather than outcomes or consequences is a practical or tenable one.

One tack often taken in this discussion is to point to the empirical evidence that human beings repeatedly act in their own self-interest (if not as individuals then as collectivities, in a race or nation). This analysis leads us to what is termed *psychological egoism*, the view that human beings are in fact motivated by self-interest. Now this may be a well supported fact, though there are clearly exceptions in human history; nevertheless, it would be fallacious to confuse this view with an ethical or normative theory. What *is* the case, is not necessarily what *ought* to be the case. So we are not so concerned here about what we term psychological egoism but rather we are interested in *ethical egoism*. In the various forms of this view the basic claim is that it is good or even a duty to act in one's self-interest.

As a personal or individual ethical philosophy, egoism is quite pervasive in our culture ("look after number one"). However, it may be refuted as inadequate and counter-productive to the associations in society which rational people hold to be essential. In Chapter Three we shall discuss further the version of the theory we call *universal ethical egoism*. It commands a more substantial claim, maintaining that *everyone* should always act in their own self-interest regardless of the interests of others although their own interests may sometimes serve others' interests. To maintain this view as a social philosophy its supporters cling to the "faith" that the individual self-interests of rational human beings, by virtue of their being rational, are generally compatible. This seems to be a dubious proposition in a world of crowded communities and limited resources where self-interests constantly conflict and where a struggle ensues to see whose interests can be served and where compromise, involving the surrender of some self-interests, seems necessary. In the end it seems that this theory is not borne out in actual experience.

Of course to many of us, egoism is unacceptable as a moral theory: if a normative approach does not include some capacity to act for others, regardless of self-interest, then it is hardly ethical. Nonetheless, we might profitably press the question as to whether altruism and egoism are so incompatible. This is especially the case if we distinguish between egoism and selfishness, because to say that someone is selfish implies something more than self-interest. It suggests a will disposed to undermine the interests of others.

We often speak of "enlightened self-interest" or "prudence" as terms to suggest that in many situations we can respond to mutual interests, the interests of others as well as ourselves. Prudence suggests that our considerations may include a balance of long-term and short-term interests. In political decisions for instance there is often a mix of motivations (and outcomes) in good decision-making. So, we are told, our overseas aid policy serves the twin objectives of helping other nations (perhaps in the short-term) while contributing to our own economy (over time). Of course, it may be another question whether what we are told and what happens coincide! In other arenas, such as management, we are counselled to employ "win-win" situations which suggest that mutual interests can be served. Of course, in these examples there may be a shift to consideration of outcomes rather than motivations. However, it at least seems possible that we can aim to protect our own self-interest while at the same time being altruistic. Indeed the Christian injunction to "love your neighbour as yourself" suggests that this possibility is not only feasible but desirable.

This proposition is unlikely to mean that we can meet the twin objectives of love of neighbour and love of self easily, without pain or cost. At times self-denial is the only way to express concern for the other, even at the cost of one's life. We should be cautious about an ethical approach which glosses over the hard choices ultimately presented by the claims of egoism and altruism. The New Testament enjoins, "Greater love has no one than to lay down one's life for friends". We see this principle at work in families and closely bonded relationships: a father sacrifices his life attempting to save a drowning child. But is this only self-interest at work because the child's survival and the parent's well-being are so closely entwined? Simply to say that is to trivialise the act of sacrifice and the fact that if the child's life is saved it clearly owes its life to another.

Nonetheless, there is something important to note in the case of self-sacrifice for one's kin. It is significant that motivation for altruistic acts is connected to one's sense of relatedness to others. Maybe the appropriate and prior question in ethics is, "how do we define our kin" or "how extensive is our sense of family"? The distinctions raised by altruism and egoism are sharpened if we have a narrow understanding of who are the members of the moral community to whom we are responsible. Arguably, those great moral exemplars of altruism who have sacrificed their life for others had a very broad understanding (if not a universalistic one) of who were their brothers and sisters. Altruism was the natural fruit of their ego and self-understanding. They demonstrate that so-called psychological or cultural egoism is not necessarily determinative.

2 *Freedom and determinism*

What freedom do we have to make ethical choices? Are our actions and choices pre-determined by prior causes? Is freedom an illusion? In what sense is our environment able to be shaped by us? Is the universe merely a product of chance or purpose? Such questions clearly have major significance for the study and practice of ethics. Indeed, if we could demonstrate that our choices and actions are pre-determined and that human freedom is an illusion, we would undermine the entire ethical domain. That domain presumes that most of us most of the time can make choices based on values we somewhat freely embrace. There would be no moral significance to our behaviour if we had no control over that behaviour; ethics would evaporate into what is sometimes termed "moral nihilism".

While we note them all too briefly here, these are obviously major issues which have exercised the minds of moral philosophers for generations. What is more, they relate to some significant issues of social policy. Social welfare policies, and their sound ethical justifications for example, take a different slant depending on whether we are inclined to "blame the victim" for social circumstances or "blame the system". Our attitudes to punishment for criminal behaviour hinge substantially on our understanding of whether criminals have the freedom to turn from their anti-social ways or whether their actions are an inevitable consequence of factors outside their individual control. After all, we do find it necessary to make a distinction in the law between cases where people can and cannot help what they are doing, that is, where their autonomy is impaired. We allow people to plead temporary insanity, we judge less harshly in cases of diminished responsibility, or in particular we distinguish between cases of shop-lifting and kleptomania where it is contended people are not even aware that they are stealing. By raising the questions of freedom (or autonomy) and determinism (or fatalism) we invite a debate about moral responsibility and the grounds for distinctions such as those referred to above.

Though we might rebut the view that for biological/genetic or socio-cultural/environmental reasons our life paths are pre-plotted so that ethical choice is virtually meaningless, there is another view to note. It is often associated with religious and divine command theory or maybe in our day with certain extreme naturalists. This view virtually claims that there is a moral blueprint in the nature of things which we must follow. Such a view implies very narrow choice as we make our lives in an ethical sense: if we have freedom, it is nothing more than the freedom to live by this blueprint or to suffer the consequences if we do not. Those who promote this viewpoint (like some conservative religious leaders or extreme environmentalists) look with suspicion on those who emphasise radical personal freedom, and who eschew external moral authority and use autonomy as the cornerstone of ethical approaches.

The discussion about determinism and freedom opens up matters of moral development and psychological learning theory. From the determinist camp, moral development theories influenced by the social psychologist BF Skinner (who in turn was influenced by Ivan Pavlov, the experimenter who extrapolated to human behaviour from experiments which conditioned animals) suggest that the major strategy for inculcating so-called moral behaviour should be one of reward and punishment. Clearly there is evidence in childhood development and in the patterns adopted by some adults that only such coercive strategies will produce moral behaviours. Similarly, it is evident that the limitations of our social location (where we live, where we are born) and our genetic inheritance are critical in our ethical formation.

However, the behaviourist or determinist account is not an adequate account of human experience and potential. Such a view downplays the role of human freedom and autonomy and overplays the pain and pleasure principle in learning. Certainly, we can point to instances of persons who, despite great odds, transform their social condition. We could cite dramatic examples in the realm of addictions: people who have decided to change life patterns and then redirected their lives. Moreover, the sweep of human history has seen enormous changes, both good and ill, which are testimony to the fact that we can struggle to improve and alter not merely social practices but whole cultural orientations. Though social movements and historical shifts such as the abolition of the eighteenth century slave trade are complex phenomena, fundamental to them was the ethical and political action of individuals and groups, like William Wilberforce and the Evangelical movement, driven by moral commitment. While there is a tendency in some human beings to accept the way things are, or even to be fearful of freedom and to dismiss responsibility by resorting to rationalisations of destiny and fatalism, there is equally a strong human need to exercise freedom and turn discontent with the way things are into an active, transformative force. After all, if social reality is socially constructed then it can be deconstructed and reconstructed – and if that is the case then at the personal level there is potential for decision, action and change also. If this premise is abandoned, the nerve of moral sensibility is cut and the unacceptable becomes acceptable.

In summary we may say that our freedom is clearly limited by what are sometimes called "life chances" (a term which covers factors affecting our upbringing) and that there may be specific occasions when our actions are not in our control (for instance, a mother stealing food for her starving children after all her possessions were lost in a devastating natural disaster). Nevertheless, though there are factors which influence and even direct our character development, over a considerable span of time we are free to shape our lives and to contribute to the well-being of the wider community. Freedom is not an illusion and ethical choice is all pervasive throughout our lives.

In concluding this section, it is useful to identify two social philosophies which are not only major movements in the study of ethics but also are very influential in contemporary cultures – *liberalism* and *existentialism*. Both are shaped predominantly by an emphasis on human freedom and autonomy. Both emerged in the wake of European civilisation's awakening to the power of humanity to reshape its destiny through scientific discovery, technological invention and democratic political reform.

Liberalism, with its many variants and adherents, is centred on the right of the individual to associate freely in society, a view which in turn is derived from the doctrine that human personhood thrives best when the autonomy of the individual is respected. The classic presentation of this case is John Stuart Mill's *On Liberty* (1859) which argued against the imposition of moral authoritarianism maintaining that restrictions on the liberty of the individual are justifiable only in so far as they are necessary to prevent actual harm to others.

Existentialism is more a philosophical attitude than a tight system. It provides an umbrella under which a number of thinkers have been grouped. Existentialists reject any notions of external blueprints in God, nature or the self as starting points of morality. For them there is no constraint (beyond physical limitations) on the person. "We are condemned to be free" writes Jean-Paul Sartre, the French philosopher who interpreted existentialism in his extensive work *Being and Nothingness*. He rejects preconceived ideas, moral laws or principles. We are what we make of ourselves. Linked to this radical notion of freedom and autonomy, existentialists arguably promote a heightened sense of personal and social responsibility.

3 *Relativism and absolutism*

There was a period in human history when village culture was the focus of one's worldview. In this context one's understanding of morality was constrained by a micro-culture which meant that there was a high degree of consent and agreement to a common ethical code. For most of us that time has long past. We live in a multi-national, multi-cultural environment, conscious of, and even experimenting with, a multiplicity of lifestyles and values. Ethical plurality is characteristic of our worldview. Views on ethics tend to be relative to the culture or sub-culture to which one belongs. This phenomenon which describes the way groups, societies and cultures differ in beliefs, customs and value systems is known as *cultural relativism*.

But what does that mean for us in the study of ethics? As we have seen already, the fact that a principle or practice *is* held by some group does not necessarily mean it is ethically justified. There is therefore a distinction between cultural relativism, which merely describes what is the case in various cultures, and *ethical relativism*. Ethical relativism is a meta-ethical view which claims that what is right or good is always relative to the particular circumstances of cultures, groups or even individuals. It denies there are objective ethical standards.[4]

None of us would concede for a minute that if a certain culture believed that the earth is flat such a belief was acceptable, on scientific grounds. By analogy, we may query whether it follows that if one group believes the practice of genital mutilation is morally justifiable in their culture, others should concede that such a practice is ethically acceptable. If we make that query we are questioning the validity of ethical relativism. We are suggesting that there are grounds which may be beyond the norms and values of a particular culture and call into question certain ethical views and practices within a culture.

Yet ethical relativism is very popular and prevalent in societies like Australia. The view is common that "everyone is entitled to their own beliefs and therefore no one has the right to make ethical judgments". "That's your ethics. These are mine. That's OK". "I don't get involved". "I'm not in her situation" – these are common responses as people in an individualistic culture like ours refuse to be drawn into ethical evaluation of issues beyond their own personal domain. Where does such a relativistic attitude lead us? At one extreme it seems to provide no way of evaluating the moral merits of practices like human slavery or bribery in politics, provided they are practised outside our neighbourhood. On the other hand, in certain matters such as sexual behaviour, at first glance there may be some support for a relativistic view that sexual preferences exercised in private are nobody else's business, although it is immediately apparent that such a view may be drawing on an underlying principle which suggests that this maxim should apply universally, and therefore ceases to be relativistic.

It is relevant to observe that when conversation is engaged around the question, "Should people be allowed to do whatever they want as long as they think it's right?" some relativists are likely to add the significant caveat "as long as they don't harm anyone else". Such a qualified response suggests that there must be certain guidelines or limits within which all humans should behave. There is more than the hint that it is impractical to sustain an unfettered relativist position throughout life: sooner or later, we encounter circumstances that we regard as totally or universally unacceptable.

Furthermore, there is also the problem that ethical relativism often rests on a logical inconsistency. Those who base their relativist position on the value of tolerance have to explain whether or not they expect everyone to be tolerant. If they do not, then they have to explain how intolerance could be consistent with their ethical position. On the other hand, if they do, they are doing something which as relativists they are not supposed to do, that is, making a claim for an ethical value which transcends a culture or particular situation.

The alternative ethical posture to relativism is generally known as *absolutism* which is related to what we term elsewhere as *universalism*. Ethical absolutism maintains that there are absolute moral truths to which all human beings must adhere if they are to be moral. The Ten Commandments or the Universal Declaration of Human Rights could be cited as examples of such truths. Such a view tends to rest on a claim about the unity of the moral community such as we made in Chapter One about the interconnectedness of all life. In traditional religious terms it may rest on the claim about the absoluteness of an all-powerful god who dispenses some moral law for all his/her creation. However, it would be fallacious to imply that absolutism or universalism is usually linked to religious perspectives. An ethic which is built on the proposition that it is always good to minimise the suffering of sentient beings (beings that feel pain and pleasure) makes universalistic claims.

To recap, in what sense is ethical relativism a sustainable position and how might we relate it to absolutism or universalism? Ethical relativism in its extreme form seems ultimately corrosive of ethical discourse and the cultivation of ethics in a communal sense. Nonetheless, inasmuch as it opens the way for the recognition that others may have a different ethical viewpoint from which we may all learn, ethical relativism, as a social practice rather than as an ethical theory, may in fact facilitate the search for so-called core, community values. Certainly, it must be granted that the intolerance of ethical difference sometimes associated with absolutist or universalist positions may lead to moral authoritarianism and coercion which is harmful and also corrosive of ethics in a communal sense. Furthermore, absolutism in its extreme form rests on a meta-ethical proposition which relativists, with some justification reject as untenable, namely that there is a single, true, universal moral code and that moral truths and justifications are not relative to factors that are culturally and historically contingent.

We can never finally shrug off the problems and challenges of relativism or absolutism in our discussion of ethical questions. They will follow us throughout the chapters of this book.

At this stage we may conclude that there are some absolute or universal ethical propositions to which we should adhere, for example, "never take human life unnecessarily", "always conduct affairs honestly", "care for the environment" or the prescriptions of the Universal Declaration of Human Rights. Absolute and universal principles are often too general to deal with specific situations, so they invite the consideration of exceptions or interpretations in particular cultural or local circumstances. In other words, though ethics is not merely relative or subjective, we cannot avoid a relativist, or more accurately, a contextual perspective in applied ethics. Though relativism is misguided, the motivation that has lead many to embrace it -

must not be discounted. There remains a place for a contextual approach in ethical decision-making, though it does not prevent us from seeking ethical agreement across cultures, religions, races or other sub-groups which points in effect to universal ethical values. In that task we will find it instructive to take an objective stance, "the viewpoint of the universe" if you like, which opens ethical issues to a critique transcending cultural norms. Indeed, the justification via moral reasons which a complete ethical system requires must be tested above all on the grounds of their universalisability as well as their application in particular contexts.

Why be Moral?

To conclude this chapter it is appropriate to return to a fundamental, meta-ethical question which pursues us through the discussions of this book: "why be moral anyway?" Many of the matters we have been discussing in these first chapters lead us back to this point. We have already outlined a case for the importance of ethics. We have argued that philosophising inevitably leads to ethical inquiry. Our discussion of egoism and altruism raised the question of motivation in the ethical life. Our examination of the key questions of human freedom and autonomy indicated that human existence is characterised by a radical freedom which requires an ethical response. Each of these discussions implies partial answers to the question, "why be moral?"

This question is in fact a two-dimensional query which, on the one hand, invites us to ask "where does human ethical behaviour come from?" but at another level invites us to inquire about the reasons we can give for our ethical attitudes and behaviours.

To the almost anthropological question "where does ethics come from?" we might get various answers. In fact, it can be demonstrated that moral practices and beliefs in many societies are transmitted across the generations through tradition, law and religion. That's where they've come from! A closer scrutiny might suggest that morality is fundamentally generated by a need for survival and to avoid social disintegration. "If our species doesn't learn to live together and in harmony with the Earth, it will die!" Perhaps a positive way of answering this almost anthropological version of the question, which at the same time does justice to the various traditions and beliefs which have been vehicles for transmitting moral codes through numerous societies, is simply to say: morality has come about because of common human needs; the living of worthwhile human lives based on friendship, love, freedom, peace, creativity and stability is best served by learning and practising a common, cooperative ethical framework. If this explanation is to be summarised crudely as the need for survival, then so be it; but it is not simply the negative response to a barbaric state of nature. It may also be seen as the response of a noble species to the desire to fashion a harmonious environment!

However, it is the other way of posing this meta-ethical question which interests us: "why be moral?" or "what reasons can we give for our ethical attitudes and behaviours?" Framing the question this way points us to that core concern in ethics, namely, *justification*, that is, the reasons or arguments we can offer for being good or doing right.

Once I asked a class the question "why be moral?" and received a very straight-forward reply: "Because if you're not, you might get AIDS". Now that answer certainly illustrated a narrow, sexually focussed understanding of what morality is, but on the other hand it was a very clear example offering a justification for what might be termed "good" or "right".

As ethicists we can begin to analyse the nature of that justification. Clearly it is one which supports the view that moral judgments should be made on the basis of the consequences of actions: one should avoid the consequence, AIDS. But is a style of moral decision-making based solely on consequences satisfactory or adequate? Does the justification hold up? Are there other types of answers that can be given which provide a better overall endorsement of the ethical life? Perhaps, the reply to my question could have been: "We should be moral because we would expect others to treat us morally". Such an answer might provide a stronger basis for a sustainable communal ethical life.

In pursuing the question of justification in this preliminary way, we are opening up a discussion on normative ethical theories, which is the subject of the next chapter. In a sense, a justificatory sense, these theories and the accompanying debates about them, are attempting to answer the question, "What is the reason for your ethical choice?" or "Why be moral?" It may be that the theories which emerge from the answers will all prove inadequate or only partially applicable, but the pursuit of a systematic normative basis for the ethical life is a necessary, desirable and rewarding task in our development as rational beings who, inevitably, choose among values.

CHAPTER REVIEW

Compose your own review:

- Identify the new terms you have encountered in this chapter. Can you explain them in your own words?
- Check the glossary at the end of the book for: egoism, epistemology, ethics, existentialism, metaphysics, meta-ethics, nihilism, normative ethics, philosophy, relativism, universalism.

FURTHER READING

Almond, B and Hill, D (eds) (1991) *Applied Philosophy: Morals and Metaphysics in Contemporary Debate*, London: Routledge.

Berg, J (1998) "How Could Ethics Depend on Religion?" in Singer, P (ed) *A Companion to Ethics*, Oxford: Blackwell Publishers.

Nuttall, J (1993) *Moral Questions*, Oxford: Blackwell Publishers.

Scanlon, TM (2000) *What We Owe to Each Other*, Harvard: Harvard University Press.

QUESTIONS FOR DISCUSSION

1. Answer for yourself the question: why should I be moral? Do I believe I should always be moral? Where do I think my own moral values come from?
2. What role does religion have in ethics? Is it possible to establish an ethical system not based on religious belief? If so, what might it be based on?
3. Some Aboriginal peoples (such as the Inuit in North America) once practised the custom of leaving their elders to die when they could no longer travel with the tribe to fresh hunting grounds. To them, this was morally acceptable. What is your view? How do you relate this case to euthanasia in our society? What are the reasons for your view? Consider this case in the light of the discussion in this chapter with respect to ethics and the law, egoism and altruism, and ethical relativism.

CHAPTER TWO NOTES

1 See, Jonsen, AR and Toulmin, S (1988) *The Abuse of Casuistry: a History of Moral Reasoning*, Berkeley: University of California Press.

2 Any reader interested to follow up the debate about varying brands of "theism" may find the work of Charles Birch of interest (eg *On Purpose*, University of NSW Press, 1990). Birch calls himself a pan-en-theist and is in the tradition of the process philosopher, AN Whitehead.

3 These three issues are very important, but to the novice reader they may also be difficult. Do not be discouraged if you find the discussion hard to follow. The general reader may scan the discussion cursorily. For the student of ethics it is time for greater concentration and persistence!

4 For a defence of ethical relativism, see Harman, G (1996) *Moral Relativism and Moral Objectivity*, Cambridge: Blackwell, chapter 1.

CHAPTER THREE

ETHICAL THEORY: AN OVERVIEW

From *Good Will Hunting*

WILL

Say I'm working at NSA. Somebody puts a code on my desk, something nobody else can break. So I take a shot at it and maybe I break it. And I'm really happy with myself, 'cause I did my job well. But maybe that code was the location of some rebel army in North Africa or the Middle East. Once they have that location, they bomb the village where the rebels were hiding and fifteen hundred people I never had a problem with get killed.

Quoted from Damon, M, & Affleck, B, *Good Will Hunting*,
Faber & Faber, London, 1998, pp 125-126.

Can we then, between this Scylla and Charybdis [dilemma] of ethical enquiry, avoiding on the one hand doctrines that merely bring us back to common opinion with all its imperfections, and on the other hand doctrines that lead us round in a circle, find any way of obtaining self-evident moral principles of real significance?

Henry Sidgwick, *The Methods of Ethics* (1907)

When we give ethical sanction or endorsement to certain attitudes or actions we are confronted, directly or indirectly, with the question: "On what basis or by what authority or for what reasons do we decide what should be on any list of moral prohibitions or ethical imperatives?". For instance, why should politicians always tell the truth or why should sexual relationships be confined to marriage?

One answer to the first question is that politicians ought always tell the truth because if they lie to the public they contribute to an erosion of the public trust on which democracy rests. Such an explanation suggests that *consequences* are the primary consideration in reasoning ethically about this issue. As we shall see in this chapter, considering consequences is characteristic of one set of normative theories. On the other hand, other types of justification can be offered. Responding to the second query about sex and marriage, one answer might be, sexual relationships ought to be confined to marriage because the God-ordained natural order requires that sex be used primarily for procreation which in turn requires a caring commitment to marriage and family. Such an explanation implies that there are *duties* sanctioned by God or nature which are the primary consideration in ethical reasoning, again suggesting a particular type of normative theory.

The range of justifications which can be offered for these moral questions is indicative of various styles or approaches to ethical decision-making, which in turn suggest a range of ethical frameworks (or normative theories). Our purpose in this chapter therefore is to identify and classify basic approaches to ethical justification. This exercise will help clarify the language of normative ethics, and may assist us not only to converse about particular issues but also more consciously, consistently and accurately to address the applied ethics topics of later chapters. In our everyday lives we employ elements of these ethical frameworks, though most of us do not fit neatly into the types these classifications suggest. We cannot expect that these theories provide precise formulae for resolving ethical dilemmas but they may indicate ways of going about deciding how to resolve them. Each of these theories has certain strengths and weaknesses which we will identify in our discussion.

We begin with the two major and diverging viewpoints which emerge in ethical theory: *consequentialism*, where ethical decisions are based primarily on calculating the *good* in terms of consequences, and *non-consequentialism*, where decisions are determined not by consequences but by some clear intrinsic view of the *right* or one's *duty*. The consequentialist approach is a version[1] of what is technically termed *teleology*: the Greek etymology of this word, *telos* meaning "a goal" or "end", indicates that these are theories in which the end justifies the means. The non-consequentialist approach is traditionally known as *deontological*: indicating, from its Greek origins, *deon* meaning "duty", that it is an approach to ethics in which a sense of duty or principle prescribes the ethical decision.

These contrasting ethical styles are often encountered in debates about controversial issues. Take for example the vexed community debate about abortion. There are those who, invoking an absolute principle of the sanctity of human life (and, quite reasonably, defining the foetus as a human individual), in all circumstances and regardless of consequences (except perhaps where there is a clash of rights between the mother's and the foetus' life), maintain that abortion cannot be ethically justified. On the other hand, there are those who believe that the ethical justification for abortion depends primarily on a case-by-case, contextual calculation about the consequences of the decision. The former is an instance of non-consequential or deontological ethical decision-making and the second exemplifies consequential or teleological reasoning.

Let us begin by examining this consequentialist approach to ethics.

Consequentialism

The best known and widely accepted form of consequentialism is *utilitarianism*. As a teleological theory, utilitarianism emphasises happiness or pleasure or utility as the desirable goal for human choice and action. Its approach is popularly summarised in the phrase: "the greatest good for the greatest number". We may distinguish two varieties of utilitarianism: *act utilitarianism* and *rule utilitarianism*. Most of the discussion here refers to the former variety which disregards rules if they are absolute, calculating happiness in terms of the consequences of acts. However, some utilitarians are prepared to nominate rules which provide beneficial consequences when they are followed. Such rules (perhaps, "never kill except in self-defence") are not absolute in the sense that they require interpretation in particular circumstances.

Utilitarianism has a long history but it was in the nineteenth century, originally through the writings of Jeremy Bentham and then later through John Stuart Mill, that it was clearly articulated. In contemporary ethics, philosophers such as Peter Singer and Jonathan Glover are well-known utilitarians. Bentham suggested a rather crude calculus for determining ethical questions based on an assessment of maximising pleasure over pain. Mill refined the theory and linked it with his political philosophy of liberalism which aimed at maximising the good for society through enhancing the freedom of individuals to determine their own good. Mill insists on disinterestedness as well as self-interest. That is, in calculating the happiness or unhappiness to result from an action, everybody with an interest in the matter is entitled to have their happiness considered equally with everybody else. Mill puts it this way in his *Utilitarianism*:

> the happiness which forms the utilitarian standard of what is right in conduct, is not the agent's own happiness, but that of all concerned. As between his own happiness and that of others, utilitarianism requires him to be as strictly impartial as a disinterested and benevolent spectator.[2]

Such a view has radical implications because it opens up for review any conventional or revealed morality which is insisted upon regardless of its consequences. Utilitarianism challenges subjectivist views based on subjective approval and disapproval; similarly it challenges cultural and ethical relativism when that implies that acts generally approved by a particular society are right and those disapproved are wrong.

It is important to recognise how utilitarianism emerged as a response to concerns about ethics and public policy. Bentham and Mill were both progressive social reformers. Bentham was alarmed at the fact that numerous citizens were punished under the criminal law for petty offences and victimless crimes and, indeed, that often moral judgments in English society of the eighteenth century had little justifiable reference to what was harmful to society. Similarly, Mill confronted the morality of his time, which promoted the subjection of women. The conventions of the time maintained that women had an inferiority to men which made it wrong for them to enter certain occupations such as law and medicine. The utilitarian calculus provided a method for assessing the social good and social harm of such conventions. Utilitarianism and liberalism in tandem offered a basis for critiquing any prevailing moral view which did not serve the interests of society.

However, it should not be assumed that utilitarianism is unquestionably enlightened. Sometimes, it is argued that, in justifying challenges to conventional morality (for instance, the vow of life-long marriage) utilitarians support the breaking of promises and even unbridled hedonism. Utilitarians may try to defend their position against these charges by claiming that the consequential calculation has been imperfectly or narrowly applied if it results in harm to a particular person. Such a defence betrays another weakness of the consequential position: is it possible to identify, know and calculate *all* the consequences of one's actions?

Another objection is that the utilitarian calculus is linked too easily with economic instrumentalism which treats human beings as means to serve the interests of the economy. Critics argue that the same view which maximises the common interest may work against the interests of minorities, groups who do not measure up to the criteria of usefulness. It is a predominantly utilitarian argument that is used to exclude from mainstream schools a disabled child who is very disruptive and difficult to manage in the classroom; the judgment to exclude is usually defended on the utilitarian grounds that to leave such a child in the classroom is not beneficial to the majority of students and is really in no one's interests. Opponents of such a decision will generally resort to an argument based on the rights of the particular individual child. In other words, the contention is that utilitarianism can justify the violation of human rights.

As an overall theory of normative justification, utilitarianism has been accused of failing a crucial test. It may not ultimately serve the cause of justice when that cause requires the defence of the vulnerable or the uneconomic, and it may lead to a spirit of cold pragmatism which offends our moral sensitivities.

Nonetheless, as we shall see in the later discussion of applied ethics topics, utilitarianism provides a persuasive argument in many debates about social policy, often leading to what many would regard as socially progressive stances. It continues to appeal as an ethical framework that is relevant and applicable to certain problems in their context. Furthermore, in a world of finite resources, mass societies and corporations, politicians, business persons, health care providers, educators, and the like will continue to draw on utilitarian justifications for policies which are arguably for the good of society.

There are other forms of consequentialism.

One that is broadly compatible with utilitarianism (especially rule utilitarianism) and with the *ethic of response* we encounter in the next chapter is *situation ethics*. Like other forms of consequentialism, situation ethics proposes that ethical decisions be made in context taking account of specific circumstances, not abstractly according to decontextualised maxims. Given its clearest expression by Joseph Fletcher, it has been inspired by a style of theological existentialism which focuses on human freedom and responsibility as the *sine qua non* of ethics. Rather than exalting utility or happiness as the *telos* for ethical action, it speaks of love as the determining, calculating principle. Love is understood in *agapeistic* terms (*agape* being the Greek word in the New Testament referring to God's love). This agape love says, "I give my love, requiring nothing in return". This is a very demanding quality for any realistic human ethic.

To summarise, in situation ethics the good is that which is lovingly intended and which maximises loving consequences. For Fletcher, only the end can justify the means; love is that end. Within Christian ethical circles (though this approach is not necessarily confined to that religious framework), situation ethics provides a challenging alternative to dogmatic moral theologies. It is therefore not surprising that it has been opposed by conservative moral theologians.

Situation ethics holds that nothing is good in and of itself except for love. Actions are good when they benefit human beings and wrong when others are hurt – this is the sole criterion. Fletcher sums up his key thesis by quoting a former Archbishop of Canterbury, William Temple: "There is only one ultimate and invariable duty, and its formula is 'Thou shalt love thy neighbour as thyself' ... this is the whole of moral duty."[3]

The critics of situation ethics regard it as a weak guide to moral action and as open to the abuse of ethical relativism. They point out that horrific acts may be justified even in the name of love. Indeed, this approach suffers from all the weaknesses attributed generally to consequentialist theories. However, we might ask whether in fact situation ethics is interested in consequences, or whether its focus on love sees ethical justification only in terms of motivation and intention. In addition, Fletcher's formulation is too individualistic. The examples he uses are invariably of personal decisions in sexual morality or medical ethics. Situation ethics is in need of a more adequate theory of justice and the substance to serve as an ethic for social morality and public policy.[4]

Finally, we need to note a contrasting form of consequentialism referred to as *ethical egoism*. As a teleological view, this approach poses self-interest as the goal of human ethical action. If I am an *individual ethical egoist* I believe that everyone ought to act in my self-interest, but as a *universal ethical egoist* I would maintain that everyone should always act in their own self-interest regardless of the interests of others unless those interests also serve theirs.

There are apparent advantages to this approach and it is probably quite popular in society generally. Arguably, it is easier to base our decisions on our own interests rather than others' because it is easier to know what they are than it is to know the interests of others. Also, as we noted in the previous chapter's discussion of egoism, some social philosophers have maintained that this view fits best with our human nature and our capitalist economies. However, when analysed, these are not convincing arguments. Ethical egoism offers no consistent method of resolving conflicts of self-interest and in the increasingly crowded and complex communities in which we live, such conflicts are omnipresent. If those communities are to be workable, they require negotiation, compromise and even self-sacrifice. In the end, though many of us, from time to time in practice, act on the basis of ethical egoism, and while it is ridiculous to promote an ethical theory which disregards self-interest, ethical egoism offends against our sense that the worthwhile ethical life involves, first and foremost, consideration of others. For that reason, utilitarianism which claims that no one's happiness is to be considered more important than anyone else's, is a superior theory to its rival consequentialist approach, ethical egoism. Despite the shortcomings we noted earlier, utilitarianism can be implemented in a way that aims at the just society; it is not so evident how universal ethical egoism can make that claim.

Non-Consequentialism

The challenge to consequentialism and teleology generally comes from the approach which we earlier identified with theories of duty, obligation or rights, that is deontology.[5] Deontology affirms that duties must be obeyed or rights acknowledged regardless of the consequences; hence the term non-consequentialism. Non-consequentialist ethics enjoin us to do the right thing simply because it is the right thing, intrinsically; no extrinsic justification is needed as with consequentialism.

Moral views based on religious belief are often deontological in character, although many ethicists of religious persuasion adopt the other frameworks of this chapter. Nonetheless, the traditional use of religious authority associated with the absolute injunctions of the Ten Commandments are expressions of a non-consequential approach. Indeed we speak of *Divine Command Theory* by which we mean that the duty or right to be obeyed is revealed by a divine authority and ought to be followed regardless of consequences. Apart from the general problems with non-consequentialism which we shall refer to later, this approach has the additional complication of verifying the existence or power of the authority in question. Nonetheless, for many people of faith such an approach provides a generally workable framework for moral behaviour.

The moral pronouncements of Pope John Paul II and the official Roman Catholic magisterium, as it is termed, provide recent evidence of non-consequentialism at work in a religious context. Because John Paul II has credentials as a moral philosopher and has weighed into the debates of interest in this chapter in a very public manner, it is instructive to note, rather briefly, his approach. There have been several encyclicals[6] on these matters which illustrate this position.

The core of the case being made by John Paul II is that there is an objective moral order. Relativism, scepticism and individualism, present even in the church, threaten this order. This official church teaching eschews consequentialism, though it derives from a form of teleology inasmuch as it sees a purpose in the natural law or order. In its Christian version natural law presumes a participation of the eternal law in the rational human being and, thereby, an ability for human beings to discern the principles which underpin the natural order, and to live to that end.

John Paul II's approach expresses what is technically known as *essentialism*, leading to a preoccupation with the abstract human essence to the neglect of its embodied situation. This type of argument allows the Pope to declare some actions such as contraception and homosexual acts, but also matters like violations of human rights, arbitrary imprisonment or dishonest business practices, as "intrinsically evil", regardless of circumstances.

There are some, even within the Roman Catholic church, who question whether the papal diagnosis and prescription for our moral malaise addresses the authentic human condition of our technological age because it tends to deal with human experience in a decontextualised way. They are questioning not only the relevance of non-consequentialism but the interpretation of "the divine command" or "truth" (*veritas*), the metaphysic (belief system or theology) which underpins the Vatican's deontology - but this is a matter beyond the scope of this chapter.

The most influential figure in our ethical tradition promoting the deontological view is *Immanuel Kant*.[7] This German philosopher of the eighteenth century sought to develop a science of morals which, though absolute in its requirements, was not based on religious premises. The authority of human reason replaced the divine command. This moral philosophy was founded on rationality around propositions that are logically consistent. For Kant the perfect moral agent is perfectly rational because it is only when we act rationally, according to rules which are perfectly general, universal and consistent, that we will act morally.

By applying the tests of rationality, consistency and universality, Kant arrives at a moral principle which is binding on all rational beings. He calls this the *Categorical Imperative* because it commands absolutely, regardless of desires or circumstances. There is nothing hypothetical, contingent or conditional about this. Expressed as a universalising principle, the Categorical Imperative declares: "Act only according to that maxim by which you can at the same time will that it should become a universal law".

The Categorical Imperative relies on a criterion of universal reciprocity and may be regarded as a restatement of the Golden Rule: "Do to others as you would have them do to you". This principle gives us a method for morally evaluating an act. Ask yourself what rule you would be following if you did something. This rule is what is meant by "maxim". If you are not willing to have this maxim become a universal law that should be followed by everyone, then the act is wrong. So, "don't lie" is a universal law according to Kant and his Categorical Imperative because you would not wish to be lied to.

Kant's moral philosophy and the character of its absolute duties was built on the cornerstone of a particular view of the human person. Not only did he place great faith in our powers of rationality, he stressed the autonomy of each individual by locating the authority for moral decision within the person, not in some external authority like God or even the law. Moreover, a key element of his ethics and of Kantian theory is enshrined in his principle about respect for persons: "Act so that you treat humanity, whether in your own person or in that of another, always as an end and never as a means only".

Undoubtedly, the Kantian version of non-consequentialism has been very influential, especially in relation to debate about rights and justice because of the high value it places on all persons and because it is not open to persuasion by pragmatic considerations.

Criticisms of Kant's approach require a sophisticated analysis of his underlying philosophical presumptions. Opponents argue, with some plausibility, that he places too much reliance on human rationality; also they argue that he makes too great a claim for the criteria of universalisability, consistency and reversibility in providing us with workable solutions to moral dilemmas.

Kantian ethics, and non-consequentialism generally, may be criticised for an inflexibility which cannot resolve conflicts between absolute rules. According to their line, "Do not break promises" and "Do not kill", are absolute moral laws. Yet, it is possible to conceive of circumstances in which those principles conflict. That is, in not breaking a promise the result may be that someone is killed. Now a Kantian might fairly want to discuss the case and provide exceptions based on the invalidity of the promise if it were made in bad faith. Such reasoning is interesting because it begins to depart from the strict line of an obligation to follow rules absolutely without regard to circumstances. The problem to be resolved is how to decide between conflicting duties, that is how to obey different but equally absolute rules. In attempting to get beyond this impasse, some adherents of non-consequentialism may be forced to resort to consequentialist modes of reasoning - indeed to refer to the consequences as justification for the rule that is absolute. So, when pressed as to why we should not break promises it might eventually be conceded that the *consequences* of not following that rule are unacceptable for marriage or for democracy or for the other fiduciary relationships of society.

Take the case of a medical doctor who is the only medico in an isolated area. This practitioner has a deontologically based conscientious objection to abortion. She is faced with a woman patient with a 15-week pregnancy who insists that, because of her isolation, if the doctor will not perform an abortion on her she will resort to assistance and methods to effect the abortion that the doctor knows could have severe medical complications. What ought the doctor do? Is she not faced with conflicting (absolute) moral demands? Can she reasonably defend her choice - either way - without giving some account that takes seriously the consequences of that choice. If the doctor proceeds with the abortion and follows the medical injunction to act for the patient's welfare she might cite as a reason "the consequential health of the mother". If she refuses to do the abortion and follows the conscientious injunction not to take the life of another (the well-formed foetus), she might cite as a reason "the consequential impact on her integrity as a doctor or the effects of abortion in the wider society". In either case the moral defence advanced resorts to citing consequences.

One prominent follower of Kant, Sir William Daniel Ross, attempted to deal with the problem of conflicts among duties. He developed a modification of Kantian ethics which really embraces elements of the consequentialist approach inasmuch as it seeks to exercise its obligation to fulfil duties by reasoning about them in their context. As a result, he introduced the notion of *prima facie duties*,[8] arguing that most moral rules such as "tell the truth" express a prima facie duty, but they have the potential to be overridden by other duties. So, to assist in working through conflicts of duty he itemised and classified duties in a hierarchical scheme which made distinctions such as those between duties "arising from my previous acts" (for example, a marriage covenant) and duties "derived from other people's acts" (such as, favours granted). Whether Ross' approach and selection of duties actually avoids the conflict of duties question is problematic, and whether he has compromised deontology to such a degree that he is inconsistent is another criticism to be considered. Nonetheless, in the case of the medico described above, Ross at least provides a framework for wrestling with the conflict, and for being faithful to what are judged to be more fundamental duties.

Ross' attempt indicates both the longstanding impact of deontology in our ethical culture and the need for moving beyond an inflexible deontology to establish a morality for the ordinary and exceptional challenges of life.

Contractarianism, Justice and Rights

Issues of human rights and social justice are topical in societies throughout the world, and they are certainly relevant to the material in later chapters of this book. The United Nations *Declaration of Human Rights* has been a powerful influence in international affairs in the past

50 years. The need for a "social justice platform", whatever its content, is regarded as important by political parties across the ideological spectrum in most modern societies. However, the terms "justice" and "rights" are often used loosely; sometimes they are even interchanged erroneously as if the granting of rights was the sum total of social justice. What then do ethicists have to say about "justice" and "rights" and what basis in normative theory can be identified to support their claims? This section contains a very rudimentary introduction to discussions of social or political philosophy.

First, what is the basis for moral rights? The view influential in the development of the American Constitution and its *Declaration of Independence* is that rights are inherent to the natural order (given by a deistic god). The English philosopher, John Locke, through his theory of individual liberty rights is the author of this approach. It results in a focus on the right of individuals to be left alone by governments and on property rights. Its contemporary proponents in political philosophy are sometimes called libertarians.

An alternative strand in the debate about rights is found in the works of Thomas Hobbes, who saw rights emerging from the contract we need to develop with a powerful ruler to protect us from the threat of the nasty and brutish state of nature which would otherwise threaten us all. From the reasonable viewpoint it is to the mutual advantage of us all to trade off some freedoms for social benefits. To live in society, people must agree to follow certain rules (don't steal, don't murder) and these rules imply corresponding rights (rights to citizenship, rights to security). Hobbes' social contract is designed to protect us from those who might harm us. Despite its other merits, it has little to say on the protection of the harmless (and vulnerable) like children or the disabled.

Both Locke and Hobbes provide minimalist theories of social obligation, concentrating on protecting the individual from harm. Locke and Hobbes predate much of the development of modern, democratic societies, though their views were important to the eventual development of democracy. They also developed their theories before Kantianism and utilitarianism and the political philosophies of liberalism and socialism. Throughout the twentieth century, progressive economic and political theorists seeking a just society which protects human rights and welfare have developed social policies which draw on liberalism and socialism for their justification often in a utilitarian context. However, in the latter decades of the twentieth century, a significant philosophical challenge to that trend was instituted by a return to Kantianism as the basis for the social contract, with ensuing implications for justice and rights. The duty-based focus on the rights of all persons who were to be regarded as of equal worth was championed by a Harvard philosopher, John Rawls, who published *A Theory of Justice* in 1971. It was a direct challenge to utilitarian or majoritarian ways of calculating just outcomes. Rawls' work has sparked an ongoing debate of relevance to social policy formation.[9]

In the tradition of contract theorists, Rawls invites us to consider a hypothetical state which he calls "the original position". Let us assume for the purposes of argument that we are on a spaceship, never to return to earth, setting out to construct a totally new society for ourselves and future generations. We agree to lay down certain principles to enable the development of a just society. That is, we agree to construct a social contract which is binding on all as a kind of template governing the future society. Rawls lays down certain characteristics about the nature of people on this quest, which reflect the liberal and Kantian assumptions he makes. The people making this contract in the hypothetical state are: (i) self-interested, (ii) equal in the sense that no one has a prior claim to power over anyone else, (iii) rational and informed so that they are able to reason about the impact of the contract, and (iv) ignorant about their future or status in the society being built. This last condition he calls the "veil of ignorance" and it is critical to his method for, he claims, it ensures impartiality or the conditions of fairness as the basis of his theory. Indeed, his theory is referred to as "justice as fairness" (whereas a utilitarian view of justice might be termed "justice as the social good"). The veil of ignorance means participants in the new society do not know their social status, whether or not they will be male or female, white or black, able-bodied or disabled and so on. This, he trusts, will guarantee rational disinterestedness in designing the principles for the just society.

Under these conditions what then will people choose? Rawls believes they will only choose a contract which would not disadvantage them - remember their self-interest - should they turn out to have some disadvantage (such as economic poverty) in the future society. In other words, whatever else they agree to, they must make sure that they could accept being one of the new society's weakest or least fortunate members.

It follows, according to Rawls, that we can define two principles on which justice can be built:[10]

(i) *The freedom principle* states:

> each person is to have an equal right to the most extensive basic liberties compatible with a like liberty for all.

This principle underpins the normal civil liberties of modern democratic societies and protects personal freedoms providing others are not harmed, in much the way that JS Mill's liberalism outlined. This principle has lexical priority, that is, it maintains that the conditions of liberty in a just society take precedence over the equality principle.

(ii) *The equality and social difference principle* states:

> inequalities of wealth, power, status and income in their new society can only be justified if they are to the greatest benefit of the least advantaged … and if they go with positions or appointments which are open to all in conditions of fair equality of opportunity …

This principle addresses issues of equality and inequality in society. It accepts that there will be inequalities but endorses equality of opportunity along with what is a potentially radical strategy for addressing these inequalities. The principle asserts that the only justified inequalities or discriminations in the society should be those that advantage the most disadvantaged. It is therefore sometimes referred to as *the difference principle*.

Rawls' liberal welfare approach, as it has been characterised, supports progressive taxation which would tax the higher incomes more and redistribute benefits via a social wage. Likewise, this approach supports special measures to enable disadvantaged groups (say, Aboriginal peoples in Australia) to have special entry rights to higher education and so on. Rawls has provided a theory relevant to moral problems associated with distribution of goods and resources, such as world hunger, welfare, job discrimination and affirmative action and other problems involving the rights of citizens.

The Rawlsian social contract has attracted considerable discussion.[11] Critique stems from what is argued to be Rawls' flawed view of human nature and society which, it is said, places too much faith in human rationality and underplays the role of social conflict and struggle between vested interests in the quest for social justice. Certain critics say his attempt to develop justice through impartiality is politically naive, for equality of worth (the basis of fairness) can only be guaranteed by equality of power. To them, Rawls fails to see social reality from the point of view of the oppressed and disadvantaged. Rawls' reliance on reason can only take us part of the way, because the cause of equality through justice often requires struggle and partisanship, which might necessitate the foregoing of individual liberties and special interests. Criticism has not only come from those who believe that justice as fairness does not go far enough in terms of social equality (the left), but also from those (on the right) who regard his view as too radical in a way that ends up compounding injustice by limiting rights.[12]

In this section about justice and rights the concept of contractarianism has been introduced. That "theory" is not really an alternative to the consequentialist and non-consequentialist approaches, but rather it provides tools for examining social, political and legal ethical questions. It is a device to be used by other ethical traditions. So in Rawls for instance, we see the contractarian device around the original position being used within a Kantian framework to develop a rights and justice theory based on impartiality. Though this superficial treatment of his views and those of his critics does not do them "justice", it provides some background to the use of the term justice or fairness in later chapters, where the term is used with a sense of appropriate partiality, recognising that social justice is forged in the furnace of competing interests.

An Ethic of Care

Coinciding with the recent debate in moral and political philosophy regarding social justice and rights, has been the emergence of a feminist perspective on philosophy and ethics in particular. The idea of a female ethic and a feminist critique of traditional ethical theories is more than a footnote to our discussions: it provides a persuasive alternative emphasis and methodology for normative ethics which irrevocably affects ethics as a study and practice. No longer does the male voice and perspective dominate Western moral philosophy the way it has since the time of Aristotle, those times when Athenians did not even include women among their citizenry let alone in their philosophical discourse.

The fundamental question provoked by the feminist "care theorists" is whether or not men and women differ when it comes to ethical approaches. Though the general answer to that question is affirmative, among feminist theorists there are varying interpretations as to the extent of that difference and the reason for it. At one extreme, writers like Mary Daly adopt an essentialist position maintaining that there are inherent differences in the nature of men and women, the consequence of which is that a male-dominated world produces violence and injustice whereas a female-run world would automatically be cooperative and peaceful. The position we elaborate in this section is not based on such an essentialist view but rather recognises that differences between men and women's behaviour and ethical outlooks reflect their different experiences of formative nurturing, socialisation, and subsequent social roles. In other words, the male/female difference in approach to ethics is more a matter of social development than innate inheritance.

The ground-breaking research which has influenced feminist ethics is that of Carol Gilligan. Gilligan reported that research in a book entitled *In a Different Voice* (1982). It was a major critique of the theories of cognitive moral development expounded by her famous Harvard colleague Lawrence Kohlberg. Kohlberg developed a model outlining stages of moral development which identified the highest (or most advanced ethically) stage as one with a highly developed sense of justice, rights and principles. Gilligan was alarmed that in his research sample, Kohlberg had a disproportionate number of males qualifying for the highest stage of moral development. Her subsequent research led to the conclusion that Kohlberg's findings were distorted because they gave greater weight to male ethical tendencies (in a Western cultural context), failing to recognise that women reasoned differently about moral dilemmas. The differences which Gilligan, and those following her, identify are as follows:

Men are more likely to:

1. think in abstract principles and,
2. see moral problems as arising from conflicts between individuals, and
3. appeal to the rights of individuals to resolve conflicts.

Whereas women are more likely to:

1. focus on particular situations rather than think abstractly;

2. see moral problems as arising from the needs of our ongoing relationships, and
3. appeal to the needs of others and mutual obligations toward them to resolve problems.

It is worth noting that Gilligan and many feminist writers point out that these characteristics are not exclusively gender specific. That is, males may adopt the so-called ethical characteristics of women and vice versa, the variable seemingly being social formation and role.

A focus on care, compassion and relationships provides the core of the feminist approach to normative ethics. We call this approach an *ethic of care*. It does not necessarily imply a complete rejection of consequentialism, non-consequentialism or contract-arianism but finds that those approaches need to be re-evaluated with a view to whether these traditional theories exemplify the male perspective to the exclusion of the care/female perspective. However, it is apparent that the feminist emphasis on making judgments in terms of their impact on relationships gives it a distinctly teleological flavour. At the same time, the ethic of care and situation ethics have a lot in common, for both elevate the injunction to care or to love to the status of a duty, applied nonetheless in specific contexts.

The contrast between traditional ethical approaches, "the justice perspective", and the feminist revisions, "the care perspective", is well summarised by Diane Meyers and Eva Feder Kittay:

> The morality of rights and formal reasoning is the one familiar to us from the liberal tradition of Locke, Kant, and, most recently, Rawls. It posits an autonomous moral agent who discovers and applies a set of fundamental rules through the use of universal and abstract reason. The morality of care and responsibility is an alternate set of moral concerns that Gilligan believes she has encountered in her investigation of women's moral decision-making. Here, the central preoccupation is a responsiveness to others that dictates providing care, preventing harm, and maintaining relationships.[13]

Of the growing number of scholars, male as well as female, writing ethics from this feminist perspective the following may be noted:

- *Alison M Jaggar*[14] who affirms that moral agents are not separate, autonomous, rational beings as Mill, Kant, Rawls and others insist. She also rejects the possibility and desirability of impartiality and its hypothetical companion, universal moral rules.

- *Virginia Held*[15] and *Nell Noddings*[16] who depart from male-inspired ethical theories based on principles like utility or a categorical imperative, maintain by contrast that a more adequate and life-affirming ethical theory, for women at least, is based on the experience of caring and particularly the mothering experience and our remembrance of being cared for in infancy. Such approaches tend to have the practical advantage of supporting ethics education and the cultivation of moral sensitivity, whereas they are weaker in the justificatory discourse which has been the traditional hallmark of ethics.

Some critics claim that the ethic of care is problematic inasmuch as it cannot be demonstrated that (a) the ethic of care can fulfil all the tasks required of a normative theory and, (b) the traditional theories necessarily and always exclude the values and considerations important to the ethic of care.

As a result, in our search for an appropriate normative theory, rather than repudiating outright the standard theories discussed earlier, we want to realign their emphases incorporating the care perspective, while accepting many of the criticisms (like excessive rationalism or reliance on impartiality). We will maintain that care and justice are two sides of the one coin.[17] Indeed, the practical quest for justice must be tempered by the relational and interpersonal concerns of care and compassion. Otherwise that quest may degenerate tyrannically into the mere imposition of social order and control.

In a related fashion, feminists remind us of the need to integrate the concerns of the so-called public and private spheres. Though the reality of this distinction may be overstated, it cannot be denied. Justice needs to be brought into the domestic or "home" context which, in the past has generally been seen as the sphere of women, just as care must find a way into the public arena. Feminists have reminded us, "the personal is political"; in turn, politics must take account of the personal. It would be a grave mistake to confine an "ethic of care" to the realm of personal life, thereby risking its subordination to the supposedly masculine "ethic of justice".

Virtue Theory

The challenge to the consequentialist/non-consequentialist dominance in ethical theory by the ethic of care has coincided with, and to an extent been supported by, the renaissance of a view which originated from Aristotle, namely *virtue theory*. The neo-Aristotelian presentation of virtue ethics points to limitations in the theories of the right and the good, theories that promote the justificatory response to the question, "what ought we do?" Virtue theorists doubt whether the ethical life is necessarily based on a set of principles or rules of reason which require deliberation and calculation. In any case, they add, this approach seems impractical for ordinary life decisions: it assumes highly developed cognitive powers and the time to exercise moral reason, whereas, in practice, we act more instinctively. The argument runs, the truly honest person does not calculate or reason about lying or truth-telling, she *is* honest.

So, virtue theory suggests that the central ethical question is not "what ought we *do* ..." but rather, "who ought we *become* ..." Here the focus is on personal disposition and character, the moral qualities of a person. It is the good person who knows and does the right thing. Such a twist on the quest for normative frameworks is particularly interesting because it provides a useful focus on the development of the moral self and the moral life - the sort of issues to be taken up in the final chapter, "Cultivating an Ethical Life". It also bears upon the concern that despite our *reasoning* about what is right or good, we may still not *choose* to do the right or good. In virtue theory, the aim is to foster living well so that good and right behaviour emanates from within the person.

In the Aristotelian tradition, the starting point for virtue theory is a prior question: "is there a goal or purpose for human living, something for which we exist, some overarching purpose for human living, a master virtue, which provides a benchmark for the good life?" Obviously, in terms of our discussion earlier in this chapter, this line of inquiry is clearly a teleological pursuit, but it is to be distinguished from the teleology associated with utilitarianism which simply promotes the best overall consequences. Aristotelian teleology is more concerned to identify the qualities that are characteristic of the life that achieves its proper end. Those qualities are the virtues which together constitute the ethical life. Aristotle's virtue-based ethics is sometimes referred to as *aretaic* ethics. *Arete* is the Greek word for "virtue", but it also means "excellence". For a knife, its aretaic quality may be "sharpness" for it is designed to cut; for a horse, "speed" or "strength" for it is designed to run fast or work hard, and so on.

Therefore, to arrive at the virtues of human living, Aristotle sets out in his *Nicomachean Ethics* by using the method (or intellectual virtue) of "practical wisdom" (*phronesis*) to identify the goal of human living. His discussion leads him to declare that "happiness" (*eudaimonia*) is that goal, but by happiness he means something more than we usually mean by that term. It is not a state of pleasurable or self-indulgent euphoria but rather a state of contentment, a life integrated happily with a sense of purpose, lived out in community. Of course, the Aristotelian way to happiness is the virtuous life.[18]

Aristotle included the following moral qualities as constitutive of the virtuous life: courage, temperance, magnificence, pride, good temper, friendliness, truthfulness, wittiness, shame and justice. This list might seem a little strange to us but we need to remember the terms may have slightly different meaning in their ancient Greek context. In other eras, using the Aristotelian method, different virtues have been added. For instance, Aquinas who adapted the Aristotelian philosophy to medieval Christian theology, saw the goal of human living more in terms of a life lived for the love of God, and modified the virtues to include faith, hope and charity.

The "excellences" of virtue theory form a total package, a unity. The virtues are linked and the good person cultivates an integrated way of life. Furthermore, these attitudes are developed habitually, through training and exercise, for this is a matter more of developing a good *will* than it is of teaching a good mind. The virtues develop in practice and arise from good upbringing and self-control. Indeed the idea of self-control and moderation is important, for virtues are "means between the extremes" (hence, courage is the mean between foolhardiness and cowardice).

One of the main contemporary interpreters of virtue theory has been Alasdair MacIntyre, though he is but one of a large number of ethicists who are exponents of virtue theory. MacIntyre's analysis of the ethical confusion in post-modern societies - pluralist polities where religious authority is largely absent and ethical discourse operates in a relativistic morass - leads him to maintain that a duty-based ethic will not work and a consequence-based ethic is fraught with too many dangers. For him, virtue-based ethics provides a way forward.

Greg Pence eloquently sums up MacIntyre's analysis that modern societies are characterised by ethical fragmentation and conflicting traditions:

> We are Platonic perfectionists in saluting Gold medallists in the Olympics; utilitarians in applying the principle of triage to the wounded in war; Lockeans in affirming rights over property; Christians in idealising charity, compassion and equal moral worth; and followers of Kant and Mill in affirming personal autonomy. No wonder that intuitions conflict in moral philosophy. No wonder people feel confused.[19]

In *After Virtue,* MacIntyre provides an extensive analysis of the concept of virtue and the variety of virtues from Homer to the late twentieth century. He emphasises how virtues arise out of a community, a profession or a tradition. So, in our era when the goal of human community is largely to maximise prosperity, the virtues endorsed are hard work, efficiency, consumption, leisure and the like. MacIntyre defines virtue as:

> an acquired human quality the possession and exercise of which tends to enable us to achieve those goods which are internal to practices and the lack of which effectively prevents us from achieving any such goods.[20]

The distinction between external and internal goods is a development of Aristotle. Wealth, status, power and pleasure are examples of external goods. The development of virtue entails the pursuit of internal goods which are available to all who engage in the practice which produces them, whereas external goods like fame and power can be possessed by a few only. In the practice of public service for instance, an example of an internal good would be "respect for the system of government" whereas an external good might be "the status of government power". The virtuous public official cultivates and practises the former.

As we have indicated, for MacIntyre virtues are practice or tradition specific, linked to a group's particular "story".[21] MacIntyre's approach is a departure from Aristotle in the sense that Aristotle's philosophy was linked more to a particular account of human nature. One consequence of linking virtues to particular practices or communities is that they change over time. Like customs, virtues can become outmoded - male chivalry is hardly a virtue in an era of gender equality. Consequently, the charge of relativism can be made against some contemporary versions of virtue theory.

There are other weaknesses in virtue theory. The critical discussion about the usefulness of virtue theory as a normative approach centres on whether it can do the full work - including moral justification - of an action-guiding ethical theory. It is not evident that

I become clearer about what I am to do, just because I have a strong sense of who I am to be. Also, like principles in a deontological framework, virtues such as honesty and loyalty can conflict. So, it is difficult to see how a virtuous disposition provides the full answer to the ethical dilemma confronting a nurse with an order not to resuscitate a terminally ill cancer patient, or a politician with a loyal disposition caught in the conflict between duty to his constituents and allegiance to his party. Because virtue theory gives us little guidance in spelling out ethical justification, it is not apparent that it is sufficient to produce good or right action.

A weaker version of virtue theory will concede its limitations as a normative theory. The stronger version which proclaims that what a virtuous person does (or is) determines the rightness of a certain behaviour, has the persistent problem of circularity and indeterminacy, sidestepping the need to provide grounds for the claim.

Despite its limitations, virtue theory is a vital part of the mosaic in understanding ethics. We shall see its usefulness in an applied sense in subsequent chapters. Its practical virtues include:

- an emphasis on character-building which can be useful in everyday morality;
- an applicability to an ethic of role and professional ethics;
- a check on the excessively cognitive style of other approaches, allowing a place for feelings, roles and relationships in line with an ethic of care;
- a tool to assist identifying core community values in pluralist societies; and
- its potential as a basis for moral education especially in extolling virtues for the young.

Universalism and Communitarianism

Virtue theory is generally regarded as a *communitarian* normative approach, especially in its interpretation by Alasdair MacIntyre, although its original Aristotelian version makes universalist claims. Communitarianism is a large umbrella category which assumes that society is more than the mere sum of its parts and that individuality only makes sense in terms of association with others, in community. That emphasis may be found across the spectrum of theories examined in this chapter, but certain communitarians disown the approaches generally labelled as deontological or teleological because of their universalistic claims, that is claims for a principle that is always applicable (as in Kantianism) or for a method that will universally produce the most ethical outcome (as in utilitarianism). These anti-universalist communitarians maintain that "the right", "the good" or "the virtuous" must be determined in relation to particular traditions or social contexts. This line of approach makes them vulnerable to the charge of relativism.

In one sense communitarianism has had a voice in Western ethical traditions since Plato's *Republic* and *Laws* placed the good of the whole city-state above that of individuals. The contemporary communitarians are severe critics of the dominant strand of universalism in our philosophical traditions which has argued that ethics involves going beyond our local interests or cultural constraints to a standpoint that is universally valid. So they are distinctly uneasy with Kant's Categorical Imperative or the utilitarian Henry Sidgwick's "viewpoint of the universe", which have hitherto been acceptable in cultures shaped by monotheistic claims that ethical obligations are universal or by the Stoic tradition which regards ethics as derivative of a universal natural law. The post-modern disintegration of that heritage combined with social movements such as feminism, some strands of which accuse universalist approaches of being patriarchically oppressive, has ensured that, at the very least, the universalist voice in ethics is tempered by a communitarian perspective.[22]

A Preferred Theory?

We have concluded our survey of ethical theories. None has been above criticism, but hopefully our understanding of the language of ethics has been significantly enhanced. The debate between these perspectives is helpful in the attempt to distil the overall strengths and weaknesses of the theories discussed. In turn, this is of assistance in the task to determine whether there is a preferred theory or whether an eclectic approach can be developed, while retaining internal consistency and practical usefulness. We have already noted some similarities and complementarities between certain theories; for instance, situation ethics and the ethics of care share a focus on loving relationships, while deontology's absolute principles and the virtues may correspond.

The most reasonable theory would surely have certain characteristics: clarity, consistency, practicality, and adequacy for the human condition. In the end, it is not helpful to ask, "which of the theories is best?" for the probability is that they all have something to offer us in certain aspects of living the ethical life. Nonetheless, in the next chapter we will try to move beyond an impasse between the theories. We will explore an integrated framework which will seek to be an action-guiding decision-making tool for applied ethics.

CHAPTER REVIEW

Compile your own review:

1. List the new terms you have encountered in this chapter.
2. Identify the major normative theories, then:
   (a) outline the key characteristics which differentiate them;
   (b) check with the summary of these terms in the glossary;
   (c) nominate the ethicists identified with these positions;
   (d) list the strengths and weaknesses of each approach.
3. Consider how the categories "universalism" and "communitarianism" may be used to classify ethical theories and ethicists.

FURTHER READING

Baron M, Pettit, P and Slote M (1996) *Three Methods of Ethics*, Oxford: Blackwell.

Mulhall, S and Swift A (1992) *Liberals and Communitarians* (2nd ed), Oxford: Blackwell. (The articles on normative ethics in this excellent reference are in Pt IV, see also no 43).

Solomon, RC (1993) *Ethics: A Short Introduction*, Dubuque, IA: Brown and Benchmark.

Singer, P (ed) (1991) *A Companion to Ethics*, Oxford: Blackwell Publishers. (The articles on normative ethics in this excellent reference are in Pt IV, see also no 43).

White, JE (ed) (1994), *Contemporary Moral Problems*, St Paul MN: West Publishing Company (chapter one contains readings drawn from the original sources of many of the theorists examined in this chapter).

QUESTIONS FOR DISCUSSION

1. Which theory (or theories) do you identify with most or which do you find most practically helpful? Why? Does

your answer reflect a pattern to your moral reasoning? Do you favour a universalist or communitarian approach?

2. Discuss: Is it possible always to balance the interests of self with the interests of others? Consider this issue with particular reference to the justice and rights theories of contractarianism, especially "Justice as Fairness".

CASE STUDIES

CASE 1 – HEINZ'S DILEMMA

In Europe a woman was near death from a special kind of cancer. There was one drug that the doctors thought might save her. It was a form of radium that a druggist in the same town had recently discovered. The drug was expensive to make, but the druggist was charging ten times what the drug cost him to make. He paid $200 for the radium and charged $2000 for a small dose of the drug. The sick woman's husband, Heinz, went to everyone he knew to borrow the money, but he could only get together about $1000 which was half of what it cost. He told the druggist that his wife was dying and asked him to sell it cheaper or let him pay later. But the druggist said: "No, I discovered the drug and I'm going to make money from it". So Heinz got desperate and broke into the man's store to steal the drug for his wife.

(Source: Kohlberg, L (1987) "Indoctrination Versus Relativity in Value Education", in George Sher (ed) *Moral Philosophy: Selected Readings*, New York: Harcourt Brace Jovanovich, p 88).

- Was Heinz acting morally? Why? or why not?
- Consider the approach you have taken in giving your reasons. Does it reflect consequentialist or non-consequentialist reasoning? Why, in what way?
- What might be the response of an ethic of care or a virtue theorist in this case?

CASE 2 – CHINESE EARTHQUAKE

After the disastrous Chinese earthquake of 1976, a man's wife and children were trapped in the rubble of their home. As he worked at digging them out, he heard the moans of the town leader beneath another pile of rubble. He stopped trying to save his family and went immediately to the rescue of the leader and his family. The leader and his family survived; the rescuer's family did not. Asked about his decision the next day, the man said that he had no regrets. The town leader was needed for the preservation of order, the direction of rescue attempts, distribution of supplies, and so forth. The leader's survival meant the survival of many other people, all of whom would have died had he saved his own family instead. It also meant a great reduction in suffering for the survivors.

(Source: Olen, J (1983) *Persons in their World: Introduction to Philosophy*, New York: Random House, pp 41-42.)

- Did this man act morally? Why or why not?
- This man acted on good utilitarian grounds. But was it the right thing? Is the cultural context a factor in your deliberation?
- What other response could he have made and what would be the ethical justification of those responses? Categorise those responses in normative theory terms.

CHAPTER THREE NOTES

1 Another version of teleology is the Aristotelian approach we encounter later in virtue theory. The Aristotelian approach is a "perfectionist ethic" because it has a view about the perfect state of humans, society and nature to which we should aim. Some religious versions of the Natural/Moral Law claim to be teleological in this sense also.

2 Quoted by James Rachels, "The Debate over Utilitarianism" in White, JE (1994) *Contemporary Moral Problems*, 4th ed, St Paul: West Publishing Co, p 31.

3 From Temple, W, *Mens Creatrix*, cited by Fletcher, J (1966) *Situation Ethics*, London: SCM Press.

4 A hybrid modification of situationism which takes seriously moral laws derived from natural law is known as *proportionalism*. This view talks of proportionate reasons for overturning otherwise firm moral rules. The proportionate reason is grounded in a particular situation or contextual circumstance.

5 Usually it is of the character of this approach to focus on rules but just as with utilitarianism we may distinguish between a *rule non-consequentialist* and an *act non-consequentialist*. We shall not discuss the latter in this section though it should be noted that *act non-consequentialists* reject the possibility of particular rules being general or universal. Decisions for the act non-consequentialists become "intuitionistic". The justification "I always do my own thing" is illustrative of this type. It has to be questioned as to whether it warrants attention as a serious ethical position, as it appears to support both absolute and relativistic positions at the same time.

6 The particular encyclicals are *Veritatis Splendor*, "The Splendour of Truth" (1993) and *The Gospel of Life* (1994). One readable assessment of Roman Catholic morality which is implicitly critical of the Vatican is provided by Australian Jesuit priest, Arnold Hogan (1993) *On Being Catholic Today*, Melbourne: Collins Dove.

7 For a list of works by Kant and about Kant's ethics see the list of references at the conclusion of Onora O'Neill's article no 14 in Singer, P (ed) (1991) *A Companion to Ethics*, Oxford: Basil Blackwell, p 184.

8 The phrase means "at first glance". Ross wrote several texts. One reference is Ross, WD (1954) *Kant's Ethical Theory*, New York: Oxford University Press. Another similar attempt to adopt Kantian ethics by developing a system of moral laws and procedural guidelines can be found in the work of Walter Muelder, the personalist moral theologian of Boston University, who in his 1966 book *Moral Law in Christian Social Ethics*, Richmond, VA: John Knox Press, details a clear structure of moral law.

9 Rawls himself has developed his views beyond *A Theory of Justice*. Because this is not primarily a text on political or social philosophy our discussion of this debate is very limited. For instance, we acknowledge the contribution of Michael Walzer who provides a social democratic alternative to Rawls in *Spheres of Justice* (Blackwell, 1983), and, in the discussion about rights, the important thesis of Ronald Dworkin. In *Taking Rights Seriously* (Duckworth, 1977) Dworkin proposes that rights are special moral facts which in social ethical disputes override like trumps do in card games.

10 The two principles are set out more fully in Rawls, J (1999) *A Theory of Justice*, (new edition) London: Oxford University Press, pp 302-303.

11 See for instance Kukathas, C and Pettit, P (1990) *Rawls: a Theory of Justice and its Critics*, Cambridge: Polity Press.

12 I refer particularly to the American libertarian, Robert Nozick, who draws on the liberty rights approach of John Locke. His view is known as an "entitlement theory" because its concern is the protection, in a negative sense, of just acquisition and just transfer of property and personal rights, and the rectification of any so-called injustice in this regard. "Justice" in these terms means little more than "legal rights". Indeed, this rights entitlement theory provides us with a good example of how a focus on *rights* alone is not likely to provide an adequate basis for a theory of justice.

13 Feder Kittay, E and Meyers, DT (eds) (1987) *Women and Moral Theory*, Maryland: Rowman and Littlefield, p 3.

14 Jaggar, AM, "Feminist Ethics: Some Issues for the Nineties", *Journal of Social Philosophy*, vol 20, nos 1-2 (Spring/Fall 1989).

15 Held, V, "Feminism and Moral Theory" in Feder Kittay and Meyers, op cit.

16 Noddings, N (1984) *Caring: A Feminine Approach to Ethics and Moral Education*, Berkeley: University of California Press.

17 See Sher, G (1987) "Other Voices, Other Rooms? Women's Psychology and Moral Theory", in Feder Kittay and Meyers, op cit.

18 We need to note how this ancient Greek philosophy has an implicit view of human nature to guide its ethics, a fact which sits uncomfortably with most contemporary worldviews, even of the neo-Aristotelian kind. It was also a view which excluded from its membership women and slaves.

19 Pence, G "Virtue Theory" in Singer, P (ed) (1991), *A Companion to Ethics*, Oxford: Blackwell, p 251. For another collection of important contemporary papers on virtue theory, see Crisp R and Slote M (eds) (1997) *Virtue Ethics*, Oxford: Oxford University Press.

20 MacIntyre, A (1981) *After Virtue*, Notre Dame, Indiana: University of Notre Dame Press.

21 Particular ethics emerge from particular stories and stories can be a way of passing on the ethical tradition. This is sometimes known as narrative ethics.

22 The dialectic between universalism and communitarianism can be a useful way of summarising and comparing the theories and themes of Chapters Two and Three. This can be demonstrated with respect to the debate about theories of justice. Rawls may be termed a universalist who has modified his views in line with communitarianism, although Rawls himself denies this. Critics like Michael Sandel and Michael Walzer, who also expound theories of justice, may be termed communitarians.

CHAPTER FOUR

RESPONSIBLE ETHICAL DECISIONS

From *Star Wars: The Empire Strikes Back*

BEN: But you cannot control it. This is a dangerous time for you, when you will be tempted by the dark side of the Force.

YODA: Yes, yes. To Obi-Wan you listen. The cave. Remember your failure at the cave!

LUKE: But I've learned so much since then, Master Yoda. I promise to return and finish what I've begun. You have my word.

BEN: It is you and your abilities that the Emperor wants. That is why your friends are made to suffer.

LUKE: And that is why I have to go.

BEN: Luke, I don't want to lose you to the Emperor the way I lost Vader.

LUKE: You won't.

YODA: Stopped they must be. On this all depends. Only a fully trained Jedi Knight with the Force as his ally will conquer Vader and his Emperor. If you end your training now, if you choose the quick and easy path, as Vader did, you will become an agent of evil.

BEN: Patience.

LUKE: And sacrifice Han and Leia?

YODA: If you honor what they fight for ... yes!

Brackett, L, & Kasdan, L (and George Lucas), *Star Wars: The Empire Strikes Back*, Faber & Faber, London, 2000, pp 102-103. © 1997 Lucasfilm Ltd

You are free, therefore choose – that is to say, invent. No rule of general morality can show you what you ought to do: no signs are vouchsafed in this world.

Jean-Paul Sartre, *Existentialism is a Humanism* (1946)

This chapter attempts to build a bridge between the realm of ethical theory and the lived reality of ethical decision-making. To achieve this we will:

(1) move beyond the differences between theories highlighted in Chapter Three to a more integrated framework which draws on the strengths of those theories while being conscious of their problems and difficulties,

(2) adapt this approach to a model for responsible ethical decision-making, and

(3) illustrate how this operates in relation to a couple of case examples.

Each of the theories explored in the previous chapter implies a certain style of ethical decision-making. For instance, deontology comes to a decision by applying some absolute rule while utilitarianism applies a calculus based on utility and what serves the best interests overall. However, it may be argued that each of these theories on their own is unable to provide the comprehensive evaluation demanded by the task of choosing among ethical options often confronting contemporary moral agents. Our quest is for a more fitting ethical response. In this quest we aim to take seriously the claims of duties, rights and principles as well as utility, together with the perspective of virtue theory and the feminist care ethic. We will label this approach an *ethic of response* because it is organised around the concepts of "responsiveness" and "responsibility", which provide a coherent justification for the special character of this approach. Although such an eclectic approach may be regarded by some as philosophically problematic, it enables us to establish a framework which does not allow important theoretical disagreements to paralyse ethical decision and action, while, at the same time it allows decision and action to be informed by theory.

The Idea of Responsibility

"Responsibility" is one of those terms used frequently in ethical discourse, even though it is a more recent addition to the ethical lexicon than ideas of duty, law, virtue and goodness. Like a musical instrument, this term can issue various themes.[1] Moral responsibility is frequently linked to the idea of autonomy and freedom and, in applied discussions, for instance, may be a critical factor in arguments about crime and punishment, environmental ethics or professional ethics. In the context of our exploration for a viable use of theory, we explore the idea of responsibility in a specific sense, one that is linked to the notion of "responsiveness". In developing this case we shall borrow substantially from the ethical approach of the American moral philosopher, H Richard Niebuhr (1900-1962).[2]

The starting point is that proposition to which this text constantly returns, that *all life is interconnected*. To reiterate, we have ethical obligations because our lives take place in a web of interdependent relationships. Consequently (to anticipate the discussion of Chapter Nine), those relationships are to be understood in a biocentric (life-centred) rather than an anthropocentric (human-centred) way. The interconnectedness of all life is the metaphysical platform on which moral responsibility rests: "all life has the character of responsiveness" says Niebuhr.[3] Because it reflects directly this fundamental characteristic of the context in which we make our ethical response, "responsibility", so Niebuhr claims, conveys a more profound clue in identifying the character of moral agency than images which lie behind the traditional deontological and consequentialist approaches which have dominated ethical theory.

Though it is something of an oversimplification, we may say with Niebuhr that *deontology* emphasises an *image of man/woman as "citizen"*, living under law by a sense of duty to certain imperatives, whereas *consequentialist approaches* highlight the human capacity to be purposeful, giving shape to things, working for a goal; in other words, it rests on a *view of man/woman "the maker"*. An *ethic of response* however, takes seriously the basic human experience of men and women as being in dialogue or conversation with themselves, with their god, with nature, with each other: *man/woman "the answerer or responder" is the key image*. According to this image, my life from birth to death is one continuous dialogue; it is from the dialogical nature of our existence that the interests of which utilitarians speak or the duties of non-consequentialists, arise; in this sense, the metaphor of responsiveness refers to a prior characteristic of the human ethical condition. Symbolising this more fundamental understanding of ourselves, "responsibility" opens the way to an ethic which is holistically responsive to the past, the present *and* the future, to the parts *and* the whole, to the self *and* the other, thus providing a perspective that has sometimes been lost in the apparently irresolvable debates of normative theory.[4]

As Niebuhr himself says:

> When the word, responsibility, is used of the self as agent, as doer, it is usually translated with the aid of the older images as meaning direction toward goals or as ability to be moved by respect for law. Yet the understanding of ourselves as responsive beings, who in all our actions answer to action upon us in accordance with our interpretation of such actions, is a fruitful conception, which brings into view aspects of our self-defining conduct that are obscured when the older images are exclusively employed.[5]

An Ethic of Response

For ethics based on responsibility, the first question is, "what is going on?" and then, "what is appropriate or what fits?", questions which include the questions, "what will result?" (consequentialism) or "what is my duty?" (non-consequentialism). The ethic of response promotes a choice of the *fitting* action, one that fits into a total interaction and anticipation of further responses. If teleology is a theory of "the good", and deontology a theory of "the right", then the ethics of response is one of "the fitting". Accordingly, what fits is alone conducive to the good and alone is right. Its justifications thereby incorporate but go beyond the teleological and deontological while preserving a contextual and "communitarian" frame of reference. To some it may appear that the ethic of response is just another version of consequentialism. On the other hand, it takes principles seriously holding that criteria such as universalisability are integral to the moral life. To that extent it may be labelled a modified non-consequentialism. In either case, as an adaptation of other normative theories, it seeks a more comprehensive ethical response, but in so doing may be subject to the flaws and contradictions attributed to their theories.

Of course the *ethic of response* is not altogether novel in its emphases: it certainly echoes some of the approaches which have been critical of deontology and utilitarianism, like virtue theory and the ethic of care. Indeed, as Niebuhr himself acknowledges, there is a note reminiscent of Aristotle in his approach, for it is concerned to decide what response *fits* the occasion, the role, the choice or what is virtuous. The ethic of response also takes seriously the prior question of virtue theory: "who am I? and what is my disposition regarding (this matter)?". Furthermore, the clear focus on being a relational and contextual ethic reflects aspects of both the ethic of care and situation ethics.

The questions of universalism and communitarianism come together in Niebuhr's analysis. Responsibility invites the question, "To whom or what am I responsible?"[6] A decision based on the ethic of response will take on a different shape depending on how that question is answered. It allows for a narrow communitarian response, such as, "My family or tribe is the only group to whom I am responsible"; but it also allows for a broad, inclusive or universal response such as, "I am ultimately responsible to all living beings in the cosmos". Because of the emphasis on life's interconnectedness, Niebuhr's ethic (and that of this text for that matter) moves in the direction of an inclusive response. The point is that however limited our frame of response, when we are open to responsiveness a universal perspective ethic becomes possible.

According to Niebuhr, four elements guide the application of responsibility: the first is *response,* the need to nurture the responsiveness built into all action and experience; the second is *interpretation,* the need to ask of all situations, in the broadest possible frame of reference, "what is going on?"; the third is *accountability,* the need to stay with our action, accepting responsibility for the consequences; the fourth is *social solidarity* and of it, Niebuhr declares that "the responsible self is driven as it were by the movement of the social process to respond and be accountable in nothing less than a universal community".[7]

Informed by this explanatory preamble, we can *outline the procedure endorsed by the ethic of response,* a procedure which if followed rigorously and faithfully creates the possibility of a *fitting* decision.

It requires:

- a response to, all facts relevant to a moral situation, all the moral agents involved, all the alternative actions available, all the possible consequences of those actions and the consequences of those consequences (including whether these actions would be acceptable if they were universalisable);
- all this is to be interpreted within a framework of social solidarity and life's interconnectedness, after consideration of appropriate values, principles, and the character disposition of the moral agent;
- and then a fitting decision is made for which the responsible self remains accountable.

Of course this outline begs many questions and criticisms. There is an absence of explicit normative guidelines in this summary.

The apparent eclectic or synthetic attempt to straddle contrasting normative positions invites critique. Furthermore, the process of decision-making indicated by the ethic of response is very demanding of any ordinary human being. Indeed, its comprehensiveness (which is one of its major virtues) surely requires super-human powers of judgment, knowledge and discernment. Yet, unless we are to adopt an unconstrained consequentialism or return to an ethically authoritarian style, where rules and behaviours are prescribed for the individual and society, is there any alternative but for us to invoke such god-like powers? In the end, such a demanding process is necessary if we are to live by an ethic which respects human autonomy and reason, as well as the complexity of the human condition.

More troublesome may be the charge that, while the definition of an ethic of response affirms the importance of "appropriate values and principles", there is no declaration of what those values or principles are. Is this a content-less ethic to be easily manipulated into relativism or subjectivism? Not every interpretation of a moral situation is responsible, for the comprehensiveness of responsiveness circumscribes and indicates value parameters within which the fitting may emerge, even though HR Niebuhr does not specify the values that go with responsibility.

In the summary statement above which outlines the ethic of response, formal or procedural values are embraced, such as the need to weigh up an ethical decision comprehensively. Integral to that comprehensive evaluation, is the concern of virtue theory, which asks "will this ethical response be consistent with the kind of person (character or disposition) I aim to be?", This is the recurring question to be addressed in deciding what is a fitting ethical response. On the other hand, the summary statement's focus on consequences suggests that utility is not to be disregarded; likewise, it enjoins consideration of the Golden Rule (or Kant's Categorical Imperative), when it inquires whether its decisions are universalisable.

To deal with the need for value parameters within which the fitting may emerge, several substantial values can be nominated which are consistent with the idea of responsibility and its emphasis on the interconnectedness of life together with its core elements like "social solidarity". These values are widely endorsed by a range of ethical approaches and they are significant to the discussion of particular issues in subsequent chapters. In brief, these three inter-related, substantial values, are:

- **The respect for life principle.**[8] This enjoins us to care for ourselves and our fellow human beings; we are not to treat others merely as means to an end but respect their rights and dignity as persons who are fellow ethical agents. Respect for life extends beyond human beings to other forms of life in our biosphere and the cosmos; such respect is especially considerate of the rights of sensate beings. This principle requires that conflicts involving choices about life (including its initiation and termination, or the environmental threat to earth's balance of life) are treated with the maximum possible care.
- **The justice principle**. This enjoins us to be fair, loving and neighbourly in public and private relationships, within our communal and societal life. The justice principle recognises that ultimately the welfare of individuals is dependent on enhancing the common good.[9] However, while it is committed to both individual freedom and social equity in the distribution of social goods, justice gives priority to considering the interests of the most disadvantaged while also being considerate of the interests of future generations. It thereby recognises that equality of opportunity is not always enough and that intervention to redress imbalances of access to power and social goods may be necessary.
- **The covenantal integrity principle**. This enjoins us to truthfulness and honesty in all our relationships. It also refers to the importance of self-consistency and inner integrity for moral agents, as well as to the recognition that our life together relies upon an implicit or explicit covenant. In pointing to the supreme importance of promise-keeping as an element of the ethical life, it suggests that promises should only be renounced in very extreme circumstances. However the notion of integrity implies that promises and loyalty should serve the purposes of respecting life and seeking justice. These purposes should give fundamental shape to our covenants. In this sense, this third principle is subordinate to the other two.

Of course, these brief definitions do not deal with the subtleties which have generated philosophical volumes on each of them. The possibility of conflict between such values must be acknowledged. The point is that these value guideposts have a claim to priority consideration as we employ an ethic of response. Similarly, it must be granted, that in the justification of this choice of values and in the weighing up of the various factors requiring our response, or in discriminating between the possible decisions resulting from an ethic of response, we will resort to those lines of argument which we identified in the previous chapter. In other words, it may be that in justifying a particular ethical decision it becomes apparent that the weight given to one's assessment of consequences is crucially significant, or that one's sense of self or disposition as a moral character outweighs any other consideration. In the former case one is applying the ethic of response with a consequentialist emphasis, but in the latter, considerations of virtue ethics weigh most considerably.

The features of the ethic of response as a process enabling and justifying normative ethical decisions include the following: (i) it is organised around the idea of responsibility and the quest for a fitting response, (ii) it supports the employment of a synthesis incorporating other normative approaches, (iii) it is amenable to practical, responsive and comprehensive ethical decision-making, and (iv) it facilitates justificatory discourse which enables others to evaluate ethical decisions, without being obstructed by the conflict between normative perspectives, although it must still confront the difficulties raised by them. As such, it is doubtful whether we can claim that the ethic of response has integrity as an alternative to the theories of Chapter Three, but it is reasonable to claim that it augments and supplements them. Notwithstanding the limitations of the ethic of response - and as we have seen no normative framework is without limitations - it provides a reasonable synthesis. This should assist us, in ways that other theories taken alone do not, as we attempt to live the ethical life within the complex, dilemma-ridden technological age which has expanded our ethical options, and confused ethical discourse as we confront those options.

A Decision-making Model[10]

Having outlined what is meant by an ethic of response and the underpinning idea of responsibility, the task in this section is to outline in a more straightforward and practical way what an ethic of response means for ethical decision-making and for community conversation about ethical matters. It is an attempt to define a process for working out in concrete and particular circumstances what is the ethically fitting course to be followed. As such, it is consistent with the Aristotelian view that living the moral life is not about reciting ethical principles or theories but engaging in "practical wisdom" (*phronesis*). Perhaps it is a process similar to the medieval tradition of casuistry, inasmuch as it is consistent with the view, expressed by Max Charlesworth,[11] that ethics, in practice, is "the art of the possible and casuistry, balancing, negotiation and compromise are inescapable".

The ethic of response is not a formula to lead us neatly from a dilemma to a resolution or conclusion, in the sense that a formula may lead to the resolution or conclusion of a mathematical conundrum which has only one right answer. Rather, it points to a method for arriving at an ethical decision for which sound moral reasons can be given, and which can be defended as a fitting ethical response. It follows that the ethic of response does not guarantee the same response by different people in similar circumstances, but it should represent a guarantee that a comprehensive and responsive approach will be undertaken before deciding, and that consequently, a framework for consultation and collaborative dialogue about ethical matters is more possible. The diagram below summarises the process simply and generally, following the outline discussed earlier in this chapter.

This responsive sequence of considerations aims at an ethical decision which is consciously justified, and one where those justifications are able to be articulated clearly. Such a decision, because it is more soundly based and is responsive to all relevant factors, is more likely to be fitting. For the same reason, it is more likely that the final decision will not only be desirable in an ethical sense but feasible in an implementational sense: impractical decisions which cannot be translated into action are hardly responsible.

The diagrammatic presentation is a general model. Greater detail can be provided as a guide to taking each step. For instance, in assessing the situation there are a host of supplementary questions one could ask of oneself to ensure greater accuracy in that assessment such as:

- What is the issue?
- How are we to interpret the facts?
- Are there special local factors, or cultural meanings which colour the facts?
- Are there different perspectives on the facts?
- Is there any source of advice on the facts?
- Are there precedents?

and so on.

Diagram One: Ethical Decision-Making Model

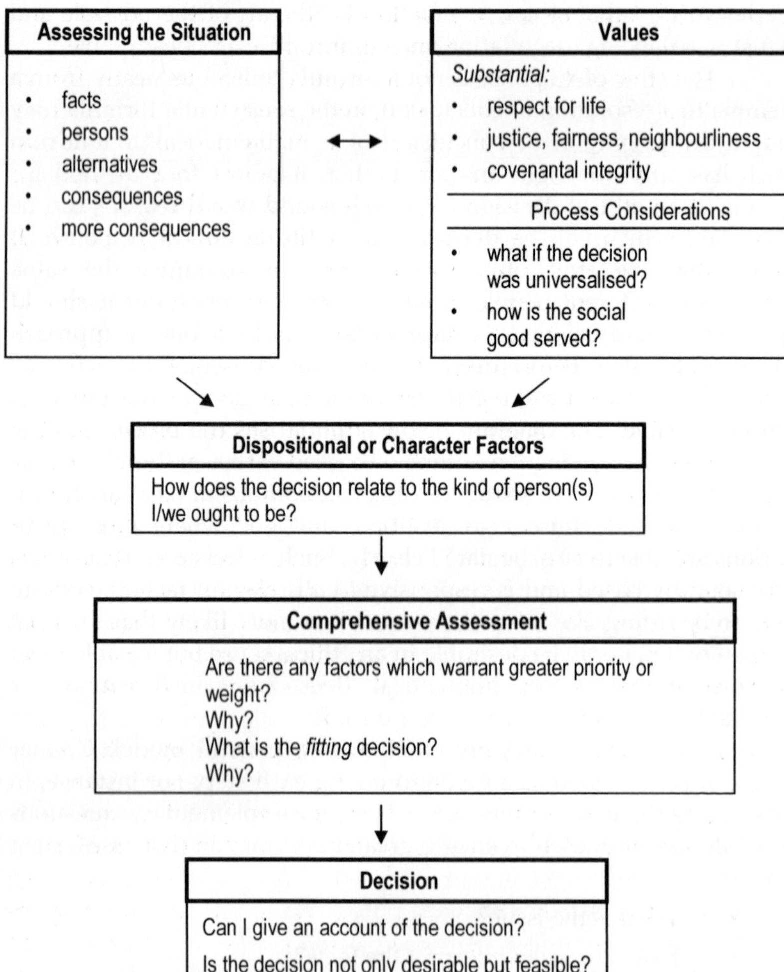

The diagram gives a central place to the dispositional factors suggesting that questions of character and ethical self-image are crucial in checking on an ethical course of action. The "comprehensive assessment" step embraces the whole model, though, quite properly it is a separate step in the sense that sound ethical decision-making requires a check on whether the assessment has been comprehensive.

Furthermore, the model is amenable to refinement for particular contexts, professions or particular roles. For example, if it were to be developed as a guiding instrument for public or government officials to enable them consciously to make better decisions in an ethical sense, it should be adapted to focus on taking the viewpoint of a public official. This would involve considerations such as duty to the employer (Government), departmental policy, the wider public interest and the like, just as it should involve considerations of specific values relevant to a public sector ethic such as respect for the law, fair dealings with citizens, careful use of public resources and the like. Diagram One could be amended to reflect the specific contextual ethical responsibilities, as in Diagram Two, below.

Here we have an example of a professional ethic or ethic of agency, and its relevant code, at work. In Chapter 8 there is a further discussion on the particular ethical character of the public sector. The different levels of responsibility and the potential for conflicting roles and value obligations becomes apparent in the diagram above. Look at the values box: it suggests the need to balance substantial and personal values (for example, "respect for life"), together with the particular values of the public service (for example, "loyalty to the government of the day"). The model must allow for an institutional or organisational response as well as an individual one; this is consistent with the idea of "institutionalising ethics" which is canvassed in Chapter Ten. Pivotal to the schema is the dispositional, self-image, character or virtue question: "What sort of public official should I be?" or "What sort of organisation do we aim to be?". It is not difficult to imagine how this might relate to an ethical dilemma for a social worker in the public service who becomes aware, in her confidential professional relationship, that a client is benefiting from a single parent allowance while living in a de facto relationship. She may wrestle with conflicting loyalties, but central to her decision will be a judgment about the expectations on her in her role as a public official. A clear and responsible ethical decision-making model should assist in enabling the public servant, as a professional, to make a defensible decision consistent with her role, despite its conflictual elements. The final step, "Document the Decision", is consistent with the demands of the bureaucracy: a good decision can be defended in a memo! It also indicates the recognition for accountability and transparency in the public sector.

Diagram Two: Public Sector Ethics Decision-making[12]

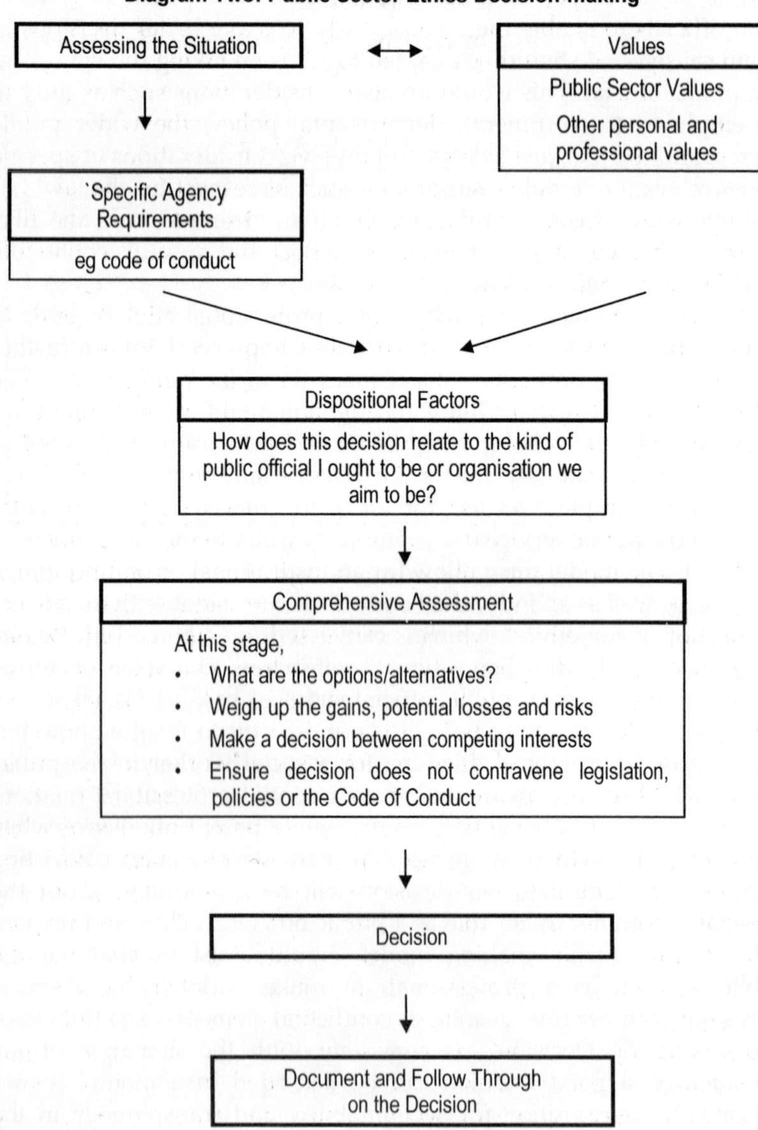

Deciding Responsibly: Two Cases

To demonstrate the ethic of response in practice let us consider two cases.

> **CASE 1 – A HARD CASE**
>
> The president of the most powerful nation in the world is faced with a most awful dilemma. His nation has developed an awesome bomb which if used could kill tens of thousands, instantly destroy a city, and have unknown radiation effects for years. The war his nation has been conducting has become protracted; casualties are heavy; many of his troops are prisoners of war on the point of starvation; if he is to use conventional methods of invasion to end the war it could take months and sacrifice many of his own troops. The bomb would probably end it all much more quickly.

We recognise that this synopsis describes the political ethical dilemma which confronted President Truman in 1945 soon after he succeeded President Roosevelt as leader of the United States. Truman's decision for the *Enola Gay* to drop the atom bomb on Hiroshima on the morning of 6 August 1945 and two days later to use this new weapon again on Nagasaki led directly to the ending of World War II and the surrender of Japan. This was not merely another strategic decision by the commander-in-chief for it signalled the dawn of a nuclear arms race whose awesome potential still threatens the peace and harmony of communities across the earth. War and international relations - to say nothing of the environmental implications - were never to be the same again.

Not only were the two cities obliterated as tens of thousands Japanese suffered deaths of appalling cruelty, but also hundreds of thousands have suffered injuries, sickness and death for decades as a result.[13] Certainly Truman's decision stands as one of the most momentous ethical decisions in human history. Was it right? Was it good? What might an ethic of response say of it, or more particularly, how might the decision be approached from that perspective?

First of all, the ethic of response seeks a full account of the facts of the situation. Of course, we approach this case with hindsight but President Truman was clearly aware of certain matters itemised in the scenario above: the effects of the bomb would be awesome, like nothing in history; the failure of Japan to surrender, though beaten, was leading to the prospect that there would be severe casualties for the allies, a fact which was becoming unacceptable to the nation Truman led. But perhaps there are other factors: this weapon had been developed in almost absolute secrecy, without knowledge or consent of the American people, a sign that democracy is a casualty of war; furthermore, the Soviet troops had begun a push East at the end of the war with Germany and threatened to demand territory in Asia after the Pacific War. Then there are "the facts" of the unknown and unintended consequences: the legacy to the community of nations of the nuclear age and the effects of radiation.[14] How are we to interpret this situation, to what do we give greatest weight in this analysis, and what alternatives or options can we then identify? An ethic of response would pose all these questions at least.

On the matter of options the President should consider (as he apparently did): (i) a conventional invasion instead of using the atom bomb, with consequential heavy loss of American military lives though nowhere near as many as the Japanese civilian casualties on 6 and 8 August, (ii) a demonstration bombing with a warning and ultimatum that if surrender did not follow it would be used, with the probable consequence that American prisoners of war would be sacrificed in retaliation, or (iii) the use of the bomb more or less as it was used.

Given this assessment of the situation, the President, according to an ethic of response, would bring to bear on these facts the values important in arriving at an ethical decision. Which option respects life most completely? How is justice and social solidarity served by the various options? Which option best serves the covenantal integrity by which the President is bound? Which decision would best carry the weight of the test of universalisability? Which would serve the greater good for the greater number (utility)? Which choice is most true to "the character" of the American presidency?

The ethic of response seeks the decision which the President can defend as fitting after employing the ethic of response. It points beyond the dutiful decision or the one with the best results. He is the commander-in-chief of his armed forces, but as President of the most powerful nation in this world he is also accountable for the hopes of all nations for an acceptable global peace, and furthermore he knows that the new weapon could change the course of history for all humanity and the environment. It is in this context that as a moral agent he faces the question critical to an ethic of response: "to whom am I responsible and in what community am I responsible?" Of course, it is possible to answer that question narrowly in this case by focussing his decision around the issue of saving the lives of American combat troops and prisoners of war. On the other hand, the idea of responsibility suggests that, though that consideration is highly relevant, there is a wider frame of reference in which a fitting decision should be made.

The ethic of response promotes a more comprehensive decision-making process grounded in the widest possible interpretation of the situation and a full appreciation of normative considerations. In this case, the ethic of response requires the fullest possible accountability toward particular considerations, namely (a) long-term consequences, (b) the dispositional factor (that is, "what will this action do to the character of the President and the American nation if it is carried through?"), and (c) respect for the life of "the universal community" (to use Niebuhr's phrase regarding the social solidarity emphasis of this approach).

The President may still come to the same decision to use the bomb which was in fact made historically, even though the approach of the ethic of response is employed. However, it is likely that the ethic of response would strongly challenge a decision to use the atom bomb. At the very least, if the decision were to bomb Hiroshima, its fittingness would then have to be justified by more substantial moral reasoning than for instance, "it is in the interests of most people that the war end" (an essentially utilitarian approach) or "it is my duty as commander-in-chief to save American lives" (a deontological approach).

The lines of this discussion could be taken further and readers are encouraged to do so. In particular, the question is left unanswered: "Even if the ethic of response leads to a better ethical decision, is it the best decision politically?". Or, "are politicians bound to make decisions based on anticipated outcomes first and then provide the ethical rationale for them subsequently?". This case study invites us to consider the particularities of ethics in political action, some of which are raised in Chapter Eight.

CASE 2- THE ACCIDENT: A CLASSIC MORAL DILEMMA[15]

You, your spouse and your three children are driving along a lonely country road one dark, winter night. You hit a wet patch and the car goes off the road and hits a tree. Everyone else seems very badly injured and the car is wrecked. You have blood on your face and hands, but are otherwise alright. You start running down the road to seek help and finally see a farmhouse with a car parked out front. You beat on the door frantically and an elderly woman and a very young child open it eventually. You explain the situation somewhat hysterically and ask to use the phone. There is no phone. When you insist on borrowing the car to go for help, the woman refuses to lend it to you. She seems very upset and somewhat afraid of you. After pleading for the keys to no avail, you begin to look for them. The woman is so frightened by your behaviour that she locks herself in a back room. You plead with her again but she won't budge. Finally, you grab the young child and threaten bodily harm if she doesn't give you the keys to the car. She still refuses so you tell her that you are going to bend the child's arm up behind its back until it breaks unless she comes out and gives you the keys.

We shall review this hypothetical case briefly, examining first how the ethic of response might view it, and then how other perspectives might approach the dilemma, and finally commenting on how the ethic of response is helpful in this case.

Assessing the facts of the situation appears to be relatively straightforward although this encounter between strangers begs more information about the elderly woman who is frightened so that we can understand, and respond to, her actions. The scenario as presented is a traumatic experience for the child and the elderly woman. Nonetheless, there has been an accident in which people are badly hurt, and in fact the moral agent faced with the dilemma is closely related to them. While this fact is significant at an emotional level, it is not necessarily an over-riding moral factor. The alternatives available are seemingly few: (a) either do nothing and return to the car to see what assistance can be provided in which case the likely consequence is that people will die; (b) proceed to plead with the occupants of the house and be prepared to take measures such as hurting the child in a way that is hopefully non-life-threatening in order to get the car for help; (c) ransack the house thoroughly in search of the keys. The scenario as presented does not suggest this latter alternative but neither is any information provided which rules it out as an option.

An assessment in the light of appropriate values rules out the "do nothing" option, because that conflicts too directly with the principles of respect for life and covenantal integrity. The other two options seem defensible on the moral consideration relevant to the ethic of response, just as they would likely be to an ethic of care (though hurting the little child is hardly caring), consequentialism (though we cannot be sure that the elderly woman will not have a heart attack) and Kantianism (though there is the difficulty of the conflicting principles of "do no harm" and "do all to save life"); a Kantian might also reject option (b) above on the grounds that we cannot know all the consequences (for instance, the car might not even start!). Perhaps a moral agent following virtue ethics who does not see herself or himself as a person of violence would be concerned about hurting the little child; however, in the role of parent or spouse, as the only one who seemingly might save other lives, the disposition of rescuer at an acceptable cost might be over-riding.

It appears that in this case there is a likelihood of agreement from various ethical perspectives that it is justifiable to take measures to obtain the car keys including hurting the child, even though differing reasons would be offered to support the decision. So, is there any distinctive contribution to resolving this dilemma from the ethic of response?

I maintain that the comprehensive approach characteristic of responsive ethical decision-making is illuminating in this case. Without it, the third option - to ransack the house - might not be considered. It is more likely to arise in the kind of audit of the moral situation which is a feature of the ethic of response, though utilitarians might claim their commitment to examine consequences implies a consideration of all alternatives. Of course, the keys may not be found and the second option - threatening and hurting the little child - within the limit of (hopefully) not threatening the child's life - may have to be pursued. Common moral sense suggests there would be great reluctance to follow this course and various styles of ethical reasoning would offer objections as noted above. Yet, it is highly desirable ethically that the victims of the accident not be left to die.

Action to prevent that is consistent with the moral agent's accountability and responsibility. The ethic of response calls for a fitting response; it eschews inaction by facilitating ethical decision and action in the face of a dilemma. The idea of responsibility takes us even further, because it implies subsequent responses to our actions, an accountability that continues. So when the episode is over, our moral agent will attempt to make reparations and reconciliation with the elderly woman and child as part of an ongoing ethical response.

What do you think? What would you do? Why? What sort of ethical perspective do your reasons contain?

CHAPTER REVIEW

1. This chapter introduced the *ethic of response* - an ethic of *the fitting* - which attempts to incorporate or synthesise the normative theories outlined in Chapter Three.
2. The *ethic of response* is built on the idea of responsibility as expounded by HR Niebuhr who nominates four elements of responsibility: response, interpretation, accountability and social solidarity.
3. The chapter promotes three substantial values, critical to the ethic of response and of core relevance to discussion of issues later in the book: the value of life principle, the justice principle, and the covenantal integrity principle.
4. The major feature of the ethic of response is that it provides a procedural outline for ethical decision-making. This is explained in the chapter and then its usefulness and comprehensiveness is illustrated in two brief case discussions.

FURTHER READING

Bowie, N (1990) *Making Ethical Decisions*, New York: McGraw Hill.

Cooper, TL (1998) (4th ed) *The Responsible Administrator*, San Francisco: Jossey-Bass.

Glover, J (1974) *Responsibility*, London: Routledge and Kegan Paul.

Jonas, H (1984) *The Imperative of Responsibility*, Chicago: The University of Chicago Press.

Pollock-Byrne, JM (1989) "How to make an ethical decision" in *Ethics in Crime and Justice*, Belmont, CA: Wadsworth.

QUESTIONS FOR DISCUSSION

1. What are the merits of an ethic of response? What are its weaknesses? How useful do you believe it can be for you in examining moral dilemmas?
2. Are the three key values listed in this chapter a sufficient statement of substantial ethical principles? What difficulties do they pose? Are there other key values you would choose? Why?
3. Could the ethics of response be developed further to be a stand-alone normative theory? How?

CHAPTER FOUR NOTES

1 For an essay on the uses of this term by ethicists see the entry on "responsibility" in Becker, LC and Becker, CB (eds) (1992) *Encyclopaedia of Ethics*, vol II, New York: Garland Publishing Co.

2 Niebuhr's statement about responsibility is contained in a posthumously published work, *The Responsible Self*, New York: Harper and Row, 1963. Niebuhr taught Christian Ethics at Yale Divinity School, but his work can be understood in a wider frame of reference than an overtly Christian one. Niebuhr is the brother of the better-known Reinhold Niebuhr, a Christian social ethicist who contributed widely to American political debates for many decades.

3 Ibid, p 46.

4 The ethic of response reflects a broadly existentialist approach. In particular it is consistent with the philosophy of Martin Buber whose "I-Thou" principle bespeaks the fundamental dialogical character of human persons. It also parallels the more recent development of discourse or communicative ethics as elaborated by Jurgen Habermas, which points to a framework for doing ethics premised on the view that human interests develop in a fundamentally dialogical manner. Similarly, it echoes emphases which are found in the writing of Seyla Benhabib.

5 Niebuhr, HR, op cit, p 57.

6 Ibid, p 68.

7 Ibid, p 65.

8 Discussions about the "value of life" are complex and abundant in ethical literature. One excellent survey of the discussions is Kleinig, J (1991) *Valuing Life*, Princeton, New Jersey: Princeton University Press. In Chapter Seven of *Understanding Ethics*, there is a further account of this principle including how respect for persons and respect for life are related.

9 The concept "common good" is elaborated further in Chapter Eight.

10 For another discussion of ethical decision-making see DP Wittmer (1994) "Ethical Decision Making" Chapter 19 in TL Cooper (ed) *Handbook of Administrative Ethics*, New York: Marcel Dekker Inc.

11 Charlesworth, M "Ethics in Public Life", No 1 *Occasional Papers in Applied Ethics*, Brisbane: Queensland University of Technology, p 13.

12 This diagram adapts a model developed by the author in conjunction with the Queensland Public Sector Management Commission in the context of implementing that State's *Public Sector Ethics Act* 1994. Terry Cooper's text listed for further reading in this chapter is an excellent guide consistent with the ethic of response written for public administrators.

13 Those who suffer ongoing trauma are known as *Hibakusha*. For a documented recollection of the horror of the atom bomb blasts, a horror beyond the understanding of the rest of mankind, see *The Witness of These Two Days*, Vols I and II, English publication 1989 by the Japan Confederation of A- and H-bomb sufferers. It records 1000 detailed testimonies.

14 Truman was briefed to this effect. A memorandum of 25 April 1945, according to Henry L Stimson, asserted that given the impact of this technology and the world's state of moral advancement, "modern civilisation might be completely destroyed". For an intimate backgrounding of this political decision, see Stimson, HL "The Decision to Use the Atomic Bomb", in Gutman, A and Thompson, D (eds) (1991) *Ethics and Politics: Cases and Comments* (2nd ed) Chicago: Nelson-Hall Publishers, pp 5-15.

15 This case is used with permission of Professor John Langford of the University of Victoria, British Columbia, Canada.

CHAPTER FIVE

TRUTHTELLING AND HONESTY

Throughout the various proceedings, former national security adviser Robert McFarlane and his attorney Leonard Garment (known in some circles as "the spin doctor" because he handles media relations for his clients so well) insisted that McFarlane might have withheld information or "put a gloss" on the truth, but that he did not lie to Congress. In what was surely a characteristic moment in the North trial, McFarlane suggested that it is customary for national security officials to be less than forthcoming in their dealings with Congress. An obviously frustrated Judge Gerhard Gesell broke in, demanding to know what *that* meant. "Do you tell the truth? Do you not tell the truth? Or do you put a gloss on it?"

His store of vocabulary words not yet exhausted, McFarlane translated: "You don't lie. You put your own interpretation on what the truth is . . ."

The Oliver North Trial in *Who's Lying Now?,* by Deborah Baldwin
in Madsen, P and Shafritz, J, *Essentials of Government Ethics,*
(New York: Meridian, 1992) p 237.

"I did not have sexual relations with that woman, Ms Lewinsky."

President Bill Clinton

Preliminary Considerations

The reason for devoting a chapter to this topic before exploring other issues is simply that truthtelling is a foundational ethical matter which impacts upon ethical discussions of sexuality, bioethics, business ethics, and political responsibility. Indeed, truthfulness, and associated taboos on lying, are a cornerstone to the association we know as society. When we are unsure about who or what is untruthful, we become distrustful, and distrust destroys not only relationships but societies as well. They *disintegrate.* Note the word. It is the antonym (the opposite) of integrate, a companion word to *integrity*. Integrity is a theme to which we will return in the final chapter. For now it is enough to observe that integrated persons and societies are wholesome or hold together because they have integrity which in turn breeds trust nurtured in an atmosphere of truthfulness or honesty.

Truthfulness is a characteristic of the moral life which reflects very directly some of the principles and perspectives we discussed in the previous chapters. The matter of truthtelling and lying illustrates the ethical importance of the universalising maxim (the Golden Rule): "do to others what you would have them do to you". Generally, we do not wish to be lied to. When it comes to lying or dishonesty the onus lies with the person telling a lie or being dishonest to demonstrate the ethical justification of that act. One eloquent essayist on the virtue of truth points out that it is those who choose not to tell the truth who must defend their actions, just as it is those who would justify saying one thing and doing another who must give an account of themselves. He continues:

> Those who dissemble under the constraint of genuine situational dilemmas should not be lumped with those who make lying and deception routine features of their life. It is one thing to decide to lie when a Nazi is at your door and you are harbouring Jews; it is quite another to routinely deceive others as to the nature of one's character.[1]

The concept of truthfulness underlies the three key values nominated in the previous chapter as being fundamental to an ethic of response and other widely accepted normative perspectives. The *value of life principle* contains within it the injunction to respect persons and their autonomy. To deliberately deny the truth to others is generally to deny them respect. Similarly the *justice and fairness principle* enshrines within it an expectation that truthfulness is supportive of the "just society" because, *prima facie,* lying is unfair; no system of justice can survive if it is undermined by cheating or falsehood. Finally, it is the *covenantal integrity principle* which directly underpins the approach taken in this chapter, for it endorses integrity, honesty and informed consent in relationships.

For all this, the question of truthfulness is not straightforward. Most of us would have to admit that we have "bent the truth" at times, sometimes even for what we believe to be ethical reasons. Consider the following brief scenarios which indicate not only how omnipresent dilemmas of truthfulness and lying are, but also how problematic they may become:

- how do you answer the waitress' question when she asks, "Did you enjoy your meal?" when the curry was overdone?
- should a parent disclose to a child that her biological father was an artificial insemination donor?
- at what age are children entitled to know there is no Santa Claus?
- should teenagers be obliged to tell their parents all the details of their first sexual adventure?
- should an unfaithful husband confess his infidelity to his wife who knows nothing of it, especially when the affair has ended?
- how confidential should the confessional or a psychiatric interview be?
- should senior bureaucrats declare conflicts of interest when they are making decisions which affect a company in which they own shares?
- how binding ought marriage vows be?
- should company directors automatically advise shareholders about financial difficulties of their company at the annual public meeting?
- is the practice of "outing" (that is, naming certain high profile people as homosexual) a justifiable way of telling the truth?

- what boundaries should be drawn around fantasy/virtual reality?
- what ought to be the limits to borrowing the ideas of others in academic research?

Given scenarios like this, it is not surprising that the literature of applied ethics abounds with debate about the morality of lying, a debate to which we return later in this chapter. The ambiguities surrounding this matter are reflected in the range of terms associated with it. We shall concentrate on the phenomenon we call "lying" but matters of honesty and dishonesty have many related terms and concerns: slander, false witness, euphemism, evasion, exaggeration or even the so-called frivolous or "white" lie. Stealing is of course an honesty issue while promise-keeping and cheating are also aspects of the same account. They in turn take many forms. Promises may be implied (as in, "stopping at red lights and stop signs") or they may be explicit (as in, "I promise not to tell anyone I saw you steal"). Cheating on one's spouse (adultery) or cheating in one's tax return are both violations of trust, often rationalised and variously accepted in the community, despite society's negative attitude to untruthfulness.

What then constitutes lying? Is it enough to define it as "a conscious discrepancy between thought and deed"? Is the crucial element the intention (to deceive) or the outcome (deception)? Surely it is a characteristic of a lie that the liar knows the truth, and the utterance we call "a lie" is known by the speaker to be false. However, if a false declaration is made in the belief that it is false, and it then turns out that the declaration is based unknowingly on incorrect fact, is it still to be regarded as a lie or is it a mistake?

Though the discussion of this entire chapter suggests qualifications to the following definition, we may describe lying as "an intentionally deceptive message in the form of a statement or piece of information deliberately presented as being true. It is meant to deceive or give a wrong impression".[2]

What is Truthfulness?

It is probably easier to identify lying than it is to nominate "the truth". Truth is stranger than fiction, so it is said, and yet it is often to fiction – rather than the evening television news – that we turn for truth. Truthful insights and commentary on human events are the hallmark of great novels.

Well might we be wary of people who claim to know capital "T" truth, for that claim may be the precursor of self-righteousness, fanaticism and tyranny. Post-modernists have been ready to seize on the legacy of the universalist pursuit of the Truth in modern and pre-modern times and to point accurately to its exploitative, and oppressive consequences. To report this is not to defend the nihilistic extremism of post-modernism which can so undermine the quest for truth that nothing is believable, and which may disregard the approximate truths around which individuals and cultures are formed.

The point is that truth is not always obvious: the so-called "facts of the matter" are open to interpretation. The drama played out in the examination of evidence in a courtroom makes this point manifestly clear: we vow "to tell the whole truth and nothing but the truth" because we apparently often deal in partial, selective or misinterpreted truth. The idea of "certainty", a concept allied to truth, can be a slippery one. There are of course certain occurrences, events or states of affairs ("the earth is spherical" for instance) the truth of which we may now not dispute, though that was not always the case. In the realm of propositions and assertions about occurrences, events or states of affairs, the certainty or absoluteness of truth is less clear. In the domain of moral propositions, as we have seen, assertions are most debatable. There is also an element of cultural relativity to take account of: to regard as deceptive or dishonest such practices as haggling at an eastern bazaar, or the evasiveness or denial of an Aboriginal person over secret sacred business, is to miss entirely the contextual and cultural limitations often surrounding matters of truth and falsehood. While we must obviously grant cultural variations in the practice of truth-telling, we can also assume (psychopaths apart) that all moral agents have what may be loosely termed "a sense of truth and honesty".

Therefore, truth is about something much more than the facts; that something more is conveyed better by the term "truthfulness", which having the character of a virtue relates more to the disposition of the moral agent than the specificity of that agent's individual acts. Truthfulness certainly eschews dishonesty, but as a dispositional characteristic it especially eschews hypocrisy (where we say one thing and do another), and more especially cynicism (where we cease to care or even pretend about these matters). To sum up, truthfulness is a philosophically, ethically and, for some, theologically grounded virtue which signifies an intention to be someone who is not deceptive, and whose actions reflect an integrated, ethical view that life is valuable, trust is important and that fair dealings are necessary. Truthfulness and a life of integrity are therefore companions. Sustaining that truthfulness and integrity is a major moral challenge, for the human capacity for self-deception is profound.

Self-deception

Self-respect (or self-esteem) is a prerequisite to the respect for others which is a *sine qua non* of the ethical life. Self-deception is the toxin which cancerously attacks self-respect because it is the enemy of the moral self; self-deception makes a mockery of covenantal integrity, for how can one keep a promise with others if one has no inner moral consistency? It is for good reason that the ancient maxims have survived: "the knowledge of self is the beginning of wisdom" and, "above all else, to thine own self be true". It follows that (alongside the question "who is my neighbour?") the fundamental prior question in ethics is the question of identity, and self-knowledge, "Who am I?" or "Who are we?"

If we get used to deceiving ourselves, eventually our personalities crumble. We do not know who we are, and we become "people of the lie", as psychiatrist Scott Peck[3] characterises the pathology of many of his patients. The following extract from *The Brothers Karamazov* is pertinent to this present discussion and illustrates the way great fiction often speaks the truth:

> Above all, don't lie to yourself. The man [sic] who lies to himself and listens to his own lie comes to such a point that he cannot distinguish the truth within him, or around him, and so loses all respect for himself and for others. And having no respect he ceases to love. And in order to distract himself without love he gives way to passions and coarse pleasures and sinks to beastiality in his vices – all this from continual lying to other men [sic] and to himself.[4]

Echoing similar sentiments, the Bible enjoins "If you know the truth, the truth will set you free".[5] The original meaning of the biblical term "to know" is much stronger than our contemporary sense of knowing as understanding. It bespeaks knowledge that is integrated into a person's self-understanding and action. In the end, being a truly free person involves truthfulness while self-deception is the pathway to an inner enslavement.

However, such a homily is in danger of missing the point of how easy it is to practice self-deception. Indeed, it is partly so easy because, paradoxically, self-deception can grow out of the necessities of life: we make excuses to avoid uncomfortable situations; we indulge in fantasy to promote pleasure at the end of a painful day; we are secretive because we have a need for privacy; we avoid the truth out of loyalty to those with whom we work. Offering excuses, fantasising, protecting privacy, and being loyal are all necessary stratagems in certain situations but they can also be the breeding ground of self-deception.

The most dramatic examples in the twentieth century of ordinary people deceiving themselves to a point where they commit extraordinary evil are found among the German Nazis. One revealing account of this process was provided by Albert Speer who was found guilty of war crimes in Nuremberg.[6] Speer was no psychopathic ogre. Many knew him as a sensitive, caring and intelligent person. In his memoirs, Speer provides an explanation of his self-deceptive pathway to gross immorality. He compartmentalised his responsibilities, selectively attending to immediate duties, cultivating emotional detachment from those affected by his decisions, refusing to reflect ethically on his role, or to be open about what he was doing. Motivated by ambition and a sense of duty, he rationalised that the questions of morality which concerned him were in the private sphere of family and personal relationships, whereas any ethical responsibility concerning the public sphere of his workplace was out of his hands. Speer's account is all the more chilling because it describes the way many of us behave who loyally obey the orders of superiors regardless of ethical consequences. I remind myself that I should not be so self-deceived as to be certain that I would not have deceived myself to avoid moral responsibilities had I worked in Nazi Germany, just as I may presently deceive myself about my responsibilities to the victims of systemic poverty and oppression in our world (see Chapter Nine).

Indeed, it is instructive to observe how self-deception works collectively in a society like ours. Race discrimination and prejudice may be outlawed but they continue to be fostered by a powerful mixture of ignorance, fear and deception which is reinforced culturally and collectively by media stereotyping or careless conversation in entertainment venues. So, for example, jokes are told about particular ethnic groups, or from time to time racist assertions are made that disadvantaged racial groups are given too many handouts. When examined, these assertions are generally found to be baseless or based on faulty information, but these falsehoods come to be believed as representing the truth. In the 1996 Australian federal election, racism and misrepresentation of the truth combined to produce an electoral backlash in favour of candidates who claimed that Aboriginal people receive too many government benefits.

The falsity of these claims is borne out by statistics which show that Aboriginal people remain the most disadvantaged group in society – their longevity is on average 20 years less than whites, birth mortality rates are much higher, and employment and education levels much poorer. There are only two areas where Aborigines are entitled to special social security benefits. One is education, where only 17 per cent of 18 to 20-year-old Aborigines participate, compared with 45 per cent of the general age group; and housing, where 28 per cent own their own homes compared with the national average of 69 per cent.

It is vital that public policy be based on the truth, free of the myths that deceive us. The High Court native title decision in 1992 known as the *Mabo* case,[7] involving a revised legal basis for indigenous peoples' land claims in Australia, illustrates the point well. The Court decision showed that the ownership of land in Australia since early colonial days had been based on a convenient legal fiction, a policy lie known as *terra nullius* which stated that the continent of Australia was "the land of no people"; that is, it was not in possession of any people when the British Crown appropriated it. The *Mabo* case indicates how discussions of national identity are critical for public policy because they provide an opportunity to confront collective self-deceptions which lead to unethical policies.

The Case Against Lying

We have already alluded to the general consequentialist arguments against lying: it has a deleterious effect on human relationships and social obligations; lying often leads to cover-up lying and means that consequent actions are influenced by false information; lying may damage the liar; lying is an unfair misuse of power. However, the strongest arguments against all lying tend to be advanced on non-consequentialist grounds. Eighteenth century religious reformer, John Wesley puts the clear, hardline non-consequentalist position, that lying is always wrong even if it is claimed that good outcomes may result.

> If any, in fact, do this: either teach men [sic] to do evil that good may come or do so themselves, their damnation is just. This is particularly applicable to those who tell lies in order to do good

> thereby. It follows, that officious lies, as well as all
> abomination to the God of Truth. Therefore there is
> however strange it may sound, in that saying of the
> "I would not tell a wilful lie to save the souls of the whole world".[8]

Deontologists maintain that lying is intrinsically wrong because it violates fundamental, universal principles. "Never tell lies" is a basic moral rule though it may encounter deontology's ongoing problem that duties and principles can conflict. So one contemporary deontologist has cause to rethink the bald assertion, "never lie", saying "Lying is wrong, while withholding a truth may be perfectly permissible – but that is because withholding a truth is not lying".[9] In his opposition to lying, Immanuel Kant attempted to deal with the limitations of a simplistic general injunction against lying. Kant's essay entitled "On a Supposed Right to Lie from Altruistic Motives",[10] argues that if we lie in an attempt to prevent a murder, we are legally and morally blameworthy for the ill effects of lying. The argument is, roughly, always follow the rule to tell the truth, because you cannot foresee the consequences of lying; they may actually turn out to be worse than if the truth had been told.

Situational (or Selective) Truth?

In contrast to the absolutist stand against lying, there is a long line of ethical analysis which is prepared to grant exceptions to the prohibition on lying. That line may be traced back to Plato in *The Republic* who used the expression "the noble lie" for the fanciful story that might be told to persuade people to accept class distinctions and thereby safeguard social harmony.

More contemporary advocates of the exceptional lie, who even question the wisdom of a rule like "never tell lies", can be found in the ranks of utilitarians and particularly the situation ethicists we met earlier. According to Joseph Fletcher:

> For the situationist what makes the lie right is its covering purpose; he [sic] is not hypnotised by some abstract law, "Thou shalt not lie". He [sic] refuses to evaluate "white lies" told out of pity and espionage in wartime as ipso jure wrong.[11]

The same sentiment is echoed by another Christian theologian, Dietrich Bonhoeffer, whose fragmentary work on ethics contains a discussion of truth-telling. For Bonhoeffer, "telling the truth means something different according to the particular situation in which one stands … the essential character of the lie is to be found at a far deeper level than in the discrepancy between thought and speech".[12] Bonhoeffer's consistent situationism is reflected in the fact that he participated in a conspiracy to assassinate Hitler, for which he was subsequently hung. Presumably, on his moral reasoning Bonhoeffer believed he faced a situation where the deception necessary to plan an assassination was consistent with speaking truth to power.

The so-called "situational" or "existential" approach to truth-telling may be accused of emphasising exceptional cases to such a degree that it undermines the integrity of human relationships, establishing a slippery slope of deception: permissible lying is likely to lead to a more permissive attitude to promise-keeping, cheating or stealing, it may be said.

Most of us can probably recall situations where we would have few qualms of an ethical nature in avoiding the truth: the social lie, for instance, telling your party host dishonestly that you have another appointment because you do not want to stay any longer with certain guests; lying to protect a friend as Huckleberry Finn does (though not without inner torment) in Mark Twain's novel, to prevent the capture of his slave companion, Jim; failing to speak the truth, which is the central dilemma of the hero and heroine in the movie of Nathaniel Hawthorne's *Scarlett Letter*, in order to outwit the evil self-righteousness of their Calvinist tormentors.

Likewise, we probably recognise that how we determine truth-telling may be legitimately governed by the level of intimacy and direct responsibility operating in a situation or relationship. In other words, for situationists the nature of covenantal integrity is conditioned by the role we are in when confronted by the demand to be truthful. Truthfulness in certain professional ethical situations may be different from those that operate in more intimate relationships: so, it may be ethically inappropriate for an accountant to disclose his client's financial difficulties to the client's wife whereas for the client the expectations of trust, honesty and mutual support in marriage suggest he should be totally honest with her.

In the medical realm, situations repeatedly occur where the dilemma of truth-telling is acute. When and how should a diagnosis that a patient is dying be disclosed? Should a child be deceived about the pain associated with a treatment to avoid anxiety? Should medical records be amended if there has been a mistake in treatment to protect conscientious medical staff? Or consider, the reflection of Tanya, who was working in a nursing home:

> I was caring for a woman who had Alzheimer's and she said: "Oh, where is my husband?" and I had been told that this lady had been a widow for about 15 years and I'd looked at this woman and said to her: "Oh sweetie, your husband died 15 years ago" and the woman's grief was instantaneous. It was like I was delivering the news for the first time about her husband's death and I felt devastated … and I thought, "Oh my God, now I have this mourning woman …" and in hindsight … if that ever happens to me again I might just say: "He's out in the garden or he's gone away or he'll be back" only because I know that they'll forget about it in a couple of minutes … If you delivered the truth to the Alzheimer patient it might be really devastating for them … I mean, I have never forgotten about that … I think I might just divert them and not answer the question next time.

The simple injunction "never tell lies" may be inadequate for such cases, just as it is necessary that clearer guidance about "truth-telling" be given to cover such dilemmas in the health care professions.[13]

The matter of truthfulness in political life is extremely vexed and topical. Testifying before the New South Wales Independent Commission Against Corruption in 1992, Dr Terry Metherell (a former cabinet minister) said: "No doubt during my parliamentary career there have been times when I have lied. Regrettably, it's part of a politician's armor". Compromise may certainly be part of the art of politics but does that include compromising the truth? The situationist, consequentialist or utilitarian may be able to find justifications for the public lie. However, Sissela Bok, the author of a contemporary ethics classic on this topic writes: "Deceiving the people for the sake of the people is a self-contradictory notion in a democracy, unless it can be shown there has been genuine consent to deceit".[14] For Bok, who wrote in the wake of the Vietnam War, Watergate and their associated political cover-ups, the examples of such consent are few and far between, yet public officials can easily convince themselves that certain deceits pass the test of the public interest or the national interest. Of course it may be that in war or in certain sensitive economic matters, a currency devaluation for example, public officials may feel constrained on ethical grounds to keep facts from the public. Another example might be where a Minister for Police, knowing his statement to be false, might deny to the media that there is about to be a secret operation against suspected drug criminals, because he believed that such a denial was necessary to protect an action which the public would support. These cases could pass Sissela Bok's test that deceit in political life is only acceptable where the people would consent to that deceit.

However, Bok's major thesis is that we have become too used to lying and paternalistic deception in personal and professional life. The kind of scrutiny her excellent study provides across a range of practices leads to the conclusion that while sometimes there may be sufficient moral reason to lie, most often there is not. Her study is an indictment of the misuse of power through the withholding of truth or the dissemination of false information in society. In the end, her study represents a distinct word of caution about a situationalist approach to lying.

Truth and Response

Our discussion has emphasised the importance of truth-telling while acknowledging that in certain situations or roles, ethical judgment may have to be exercised about whether, how or when the truth can be spoken. The implication of our discussion is a practical guideline: *honesty is generally the best policy and if we have doubts in particular cases about this policy, honesty is still the best policy, for it is only when we believe (and can advance to ourselves and others sound ethical reasons for that belief) that honesty will lead to greater harm, that truth may then be denied or hidden.*

This is an approach which could receive general support from utilitarianism, the ethic of care and, in a different sense, from virtue theorists. However, I maintain that it is to the ethic of response that we can turn to spell out in a fuller way the approach to truth-telling we have been advancing. First of all, the ethic of response counsels us to take full account of principles (like that of *covenantal integrity*) which value truth-telling as a duty and to interpret the situation responsively and comprehensively. An ethic of response enjoins us to confront an ethical decision about lying or honesty in terms of self-knowledge or character: "If I am to be a truthful person what does that require in this context?" Then, in doing all that, the ethic of response focuses us on the appropriate question for addressing situations where truth-telling becomes a dilemma: "What is the *fitting* response?" This is the question Tanya, the nurse of the Alzheimer's patient, had to grapple with, just as it was for Huckleberry Finn agonising over a fitting way to answer the question which would have betrayed his slave friend. That "fitting-ness" implies accountability for the consequences of one's response. Furthermore, it suggests the need to be ready to follow up on the truth with action, to ask the subsequent question, "When I know and speak the truth what do I *do* about it?" For the responsible moral self, the truth is not merely spoken: it must be lived. The one who follows this pathway consistently, in whatever role in life, fashions a life of integrity.

CHAPTER REVIEW

The major points considered in this chapter are:

1. Truthtelling (like promise-keeping) is a foundational ethical matter, related to the principle of covenantal integrity introduced in Chapter Four.
2. What exactly constitutes truthtelling is not always clear.
3. The concept of "truthfulness" was examined to help clarify the matter. We concluded that "truthfulness" signifies an intention to be someone who is not deceptive and whose actions reflect an integrated, ethical view that life is valuable, trust is important and fair dealings are necessary.
4. However, the human capacity for self-deception bedevils our ability to be truthful.
5. Ethicists present a range of guidance about lying ranging from the deontological prohibition on all lying to a view which allows for situational or exceptional cases.
6. A practical guideline which is best interpreted in terms of the ethic of response's notion of *the fitting* was offered.

FURTHER READING

Bok, S (1989) *Lying: Moral Choice in Public and Private Life,* New York: Random House.

Bok, S (1982) *Secrets: on the Ethics of Concealment and Revelation,* New York: Pantheon Books.

Giannetti M, (1999) *The Lies We Live By: The Art of Self-Deception,* London: Bloomsbury.

Nyberg, D (1993) *The Varnished Truth: Truthtelling and Deceiving in Ordinary Life,* Chicago: University of Chicago Press.

QUESTIONS FOR DISCUSSION

1. Discuss the idea that it's all right to lie, cheat, break promises, steal or deceive yourself, (i) "as long as no one is hurt" or (ii) "as long as you don't get caught". Do you support these contentions? Make your reasons clear.

2. Does our responsibility to our close friends and relatives over-ride our responsibility to honesty and truth? Identify instances where this has been an issue in your own experience. How do you justify your position?
3. Is there an acceptable moral justification for stealing from the rich to give to the poor? Should people who have been unemployed for sometime through no fault of their own feel justified in shop-lifting at the supermarket? Give reasons for your views.
4. Someone once said, "All wealth is a theft from the poor". What does this suggest about (a) whether our global economy is built to some degree on cheating and stealing, and (b) the integrity of those who are among the affluent in global terms?
5. Consider the cases referred to throughout this chapter – especially the brief scenarios listed in the first section of the chapter, and those referred to in the section, "Situational (or selective) Truth". How do you respond to them? How might an ethic of response guide your ethical decisions?

CASE STUDY

PLAGIARISM OR ACCEPTABLE CUSTOM?

A science student discovers that two of his classmates who are international students are copying a chapter of a book to be submitted as a semester assignment. When he confronts them, he discovers they do not believe that they are doing anything wrong. They claim that in their home country, copying (without attribution) for such assignments is acceptable.

- Is this cheating? How are the rules about plagiarism and referencing related to the issue of honesty?
- Consider the question of ethical relativism. Should copying material out of a book and handing it in as a paper be acceptable in any country? Should these scientists

as graduates accept bribes while doing work in countries where bribery is an acceptable way of doing business?

- In what sense can we speak of honesty (and covenantal integrity) as a universal moral value?

CHAPTER FIVE NOTES

1 See Jordan, T (1995) "Truth" in Fitzgerald, R (ed) *The Eleven Saving Virtues*, Melbourne: Minerva Books, p 54. Trevor Jordan's essay on this topic is well worth reading. It is all the more potent because of the writer's personal history as an adopted child who was 24 years old before he learnt of his family's "elaborately sustained fiction".

2 Taken from Thiroux, JP (1990) "Ethics: Theory and Practice" (4th ed), New York: Macmillan Publishing Co, p 297. The other cognate definitions he offers are: *Cheating* is deceiving by trickery, swindling, misleading, and acting dishonestly or practising fraud. A *promise* is a declaration or vow that we will or will not do something, and breaking a promise is to fail to conform to or act contrary to or violate the promise. *Stealing* is taking something without right or permission, generally in a surreptitious way.

3 Peck, M Scott (1983) *The People of the Lie*, London: Arrow Books.

4 Doestoevsky, F (1957) *The Brothers Karamazov*, trans. C Garnett, New York: New American Library, p 49.

5 John 8 v 32, *The Bible*.

6 I am indebted for this report on Speer's memoirs to Mike W Martin (1989) *Everyday Morality*, Belmont, CA: Wadsworth Inc, especially the Chapter 6, "Self Deception".

7 *Mabo v Queensland (No 2)* (1992) 66 ALJR 408. The Full Court of the High Court handed down the decision on 3 June 1992.

8 From one of John Wesley's *Forty-Four Sermons*.

9 C Fried quoted in Nancy (Ann) Davis, "Contemporary Deontology", in Singer, P (1991) *A Companion to Ethics*, Oxford: Blackwell, p 208.

10 Immanuel Kant, (1949) "On a Supposed Right to Lie from Altruistic Motives", in Lewis White Beck (ed and trans) *Critique of Practical Reason and Other Writings in Moral Philosophy*, Chicago: Chicago University Press, pp 346-350.

11 Fletcher, J (1966) *Situation Ethics*, London: SCM Press, p 65.

12 Bonhoeffer, D (1955) *Ethics*, London: SCM Press, pp 363-371.

13 This extract comes from the research into lying in the nursing profession of a graduate student of mine, Anthony Tuckett.

14 Bok, S (1989) *Lying: Moral Choices in Public and Private Life*, New York: Random House, p 172. Another classic critique of the way the powerful, ruling groups of society including the mass media, practice deceptions on the people is put forward by Noam Chomsky. See Chomsky, N and Herman, ES (1988) *Manufacturing Consent: The Political Economy of the Mass Media*, New York: Pantheon Press. See also Hausman, C (2000) *Lies We Live By: Defeating Double-Talk and Deception in Advertising, Politics and the Media*, London: Routledge.

CHAPTER SIX

SEX, LOVE AND MORALITY

From *Looking for Alibrandi*

JOSIE: You two did it in a car, didn't you?
MICHAEL: I don't think this is the time or the place.
JOSIE: What type? Tell me.
Michael looks at her, defensively.
MICHAEL: A Charger.
JOSIE: Were you in love with her?
Michael is taken aback.
MICHAEL: I was a bit in awe of her. She wasn't like any of the other girls I knew.
JOSIE: In what way?
MICHAEL: She was smarter than me. She was going to go to university and study poetry.
JOSIE: My mother? A poet?
MICHAEL: I never thought that she would be interested in me. I had to use my brains for the first time. [...]
MICHAEL: I used to hang out here after school ... and your mother would walk by with Katia, who'd be clutching Christina's arm as if she was frightened of letting her go.
Michael gives a secretive smile.
Christina and I were experts at keeping it quiet. If Katia knew what we were getting up to she would have killed me.
JOSIE: I think she still wants to.

Marchetta, M, *Looking for Alibrandi*
Currency Press, Strawberry Hills, 2000. © Belle Ragazze Pty Ltd, 2000.
[Annotations to the script showing dialogue deleted from the final film omitted.]

In short, there are three things that last: faith, hope and love; and the greatest of these is love.

St Paul writing to the Corinthians

Setting the Scene

Sexuality is fundamental to our sense of identity and self-esteem. The idea that the expression of our sexuality has ethical implications seems indisputable, although whether sexuality yields its own ethic is a matter of dispute. In recent decades, the ethical implications of sexual activity have multiplied. The so-called sexual revolution, ushered in by the advent of the contraceptive pill, continues, despite the AIDS scare and the associated need for safe sex practices, as new sexual experimenters surf the Internet and engage in the virtual reality of cybersex. The enormous variety of sexual inclination, practice and custom across human cultures and sub-cultures presents such a complex mosaic that, to some, the area of sexuality defies normative prescription, creating a domain in which ethical relativism is rampant. The quest for a universal sexual code seems futile.

However, incest taboos are enforced widely across cultures while most societies channel sexual expression through some form of marriage, not necessarily monogamous, for 75 per cent of recorded human societies have been polygamous. In some societies the young are formally instructed in sexual acts by older women, while in others sexual initiation is furtive, secretive and random. The sexual preferences of human beings take on many names.[1] At the same time, for some, abstinence from sexual activity (celibacy) is a viable lifestyle which can rechannel sexual energies into other creative pursuits, while many express their sexuality through a marriage in which the fostering of a family is paramount.

To set the scene further: what are we to make of the array of sexual options now openly practised in societies like ours? Have we gone overboard in demythologising and demystifying sex by challenging the romanticism and puritanism which shaped sexual ethics before the sexual revolution? The divide between baby-making and love-making may be liberating, but are the popular culture's demands for sexual performance creating another kind of enslavement? While we might agree that in the privacy of their bedrooms people can do what they want "as long as they don't do it in the street and frighten the horses", we might also ask whether sexual expression is a purely private affair?

The clearest ethical response to the confusing messages about sex is the *conservative view that sex is morally permissible only if it occurs within the institution of marriage*. One version of this view is the Roman

Catholic position reaffirmed in many papal encyclicals. Based on a particular interpretation of natural law which says that sex is essentially for procreation, all sexual expressions that occur outside the institution of marriage, and all sexual activities that are incompatible with reproduction, even in marriage (including the use of contraception, oral and anal sex, and masturbation) are termed "contrary to the law of nature" and therefore immoral or "intrinsically evil".[2]

This so-called conservative view can be supported on secular utilitarian grounds. However, in the secular form the natural law taboo on sexual acts within marriage that are incompatible with procreation does not usually apply. Nonetheless, the argument for sex to be practised exclusively within marriage, on grounds of social utility, maintains that this limitation will contribute to the development of stable family units which in turn are essential for the proper nurturance of children and the consequent welfare of society. Of course, this consequentialist argument is open to question because its assumptions about the consequences (for example, that non-marital sex clearly undercuts family life) may be challenged. In this sense the conservative proposition based on a social utility argument is very different from the natural law (deontological or essentialist) approach which attempts to ground sexual behaviour in a fixed moral order. Both the natural law and secular utilitarian approaches take seriously the union between persons involved in sexual expression, as well as the important link between sexuality and the nurturing of a family. However, the conservative view labours under the grave practical (but not ethically fatal) difficulty that the proposition of confining sex to marriage is no longer accepted even in principle by a large proportion of the community.

The conservative approach makes claims about the nature or meaning or purpose of sexuality. In the natural law version there are strong and explicit claims that sex is fundamentally and exclusively for procreation; in the social utility approach the implicit, if weaker, claim is that sex should contribute to human happiness, well-being and social stability through the nurturance of the young. Both approaches therefore invite a consideration of the nature, meaning or purpose of sexuality as the starting point for any ethic of sexual practice. It is this matter which underpins the discussion of this chapter.

However, rather than discuss the meaning of sexuality, it is appropriate that we first explore the human experience of "love" which may be both a pre-requisite for, and a consequence of, sexual expression. Certainly, the intimacy and bonding often associated with sexual attraction and expression suggests a link between sex and love. Even in the sexual interaction of a client with a prostitute it is not unknown for the sexual partner(s) to "fall in love"; it is for good reason that we sometimes refer to "*having* sex" as "*making* love".

What is the Meaning of "Love"?

Love - whatever we mean by it - is important in the ethical life. It is the virtue which finds a correlative in Kant's core maxim, "respect persons as ends not means", just as it is pivotal in the ethic of care and situation ethics. "Love" not only "makes the world go round" as the song says, but it also makes the ethical life possible and necessary. It is some concept of "love" which resides within the substantial values of the ethic of response: valuing life, justice and covenantal integrity. Indeed, though the focus of this chapter is on the link between "love" and "sexuality", the connection between "love" and "justice" is a vital and noteworthy one. We normally understand love to be a virtue within interpersonal relationships, but it has its implications for groups, organisations and societies, implications which point to distributive or social justice. In this sense, justice is the social expression of love. If the necessary quality of compassion is to be developed in social and public policy, then the dialectic between love and justice must be maintained.

Of course, many meanings are conveyed by the word "love". The Greek language, which is so formative in our intellectual culture, accommodates these diverse meanings by having different words for different forms of "love". One form of love refers to filial, mutual or friendship love - *philia*. This ordinary love between friends or family members nurtures our need to belong to a group of fellow human beings in whose welfare we have an interest, just as they do in ours. A more demanding and extraordinary form of love refers to sacrificial or divine love - *agape*. In the human condition it functions as a kind of impossible possibility. Agapeic love is transcendent, it knows no bounds, it is for all (even one's enemies), it is ready to sacrifice the self for the sake of others with whom there is no filial kinship; it says, "I will give of myself, requiring nothing in return".

The other Greek word for love is *eros* which signifies the erotic, desiring, lustful exchange, which leads in the direction of sexual activity. Erotic love may enable us temporarily to transcend our personal ego's limitations but it remains dependent on arousal by another, fantasised or real.

"Love" may refer to any of these dimensions of human experience or all of them, interacting with each other; *eros* without *philia* may become a consuming passion, just as *agape* can enrich and nurture both *eros* and *philia*. In our embodied human wholeness we are potentially agents, and objects, of all three dimensions of love.

Given this preliminary analysis of what we may mean by love, it is apparent that "true love" (to cite that over-used expression) is more than a feeling. It is certainly more than physical desire which can either be the spark which attracts us to another or a preoccupation with a sexual object. A person may lust after Mary's body, indeed her buttocks or her breasts, but that is not the same as saying, "I love Mary (the person)". "True love" is a state beyond mere "falling in love"; after all, it sometimes happens that people keep falling in and out of love, moving from one love affair to the next. Indeed "true love" may sometimes grow even when people have not romantically fallen in love, as the experience of some pre-arranged marriages in certain epochs or cultures indicates. "True love" suggests a state of being in love which, while it involves attraction, is followed by a decision which harnesses the feelings of love (*eros, philia,* and even *agape*) to be with and for the other whom one loves. *Commitment* is fundamental to true love, commitment which takes seriously that interdependence which is characteristic of life itself, while also taking seriously our limitations, the ambiguity of the human condition, to which we alluded in the first chapter. Given these limitations and this interdependence, love as commitment exercises self-discipline and respects the autonomy of the other to whom love is given. Such an approach is an expression of what we have termed *covenantal integrity*, and is arguably essential to marriage, though it is not our purpose here to develop an analysis of marriage.

So, love has a quality of steadfastness which is captured by the Shakespearean sonnet:

> Love is not love
> Which alters when it alteration finds,
> Or bends with the remover to remove:
> O no; it is an ever-fixed mark,
> That looks on tempests, and is never shaken;[3]

Though love is hard to define, one of the most influential accounts of love in contemporary literature comes from the psychiatrist,

M Scott Peck who in his book *The Road Less Travelled*[4] defines love as: "The will to extend one's self for the purpose of nurturing one's own or another's spiritual growth".

Peck focuses his discussion of love on the mutual growth and development of the lovers. This involves "a progressive enlargement of the self" which can eventually, though rarely in practice, lead to a mystical state where "the distinction between the self and the world" become blurred, just as when we "fall in love" our ego boundaries fall. It is our ego boundaries which protect our sense of self from vulnerability; in the process of falling in love we lose that protection as another merges with our intimate space. Peck draws a comparison between this heightened state of love and the momentary ecstasy (literally, *eks – stasis,* standing outside oneself) of sexual orgasm. The suggestion is, and it has been taken up by others, that sexual union prefigures the potential sense of union with all life, a state of spirituality which is rare but can be fostered and practised. In other words, the experience of love, as Peck promotes it, synchronises with a belief that one is all and all is one, the consciousness that reality is oneness, which produces a sense of universal love.

Erich Fromm is another who has explored the meaning of love in a profound way. In language that may seem far removed from young lovers, he concludes:

> Love is not primarily a relationship to a specific person; it is an *attitude,* an *orientation of character* which determines the relatedness of a person to the world as a whole, not toward one "object" of love … If I truly love one person I love all persons, I love the world, I love life.[5]

There is a prima facie difficulty in relating this view of "true love" to erotic love however. While "true love" so defined is "*in*clusive" or even, universalistic, erotic love is "*ex*clusive" focussing attention on one person (or at least, not many). In the above we are in danger of idealising and disembodying love. We might end up reinforcing the dualistic view that sex is merely a physical act of relief, pleasure and procreation, while love is a spiritual, almost out-of-body experience. Surely, erotic love and true love belong to the same realm of human experience. When we examine erotic love a little more closely, the distinction is not so sharp. Erotic love creates a process of union and re-union between individuals. It opens the way for an intermingling not only of bodies but of persons (though in the case of prostitution or the most casual sex this is less likely). Arguably, a context of commitment will sustain that intermingling most effectively.

We are not yet ready to declare the ethical parameters which arise from the nature of love and sex but we may offer a tentative hypothesis: *while love may enhance sexual expression, sexual expression can enhance love, though not necessarily so*. Scott Peck summarises the dynamics of how this may occur:

> the temporary loss of ego boundaries involved in falling in love and in sexual intercourse not only leads us to make commitments to other people from which real love may begin but also gives us a foretaste of (and therefore an incentive for) the more lasting mystical ecstasy that can be ours after a lifetime of love. As such, therefore, while falling in love is not itself love, it is part of the great and mysterious scheme of love.[6]

Whatever we think of the metaphysical assumptions Peck's statement implies, his analysis suggests an approach to the morality of sexuality which begs our serious attention: one that fosters the expression of sexuality in a way which nurtures maturing, loving persons.

The Purpose of Sex

Our discussions so far have identified several answers to the question: "what is sex for?"

- procreation
- an expression of power
- pleasure
- an expression of affection or love

In this section we will explore in greater detail how these are expressed in sexual activity. Sometimes all four may be present in a sexual relationship and it can be plausibly claimed that for a sexual relationship to enhance psychic health, a balanced expression of all four is necessary. However, our purpose here is to examine them in turn to assess whether each so-called purpose or outcome of sex is necessary or sufficient, in an ethical sense, to sexual expression. This examination will provide a basis for indicating whether or not there are ethical guidelines which especially apply to sexual activity.

(a) Procreation

It is self-evident that heterosexual intercourse can result in pregnancy and children. At the same time, current reproductive technology provides devices which can control this outcome. Specifically, modern contraception and sterilisation break the necessary nexus between heterosexual intercourse and procreation so that the fear of pregnancy need no longer dominate sexual ethics. In addition, the techniques of in vitro fertilisation, artificial insemination by donor, sterilisation or surrogate motherhood exemplify the way procreation as an outcome of heterosexual activity is being modified. However, the effect of these technological options is to create other ethical dilemmas.

The normative argument which links sexual activity to the need always to preserve the possibility of procreation depends on a worldview which says there is a law of nature (natural law) which is binding (in a deontological sense) on sexual behaviour. Consequentialists can find any number of sound moral reasons, including the prevention of human pregnancies in an over-populated world, for rejecting the view that sexual activity ought always be open to the possibility of procreation. In any case, invoking "the natural" is a dubious factor where sexual expression is concerned because human beings seem to express themselves naturally in various ways. Indeed, some ethicists argue that "nature" is generally a doubtful and even fallacious guide to morality. They point out that in many areas of life, especially in medical practice, we intervene in what *is* a natural process, for example, disease, because we believe *ought* to. When the argument is offered that some sexual activities are morally wrong because they are unnatural, it is wise to check whether that view is based on some preconception that sex, in itself, is wrong, and that it can only be the propagation of the species which would over-ride its intrinsic evil. So what needs to be demonstrated, in order to defend the view that procreation ought to be an essential part of sexual activity, is why sex should be seen as being, in itself, wrong or deficient and why particular instances of sexual intercourse need a superior reason, like procreation, to be morally permissible.

Obviously, the notion of procreation as one purpose of human sexuality remains, and points to a serious responsibility associated with sex, namely the obligation to care for children. However, the claim that procreation provides the sole, or necessary moral reason to express sexuality is not sustainable.

(b) Power

The term "potency" (which is cognate to "power") is often linked with sexual expression. Sexual interaction often gives partners a sense of empowerment and well-being. Indeed, "power" is a factor present in all relationships. However, the thrill of seduction and a sense of dominance sometimes associated with sex can lead to coercive relationships in which the power relationship of sex is unequal. The sexual abuse of clients in a professional context is an instance. Rape is the most explicit example of the misuse of power in sex, while sexual harassment in the workplace is another.

The exercise of power through sexual expression may be inevitable and relatively harmless in many circumstances; indeed it may be part of the pleasure of sex. However, there is plenty of shocking evidence, especially in the testimony of female victims of domestic violence and incest victims, that the urge to power combined with sex can result in coercion and physical domination which amounts to a violation of a sexual partner that is not ethically justifiable. Some feminists even suggest that genuinely equal personal relationships in a class-structured sexist society are not possible. As a consequence, they claim that, because of the power factor, sexual harmony between men and women is fundamentally threatened. The complex and harmful consequences of treating sex as an exercise of power alone prevent us from allowing "the expression of power" as an essential, necessary or sufficient moral justification for this activity.

(c) Pleasure

As a gift available to most healthy adults, sexual activity is one of life's freely given joys. Foreplay and sexual orgasm are re-creative and a relief from tension. However, as with other pleasures or appetites craving satisfaction, there can be a fine line between pleasure and an indulgent self-gratification which is narcissistic and addictive in a way seemingly self-abusive to persons.

Pleasure seems to be intrinsic to sex, although the nature of what is pleasurable may differ between persons. Nonetheless, it is possible to envisage circumstances where pleasure is absent from sexual activity: in rape, for the victim that is clearly not the case; in a loveless marriage, the sex act might lose all sense of pleasure; a sexually addicted person, driven by undisciplined gratification of needs, may eventually come to the point where sex is no longer pleasurable. Regardless of these extreme cases, pleasure as a goal for sexual activity makes a fair claim to be an adequate and morally justified basis for sexual expression. Indeed, the case may be plausibly made (as in Russell Vannoy's *Sex Without Love*[7]) that the demands of love or procreation can burden sex and mar the unfettered excitement which is important to sexual well-being. However, the weakness of this claim is that it may isolate sexual activity from the development of the whole person who has needs other than the sexual, and from the whole gamut of relationships and responsibilities around which mature human existence is formed and sexuality expressed. While granting that for a period in one's lifetime, or in particular circumstances, the pursuit of sex for pleasure alone is morally permissible, it is not so clear that, across a lifetime, pleasure alone is the most desirable or justifiable expression of sexuality.

(d) Love or affection

As we have already said in our discussion of love, sexual intimacy can cultivate a bonding, or thoroughgoing union of interests between persons. Sexual expression is a way of sharing mutual pleasure or the mutual intention of procreation or a mutual sense of empowerment which directly communicates emotions of affection, caring and love. To those who endorse this approach as fundamentally desirable (without necessarily making the link to the mystical terrain chartered by Scott Peck), this loving bond is a liberating discovery of individuality within sexual interdependence. Sex with love is more able to sustain the conditions of voluntariness, caring love and commitment which some maintain is more likely to nurture pleasurable sexual expression over a period of time, and which also can support the task of parenting a family. Whether this implies monogamy is a further question. Human experience in certain cultures suggests that love implies sexual exclusivity (or monogamy), though not always for a lifetime. Likewise, a concern for justice and fairness (or equal power) in a sexual relationship could also be interpreted as affirming monogamy.

In summary, we have argued, that, (i) power is neither a necessary or sufficient justification for sexual activity, (ii) procreation is not a necessary reason, (iii) pleasure and love may be sufficient reasons, taken together or alone, and, (iv) love and pleasure are most desirably expressed in an environment of commitment to enhance personal growth. Under these conditions, sexuality is more likely to be an instrument of the values of *respect for persons, justice* and *covenantal integrity*.

Before we take these conclusions any further we need to address a view which, while possibly being advanced in conjunction with any of the above purposes, is more particularly advanced for a position which sees no necessary ethical requirement for the nexus between sex, love and commitment.

Are Honesty and Consent Enough?

In advocating *a liberal approach to sexual relationships based on pleasure alone* and where sexual expression is not necessarily linked to love and commitment, the following moral guideline is often invoked: "Any sexual relationship is alright providing you are honest with your partner and don't use or manipulate them". This honesty is taken to refer to revealing any other sexual commitments, and whether, if married, one's partner will object to the liaison. Also, in this era of safe sex, it refers to disclosing any history of sexually transmitted diseases. Overall, this guideline simply means, "Sex is fine providing you are open with your partner about any potential problems and the status of the relationship – and then he or she voluntarily agrees to go ahead". This section questions that rationale.

In an important essay which canvasses such matters, Thomas Mappes argues that, in general, another person is not being used sexually whenever there is voluntary informed consent to the sexual interaction. However, as Mappes shows through the analysis of several hypothetical situations there may be violations of an apparent informed consent through coercion and deception.[8]

Mappes cites the hypothetical case of Mr Troubled, a young widower who is raising three children. Mr Troubled has been retrenched and cannot find another job; he believes he should not move to another town because his children need the stability and emotional support of their environment. Financially, he is in grave circumstances: he is no longer eligible for unemployment benefits, his relatives are in no position to help, and if his mortgage payments are defaulted, he will lose his modest house. Ms Opportunistic who lives in the same town has been making sexual overtures to Mr Troubled. Mr Troubled has previously made it clear to Ms Opportunistic that he is not interested in a sexual relationship with her. However, aware of his present difficulties, Ms Opportunistic offers to make mortgage payments for Mr Troubled on a continuing basis provided he consents to a sexual affair. Ms Opportunistic's attempt to use Mr Troubled sexually by taking advantage of his desperate situation is a case of manipulation, which effectively precludes Mr Troubled from the voluntary consent necessary to an ethically justified liberal approach to sex outside marriage.

Cases such as this point to the fact that in matters of sexuality, where powerful urges, needs and desires operate, we may be especially vulnerable to deception about what is honest or when we are acting voluntarily. The phrase, "taken advantage of" is often used to refer to sexual liaisons where apparent honesty and consent turned sour. There is no doubt that honesty, voluntariness and informed consent in sexual relationships are morally important, as the liberal approach emphasises, but they are overstated when they are presented as sufficient ethical justifications on their own.

Responsible Sex

This chapter has adopted an approach to the ethical justification of sexual activity which emphasises a desirable, preferable, though not essential, linkage of that activity to love and commitment between persons. Nonetheless, it is in keeping with the ethic of response to be open to a contextually based fitting judgment about what is "the best available action" even if it does not conform to what has been presented as desirable or preferable. Sexual expression consistent with the ethic of response does not respond simply to narrow self-interests. Rather, it responds to a comprehensive appreciation of the total moral situation and with special care to act in ways that are consistent with the kind of person we seek to be, conscious of how fundamental to personal growth and identity sexuality is. At the same time, the *fitting response* is not bound by pre-conceived rules such as, "sex outside marriage is forbidden".

The argument which chooses to stress the link between sex and love is in line with that of Vincent Punzo.[9] Punzo speaks of "existential integrity" as being a necessary condition to ethical sexual activity. Existential integrity requires attention not only to matters of covenantal integrity, the bonds between people, but to the dispositional question of personal character. In other words it asks: "how can I be true to myself in my sexual activity?" In Punzo's view, sex for pleasure alone, when it means casual sex without commitment, involves actually separating the self from one's existential integrity as a sexual being – "an alienation that makes one's sexuality an object, which is to be given to another in exchange for his [sic] objectified sexuality". For Punzo, there is a morally significant difference between sexual intercourse and other types of human activity because it is "not simply a union of organs, but is as intimate and as total a physical union of two selves as is possible of achievement".

Punzo believes it is necessary to link sexual activity and loving commitment. This leads him to argue that sexual unions apart from the framework of marriage (which may include pre-marital commitment, though not exclusive homosexual commitment apparently) are "morally deficient because they lack existential integrity". However, I maintain that the thrust of Punzo's argument can be accepted without taking it to the precise conclusion he draws.

We may summarise the discussion to date: a morally preferable, though not morally essential, approach to sexual activity is that it be developed within a relationship of long-term commitment in which the nurturance of a mature love is valued. In other words, sexual activity is best directed morally when it is true to the covenantal integrity of which we have spoken earlier. In response ethics terms that approach is most fitting to the human condition. However, the circumstances of life and human contexts vary so much that this "ideal" is not always possible nor appropriate nor fitting at all stages of life. It is always problematic to define the exceptional cases. One thinks of a person who, for whatever reason, has little prospect of a long-term partner, perhaps a widow in mid-life whose commitment to her adolescent children limits the prospect of marriage, or the young person at an experimental stage of life not ready to settle down. In such cases, and undoubtedly in others, it may not be appropriate to judge this sexual activity (which is primarily for pleasure and outside the framework of commitment) unethical, providing there is care taken not to be coercive or manipulative but to be honest with one's partner about the limited context of the activity. Of course, as we have seen, even the caveat of honesty and non-coerciveness is more problematic than at first might seem the case.

It is appropriate at this point to consider one of the vexed areas of sexual ethics: *homosexuality*. How would an ethic of response approach the question of when, if ever, homosexual acts are ethically justified?

First, the ethic of response is not shackled by the natural law argument which concludes that homosexuality is contrary to nature. Secondly, the focus for an ethic of response is on the quality of relationships rather than the specificity of sexual acts: the question is not, what do sexual partners *do*? but, how does what they do contribute to personal growth, loving interdependence and the other goals which sex can serve? This is not to say that "the nature of acts" is irrelevant to ethical judgment: particular acts, especially when they are repeated, certainly refashion the character of a person for good or ill. However, except in the case of sexual violence,[10] there is no ethical reason to question any sexual act *per se*. We conclude that homosexuality, while it has limitations in terms of serving that optional goal of sexuality, procreation, can promote ethical ends just as heterosexuality can. In the terms argued in this chapter, responsible homosexual expression preferably links sex with love and aims to cultivate faithful, committed relationships, analogous to heterosexual marriage. As with heterosexuality or bisexuality, the ethic of response would challenge (if not prohibit) promiscuous, casual homosexual activity.

Because of the confused attitudes towards homosexuality in our culture, persons of gay and lesbian orientation have often suffered deeply as they struggle to find appropriate ways of expressing their sexuality.[11] So too have trans-gendered individuals who often live in a tortured "no person's land" of shattered identity. The experience of homosexual and transgender persons reminds the community at large how troublesome it can sometimes be to direct our sexuality in creative and ethically justifiable ways. This chapter itself has demonstrated that it is very difficult to be clear and prescriptive about an area of human experience which so directly reflects the ambiguity of our human condition.

All in all, if any topic of applied ethics should be approached with compassion, it is the domain of sexual passion. We cannot be who we are, nor can we collaborate to build livable communities without keeping our passions alive, but an unbridled, undisciplined expression of passion can be destructive. Furthermore, our sexual passion is most vulnerable to the human capacity for self-deception spoken of in the previous chapter. One antidote to self-deception is self-discipline. So, in this chapter, we have affirmed that the passion of sexuality is best disciplined by the bridle[12] of love.

Sexuality and Public Policy

The discussion throughout this chapter has concentrated on ethical considerations within the personal and interpersonal dimensions of expressing sexuality. However, an activity so important to human beings as sex, necessarily has serious social and communal implications which create ethical dilemmas in public policy. Society has a major stake in how its members express sexuality. There can be no denying that marriage and family patterns in society generate issues that require a collective responsibility, especially in terms of the rights of children. Developments in reproductive technology are raising legal, ethical and social policy dilemmas. In Vitro Fertilisation techniques make surrogacy possible but may raise difficulties of identity for child and parents alike.

Central to considerations of sexuality and public policy is a major plank of liberal democratic societies: the Millian (JS Mill) principle that the private behaviour of citizens should only be regulated by the state when there is demonstrable harm to citizens.[13] An allied half-truth raised on matters of policy involving sexuality is that you cannot legislate morality. Consequently, there is often reluctance in societies such as ours to adopting interventionist public policies in areas related to human sexuality. At the same time, it seems that matters of sexuality and public policy often involve issues of social ethics. Each of the following items enshrines questions which are ethically disputable, questions which revolve around the interpretation of the principles of respect for persons, justice, and social obligation:

- Adultery is subject to the criminal law in some countries.
- In Australia divorce is automatically granted after a 12-month separation of a married couple.
- The ethical responsibility of the medical profession to advise unsuspecting partners that their spouse is HIV positive is a hotly debated public issue.
- The provision of condoms in a male prison population is a matter raised regularly in the media.
- The procurement of sex for disabled clients is a real concern for some welfare workers.
- The open promotion of sex in advertising is a feature of many societies.
- The availability of anonymous, sexual relationships across the Internet.

An aspect of public policy which has received increasing attention recently is *sexual harassment and discrimination.* Statutory endorsements of equal employment opportunity, workplace sexual harassment procedures, homosexual law reform, abortion law review and laws against rape in marriage are major instances of social policy reform in areas related to sexuality. These are generally presented as social justice issues, which they are, but they also involve complex ethical justifications, set within an analysis of the sexist nature of society. The practical application of these policies can be difficult and demonstrates the value of an ethical decision-making process based on an approach like the ethic of response.[14]

What follows is a very limited and introductory discussion of two other topics around which considerations of sexuality and public policy converge.

(a) Prostitution

Whether or not prostitution is "the world's oldest profession", societies have invariably failed to eradicate the practice of people paying others, male or female, to have sex. This suggests that prostitution meets some fundamental social need, and could even therefore be regarded as a social service. Saint Thomas Aquinas reportedly, if crudely, made the point by saying, "Even the palace must have its sewers".

Utilitarians are concerned to determine whether meeting that need creates more social harm than benefit while Kantians might conclude that prostitution is a clear case of persons being used as a means and is therefore morally dubious. Certainly, within the ethical view that sex and love should ideally be linked, prostitution is most questionable; on grounds of sex for pleasure alone it might be justified, though within the ethic of response such a consideration will probably be qualified by the requirement to respond comprehensively to facts about prostitution in society, including undesirable health hazards for example.

Defining what prostitution is, is not always straight forward. Some want to present the industry conducted by sex workers as a commercial activity, more the concern of business ethics than the ethics of sexuality. The complexity of this phenomenon is further illustrated by the emerging trend to use sexual surrogates in certain forms of sex therapy. Though money exchanges hands for this service, is it prostitution when the motivation is therapeutic?

Within the public discourse over whether the state should take a stance on prostitution, major issues include, (i) are there victims to be protected, when the activity is between consenting adults? and (ii) are prostitutes under coercion to ply their trade, including the coercion of economic necessity? Some take the view that it is not up to the state to enter into the question of personal morality associated with prostitution and that though the practice is not to be legalised, it is only the linkage between prostitution and other crime like the illegal drug trade, or the involvement of minors, which should be policed.

Certainly, from the perspective of social responsibility, a critical ethical concern is the underlying conditions which give rise to prostitution. These may include economic hardship, drug addictions, sexual abuse and low self-esteem, together with a culture and pattern of sexual socialisation which encourages the commodification of sex. A most serious ethical issue associated with prostitution law reform is the relationship between female prostitution and the place of women in society. It is certainly the case historically that women have been the chief victims of prostitution. Women may be divided about the appropriate public policy on prostitution, but from our ethical perspective it is essential that any policy should not exacerbate injustices between the sexes in society, but should seek to reduce them.

(b) Pornography and censorship

Pornography is a multi-billion dollar industry within many societies influencing the sexual appetites and expressions of countless individuals. Its recent promotion through the medium of the Internet is disturbing because it makes pornography more accessible to the young. Pornography can be defined as "sexually explicit material intended to be sexually arousing", although many would question the usefulness of such a general definition, drawing a distinction between erotica and so-called "soft" or "hardcore" pornography. Furthermore, that definition's focus on the intention in producing the materials suggests that works of art or novels or even medical textbooks which depict sexually explicit material are not pornographic. Analyses of pornography raise a dimension of sexuality which merits closer examination than we have provided thus far, namely, the morality of fantasy.[15] Yet pornography involves more than fantasy and images: the storylines of an X-rated video convey very explicit values about interpersonal relationships. The subtle impact of these values on the viewer as well as on the participating models or actors raise considerable moral doubts about pornography.

In many ways pornography is akin to prostitution as it involves the commercialisation, objectification and commodification of sex. An ethical critique of pornography is therefore likely to raise similar arguments to those used against prostitution in the previous section. Depictions of sex with violence or the use of children are widely condemned from various ethical perspectives. Certainly, most utilitarians would take this line although the argument about pornography from a social utility basis is bedevilled by contrary, conflicting and inconclusive evidence about the social harm caused by pornography. Even the argument that pornography is demeaning of women (for overwhelmingly, though not exclusively, it is women who are depicted as sexual objects) is sometimes contested. The responsible use of sex we have outlined earlier in this chapter would almost certainly find the production and use of pornography ethically unjustified although an argument could be made for certain cases where pornography is sexually therapeutic, for example where its use revitalises and enhances a committed couples' love-making. However, not even this justification overcomes the doubts about such an exploitative industry.

While pornography might fail the ethical test, it is another question as to how it should be treated in public policy. Until there is incontrovertible evidence of the harmful effects of non-violent, adult pornography, it is improbable that liberal democratic states will impose anything but minimal regulation on this industry, because to do so appears to limit a principle central to liberal democracy, namely freedom of expression. Of course, it can be argued that in matters of sexuality the human capacity for self-deception makes unfettered freedom a doubtful quality (that is, freedom without discipline). The question remains, however, whether it is the state or the individual who should impose limits on personal freedom, although there are clearly some matters of wrongdoing or criminality where that freedom must be restricted. In any case, it is around pornography that major debates on the ethics of censorship have arisen.[16] Even if it were accepted that pornography is harmful in society, there may still be insufficient grounds for instituting censorship. An ethic of response is likely to be influenced by the utilitarian considerations that on balance, the censorship of non-violent adult pornography may create more harm than good. Because censorship could create a pornography blackmarket, it would present administrative nightmares and could open the way for censors to abuse their powers. As with some other moral questions involving potential censorship, a responsible approach indicates that it is preferable for society to promote educational campaigns along with minimal censorship to curtail social harm.

CHAPTER REVIEW

The major points considered in this chapter are:

1. Human sexual practice is very diverse.
2. An analysis of the nature of love and its relationship to sexuality led us to the view that the expression of sexuality should ideally foster and nurture maturing, loving persons.
3. Our analysis of the nature of sexuality defined four possible functions of sex: procreation, power, pleasure, love.
4. The conservative view that sex is primarily and necessarily for procreation, was outlined and rejected. We also outlined and rejected the liberal view that honesty and consent between partners are a sufficient ethical basis for sexual relationships.
5. We argued for the view that a morally preferable, though not absolutely essential, approach to sexual activity is that it be developed within a relationship of long-term commitment in which the nurturance of a mature love is valued. We noted that homosexual relationships may meet this criteria.
6. However, following the emphasis on a fitting response, we (a) claimed there can be circumstances in which this "ideal" is not possible, and (b) granted, with caution, that there are cases where sexual activity primarily for pleasure outside the framework of commitment might not in itself be labelled unethical.
7. Finally, we considered briefly a range of public policy matters in which sexuality is significant: sexual harassment and discrimination, prostitution, pornography and censorship.

FURTHER READING

Belliotti, R (1991) "Sex" in Singer, P (ed) *A Companion to Ethics*, Oxford: Basil Blackwell.

Gaita, R (1999) *A Common Humanity: Thinking About Love and Truth and Justice,'* Melbourne: Text Publishing.

Jeffreys, S (1997) *The Idea of Prostitution*, Melbourne, Spinifex.

Scruton, R (1986) *Sexual Desire: a Moral Philosophy of the Erotic*, New York: Free Press.

White, JE (1994) *Contemporary Moral Problems* (4th ed) St Paul, MN: West Publishing Company (Chapter 6 "Women's Issues"; Chapter 7 "Sex, Testing and AIDS").

QUESTIONS FOR DISCUSSION

1. What do you think?
    - Love, commitment and the potential for sex to nurture family bonds are the main considerations in the ethical expression of sex.
    - The questions, "do you want to have sex?" and "do you want to play tennis?" are not necessarily significantly different in ethical terms.
    - Does the institution of marriage enhance sexual expression and the growth of love? What are the arguments in support of marriage – identify the ethical theory supporting the arguments.
    - If it is morally preferable to have sex in a monogamous context, does it make any difference whether that context is heterosexual, homosexual or bisexual?
    - Can we ever get away from the "power factor" in sexual relationships? Is it naive to suggest that all that matters in sexual relationships is honesty?
2. "Sexual expression is a purely private affair, it only raises questions of morality when it involves harm to others". Debate.
3. "The ethics of sexuality hinges on the quality of relationships not on the nature of acts". Discuss generally, but illustrate your views with particular reference to gay and lesbian relationships.
4. "Gender and reproductive roles are naturally ordained not socially constructed". What is your view? Why?
5. What are the considerations an individual or couple may need to identify in deciding to use contraception or proceed with sterilisation? In particular, when are these decisions ethically justified, and for what reasons?

6. Legal discussions to ratify the rights of same sex couples to "have" children have recently proved controversial. One commentator asked: "Are we really happy to have fatherhood regarded as the supply of sperm, and that is all?" What do you think? Why?
7. How do you define "prostitution" and "pornography"? Do you think these activities are moral or immoral? Why? Should these activities be subject to censorship or government regulation?

CASE STUDIES

CASE 1 – GAY MARRIAGE

On December 31, 1999, *Time Magazine* contained the following report:

Four years ago, a group of lesbian and gay Vermonters got together in the basement of an Episcopal church to plot the redefinition of marriage. Among them were a nurse, a few lawyers and a pair of Christmas-tree farmers. They thought the state should treat their relationships no differently from those of heterosexuals, and they eventually brought a lawsuit.

Last week the Vermont Supreme Court agreed with them, sort of. The court ruled, as no appellate court ever had, that gay couples have a right to the same benefits as heterosexual couples – with one monumentally symbolic exception. Same-sex couples still cannot obtain a marriage license.

- Is there any ethical difference between a homosexual marriage and a heterosexual marriage? Are there grounds for the State to differentiate between the two?
- What kinds of ethical reasons (consequentialist, non-consequentialist etc) have you used in arriving at your judgment? Use the comprehensive approach of the ethic of response to check whether you have considered all relevant factors.

CASE 2– PATRIOTIC PROSTITUTION AND PERSONAL INTEGRITY

Joseph Fletcher, an Episcopalian priest, recounts the following encounter with a young woman on a plane who sought his advice about an ethical dilemma.

I learned that she had been educated in church-related schools, a first-rate college, and was now a buyer in women's shoes for a Washington store. We agreed, however, to remain mutually anonymous. Her problem? "OK This is it. One of our intelligence agencies wants me to be a kind of counterespionage agent, to lure an enemy spy into blackmail by using my sex". To test her Christian sophistication, I asked if she believed Paul's teaching about how our sex faculties are to be used, as in First Corinthians. Quickly she said, "Yes, if you mean that bit in the sixth chapter - your body is the temple of the Holy Spirit. But," she added, "the trouble is that Paul also says, 'The powers that be are ordained of God'."

The defence agency wanted her to take a secretary's job in a western European city, and under that cover "involve" a married man who was working for a rival power. Married men are as vulnerable to blackmail as homosexuals. They did not put strong pressure on her. When she protested that she couldn't put her personal integrity on the block, as sex for hire, they would only say: "We understand. It's like your brother risking his life or limb in Korea. We are sure this job can't be done any other way. It's bad if we have to turn to somebody less competent and discreet than you are".

(Taken from Fletcher, J (1966) *Situation Ethics*, London: SCM Press, pp 163-4.)

- Is this prostitution?
- What should the young woman do? Why?
- What purpose would sex serve in this case? Is it a morally legitimate purpose? Does your reasoning reflect any normative approach?
- How might the values of respect for persons, justice and covenantal integrity relate to this scenario?

CASE 3 – SISTER ACT

You are a counsellor approached by a young married woman with a family problem. The woman's sister cannot bear a child because of endometriosis, a disease of the uterus, but she can make eggs and her husband's sperm is healthy. The sister is asking this woman to receive an implanted embryo from them, bear the child to full term, and hand it over to them. She is very close to her sister, but is worried about any ethical implications.

- What are the issues you would raise with this woman?
- What are the ethical considerations? What does the concept of "love" (as discussed in this chapter) or the principle of "covenantal integrity" (as in Chapter Four) contribute to the consideration? Note also, this case involves issues alluded to in the next chapter on bioethics.

CHAPTER SIX NOTES

1 Certain issues will not be examined in the brevity of this chapter: incest involving children, paedophilia, bestiality, and rape. These sexual practices do not qualify for ethical justification because they are patently exploitative of others, and violate the previously declared substantial principles (valuing life, justice and covenantal integrity) particularly as they are not acts between consenting moral agents of adult age. There is another sexual practice, which we will not discuss - masturbation - because it is morally problematic to very few in society even though under some codes it is proscribed. An example of such a code is *The Declaration on Sexual Ethics* issued by the Vatican in 1975.

2 See ibid, and in several more recent papal encyclicals. There is widespread disaffection with the official church stance against contraception led by moral theologians such as American Fr Charles Curran.

3 Shakespeare, W (1991) *Complete Sonnets,* Dover Publications, Sonnet CXVI, p 51.

4 Peck, M Scott (1978) *The Road Less Travelled,* Melbourne: Rider, p 81. Pages 81-182 are instructive for this discussion.

5 Fromm, E (1956) *The Art of Loving,* New York: Harper and Row, pp 38-39.

6 Peck, op cit, p 97.

7 Vannoy, R (1980) *Sex Without Love: a philosophical exploration*, Buffalo, NY: Prometheus.

8 Mappes, TA (1992) "Sexual Morality and the Concept of Using Another Person" in Mappes, T and Zembaty, J (eds) *Social Ethics*, New York: McGraw-Hill Inc, pp 203-216.

9 Punzo, VC (1992) "Morality and Human Sexuality" in Mappes, T and Zembaty, J ibid, pp 217-222.

10 This exception effectively embraces "unsafe sex practices", as well as sado-masochistic practices.

11 Abelove H, Barale MA and Halperin, DM (1993) *The Lesbian and Gay Studies Reader*, New York: Routledge.

12 This imagery comes from the medieval mystic, Meister Eckhart who says, "If you want to treat your passions well, don't go into asceticism, don't mortify your senses and kill them. Rather, put on your passions a bridle of love". What an image for those who have experienced the glorious stallion (or mare) of craving desire. As Matthew Fox, to whom I am in debt for this note, adds: "We can't go any place important without our passions but we need to bridle them".

13 "Harm" is used in law, jurisprudence and liberal political philosophy to articulate the proper nature and function of the law. Specifically, that the only purpose for which the law may use its coercive powers is to prevent an individual doing harm to themselves or to others. John Stuart Mill proposed we understand the concept as a guide for determining the limits of legal intervention. See Mill JS, (1989) *On Liberty and Other Writings*, Cambridge University Press: Cambridge. A contemporary defender of the harm principle is Hart HLA, (1963) *Law, Liberty, and Morality*, Oxford: Oxford University Press. A recent extension to the concept of harm is made by liberal political philosopher Joseph Raz who suggests that the concept should be used to define how government ought to conduct its interventions in a society which values autonomy. "So if the government has a duty to promote the autonomy of people, the harm principle allows it to use coercion, both in order to stop people from actions which would diminish people's autonomy, and in order to force them to take actions which are required to improve people's options and opportunities". See Raz J (1986) *The Morality of Freedom*, Oxford: Clarendon, p 416.

14 An excellent set of readings on these topics is found in White, JE (1994) *Contemporary Moral Problems* (4th ed), St Paul MN: West Publishing Co, Chapter Six.

15 For a discussion of the question of fantasy and pornography generally see Martin, MW (1989) *Everyday Morality*, Belmont, Calif: Wadsworth, Chapter Sixteen.

16 For a good review of the case for and against censorship see Mappes, T and Zembaty, J, op cit, Chapter Six.

CHAPTER SEVEN

MATTERS OF LIFE AND DEATH

From *Dead Man Walking*

MATTHEW PONCELET: The boy. Walter.
SR HELEN PREJEAN: Yes ... what?
MATT: I killed him.
Helen sighs.
HELEN: And Hope?
MATT: No ma'am.
HELEN: Did you rape her?
MATT: Yes ma'am.
HELEN: Do you take responsibility for both their deaths?
Matt begins to cry.
MATT: Yes ma'am.
HELEN: Oh Matt. There are spaces of sorrow only God can touch. You did a terrible thing, a terrible thing. But you have a dignity now. Nobody can take that away from you. You are a son of God, Matthew Poncelet.
MATT: Nobody never called me no son of God before. Called me a son of a you-know-what lots of times, but never no son of God. I just hope my death will give their parents some relief, I really do.
HELEN: Maybe the best thing you can give a person ... is to wish for their peace
MATT: I never had real love myself ... It figures I'd have to die to find love.

quoted from Robbins, T, *Dead Man Walking,*
© Tim Robbins & Polygram Filmed Entertainment, 1995.

There is no question of his life being worth living or not being worth living because the stark reality is that Anthony Bland is not living a life at all. None of the things one says about the way people live their lives – well or ill, with courage or fortitude, happily or sadly – have any meaning in relation to him.

Lord Justice Hoffman, *Airedale NHS Trust v Bland* (British Court of Appeal)

To Be or Not to Be

That we will all die is a fact of life, but how we are to die or whether we are to live may become a matter of ethical dispute. The incredible advances of medical technology that enable us to extend and maintain life in ways previously unknown, as well as to diagnose and forecast debilitating diseases, have compounded these life and death ethical dilemmas. The questions and the issues abound. The cases cited below may be the more unusual, but they sharply illustrate how matters of living or dying may revolve around ethical decisions. In addition, as human dilemmas they also evoke the need for sensitive pastoral care, a further dimension of ethical responsibility.

The traumatic case of Karen Ann Quinlan who lay in a New Jersey hospital in the mid-1970s after she had collapsed into an irreversible comatose state focussed world-wide attention on the dilemma between terminating or prolonging the life of such patients. The Quinlan decision became a matter of protracted legal dispute between Karen's parents, who wanted the life-support extinguished, and the hospital authorities, who opposed the parents' request. When a higher court ultimately ruled that the mechanical life support be withdrawn, she did not immediately die, but remained in a vegetative state for a further ten years, after being secretly weaned off the life support. Was Karen's a life worth living? Was Karen living? Who should decide her fate?

Ethical dilemmas regarding the ending of life sometimes occur at the beginning of life. In Britain during 2000,[1] there was a very difficult public legal and ethical controversy over a decision to separate Siamese twins joined at the lower abdomen. Doctors believed that an operation to separate the twins would result in one sister having a good chance of a normal life, while the other, who relied on her twin for her blood supply, would die. Furthermore, doctors maintained that without an operation, both girls would perish within about six months because of the strain imposed on the one heart that was keeping them both alive. On moral and religious grounds, the parents opposed the proposed operation. Medical authorities successfully appealed to the courts for permission to separate the twins. The operation proceeded with the outcome anticipated by the surgeons. Should the law intervene in such cases? On what ethical grounds should the right to life of one newborn child take precedence over the right to life of another?

The possibility of genetic testing and ante-natal screening (diagnostic tests on the foetus during pregnancy such as amniocentesis) provoke other dilemmas about life and death. Corinne was a 42-year-old mother-to-be when ante-natal diagnostic tests revealed that her foetus of several months had the chromosomal disorder, Down's syndrome. According to the doctor, this meant Corinne's child would need a major commitment of care throughout a life which was likely to be shorter than the average. While it is difficult to calculate how abnormal the child would be, it certainly would be intellectually handicapped. Notwithstanding this, many with Down's syndrome are warm, loving, cheerful and have relatively fulfilling active and creative lives. Considering her 19-month-old son's future as a priority, Corinne decided for an abortion. She admits, "It was the hardest thing I've ever done". A funeral was held for the foetus named Madeleine. On the way to the funeral, Corinne wrote a farewell to Madeleine: "Darling girl, you knew it had to be this way. You didn't want to live half a life in this body. And we didn't want you to live with less than you deserve. Better luck next time, little one."[2] Does Corinne have the right to end the life of an unborn child with potential to develop into a happy human being? Does it make any moral difference at what stage of the pregnancy the decision to abort is made?

Suicide is another form of active termination of an individual's life which involves ethical decisions. Consider the case of those who, suffering a terminal illness, seek assistance to suicide. This is what Ricky Brooks who was suffering with the HIV virus sought of his lover, Leslie Hoddy, in Sydney in October 1994. A charge of manslaughter was dismissed against Hoddy though he admitted to crushing 15 tablets of codeine phosphate into a glass of orange juice for Brooks when the distraught terminally ill man made a failed attempt to commit suicide. Some might prefer to term such messy and unhappy cases as euthanasia, though Hoddy's acquittal suggests that the magistrate regarded the incident technically or legally as suicide. In any case, suicide provokes questions like: is life a gift? In which case, who is the giver and is it only the giver who should take it away from any individual? Does life have a purpose, regardless of whether the one living the life has a sense of that purpose? Where an individual has no sense of purpose, is there any rational reason which could be offered for that individual to cling on to life?

The more we examine cases such as these, the more we realise that as individuals and communities we cannot avoid thinking about the unthinkable: while the mystery of death confronts us, we often have the capacity to control our dying. The exercise of this responsibility highlights the need for an ethical framework for our decision-making, which is supported by substantial values such as those linked to the ethic of response. Though they may provide guidance for decision-making, of themselves they do not provide answers. Indeed they beg interpretation. For instance, in the case of abortion, the *respect for life principle* invites the further question: "can respect include the termination of a life?" the *justice principle,* the question "how are we to resolve the competing rights say between mother and the unborn?" or the *covenantal integrity principle,* "does conception carry with it an obligation to nurture a potential child?"

Embedded within these cases and the broader issues they signify are complex philosophical and technical questions beyond the scope of this chapter, though they are critical to the study of human bioethics.[3] While the discussions of this chapter are introductory and far from exhaustive, we can identify three key prior questions which are raised by the cases cited above and which beg examination when we consider matters of life and death.

Persons, Quality of Life and Social Values

Samuel Linares[4] was a seven-month-old child who, in 1989, swallowed a balloon that stuck in his windpipe leaving him irretrievably comatose but still breathing with the permanent aid of a respirator. The hospital refused to disconnect Samuel's respirator despite his parents' wishes. Eventually, Samuel's father took matters into his own hands. After a hospital visit, Rudy Linares produced a gun and told the nursing staff to keep away while he disconnected the respirator; he did that and then cradled his baby. After 30 minutes there was no heartbeat. When Rudy Linares was sure Samuel was dead, he broke down, crying, and surrendered to the police. Rudy Linares was finally granted a suspended sentence relating to his unlawful use of the gun after a grand jury refused to indict him for homicide.

In the court case, the medical opinion as to whether Samuel was already "brain dead" was critical. Dr Robert Stein, the medical examiner for the county, took the view that Samuel effectively died when he went into the irreversible coma. His statement is pertinent to the point at issue, "The person was dead. The only thing you kept living was the organs".

Can persons die before their body ceases to function? What constitutes personhood? Are all human beings persons? Is it only persons who have moral rights? Do person rights give us a basis for addressing life and death ethical dilemmas?

To some it might come as a surprise to learn that the term "person" is not a synonym of "human being". However, if we encountered extra-terrestrial beings of similar or superior intelligence to us, we might easily attribute the character of "personhood" to them. Perhaps "person" never really has been simply equated with "human" in our language. Some Christian believers speak of the "three persons" of the Trinity and the members of the Trinity are certainly not understood as human beings. The Latin origin of the term comes from a word which referred to a mask worn by an actor revealing the character played by the actor. There is then a strong sense in the etymology of the term, "person", of certain characteristics which go beyond or mask a particular species form. So, human beings are not by definition persons though they are all potentially persons. In Chapter Nine we shall return to the argument that other non-human species may possess personhood. The immediately relevant question is whether any members of our human species should not be regarded as persons. In turn, this question invites us to nominate some characteristics of personhood.[5]

If the concept of personhood is to be linked with moral agency then there is more than a suggestion that autonomy, independence or viability - at least to the extent that the person has a sense or awareness of themselves as an individual - is important, if not essential. Consciousness, awareness and rationality could also be regarded as pre-requisites for personhood, though of course, that may leave uncertain the status of new-born babies, the intellectually disabled, or those who suffer illnesses such as Alzheimer's disease or delusory mental states. To avoid the problems associated with defining personhood, some include as persons all those human beings with measurable brain activity. The idea of linking life and death judgments to brain activity which signals either the prospect of consciousness or the end of it is now widely accepted, though precision about brain activity is a complex question in itself.[6] At the foetal stage of development, measurable brain activity probably begins around the tenth week of gestation, a factor which could be regarded as ethically relevant to the decision to abort. A view of personhood closely linked to brain activity presumably excludes anencephalic new-borns from the category of persons. Similarly, on this consideration those with severe brain damage (like Samuel Linares or Karen Quinlan) who will never be conscious are no longer persons though some of their vital organs still live, as Dr Stein said.

There is reason to challenge a view of personhood which focuses narrowly on measurable mental states and consequently fails to grant moral significance to the severely brain damaged. Severely brain damaged human beings are members of a species whose capacity for consciousness is a clear indication of personhood. By that membership they are relatives with other persons. Arguably, the "relational factor", the sense of belonging to a moral community, is an important aspect of personhood, for without it we are de-personalised.

To summarise: the factors which have been emphasised in this discussion of personhood are awareness and consciousness, associated with a sense of being an individual who is related to other persons. These criteria incline us to a broad definition of personhood to include all human beings. At this stage we suspend judgment on whether non-human species possess personhood though an appropriate respect for life takes seriously the moral rights of animals as sentient beings and as companions with human beings in the web of life.[7] In the case of human beings, it might no longer be relevant to use the criterion of personhood as a justification to keep alive those in a permanently unconscious, vegetative state. Others might add also pre-natal cases where the foetus is clearly not a viable[8] individual. What would this understanding of personhood mean for Corinne's Madeleine, the unborn foetus with Down's syndrome? As a Down's syndrome child, Madeleine would certainly have awareness and consciousness and a sense of individuality. Furthermore, she would clearly have a capacity to relate and to be a relative in the moral community. This factor was recognised by Corinne through her letter to Madeleine and the funeral; that proper recognition by Corinne underlines the ethical doubt about the decision to abort in that case. Corinne's story calls to mind how parents of a baby who is stillborn often name the child, bury it and cherish its memory as if it were "a person" for the rest of their lives.

While our description of personhood remains imprecise and invokes notions which require further explanation, it provides a background for considering matters of life and death. It also introduces the question as to whether ethical decisions about life and death should be determined only by *quality of life considerations*.

In the Siamese twins case, both quality of life and sanctity of life considerations were clearly involved. Though questions of personhood were crucial in the Quinlan and Linares cases, for Corinne and Ricky Brooks, *quality of life* considerations were paramount. Corinne made the judgment that the impact on the quality of life of her 19-month-old son particularly was the dominant consideration, while Ricky presumably concluded (how rationally we cannot be sure) that the circumstances of his life as an HIV sufferer so lacked quality that it was not worth living.

In *Rethinking Life and Death* Peter Singer maintains that medical practice and the law have effectively moved to a position where quality of life considerations outweigh the so-called sanctity of life principle in determining the hard cases about whether an individual's life is worth living and should continue.[9] The principle of selective non-treatment which is widely employed by the medical profession is, Singer says, a concession to the quality of life ethic. In his view, we have to move from lip-service to an old ethic which proposed: "Treat all human life as of equal worth", to a new ethic which proclaims: "Recognise that the worth of human life varies". The contrast here is between a principled, if not deontological, approach (as in sanctity of life) to a calculating, utilitarian approach (as in quality of life).

It would be naive to disagree with Singer's contention that contemporary bioethical practice involves quality of life judgments. But are considerations of quality of life inconsistent with a profound respect for life, or with what some speak of as "the sanctity of life"? In line with Singer's claims, "sanctity of life" is often presented as a rigid, absolute defence of the individual's right to life. This interpretation is an overstatement. For a start, there is no necessary connection between a so-called "sanctity of life" position and religious belief, although the connection is often made. The doctrine has been explained by Elizabeth Hepburn, an interpreter of Catholic bioethics, as follows:

> Properly understood, the sanctity of life doctrine holds that life is a sacred gift and that we are not at liberty to dispose of it at will … The doctrine does not, however, commit us to regarding life as an absolute good or to ignoring the interests of the individual.[10]

She cites the support of Robert McCormick, who says: "Quality-of-life assessments ought to be made within an overall reverence for life, as an extension of one's respect for the sanctity of life".[11]

Unless we situate quality of life assessments within a wider reverence for life, we become vulnerable to the subjectivity and relativity of quality of life criteria. Julie Reiskin[12] illustrates this danger by citing the case of a woman with a degenerative disease. This person claimed she had drawn a base line, beyond which she did not want to live. She found, however, that as she got closer to the base line, she shifted it.

> Three years ago my line lay at not being able to run. Then it moved to not being able to climb the stairs. It moved again, to: not being able to walk, then to: not being able to drive ... Seeing as how I am writing this and I can no longer do any of these things, it's clear I've changed my line again.

Nonetheless, she apparently accepts that there is a quality-of-life continuum and that individuals negotiate that continuum flexibly, depending on their circumstances.

The respect for life principle within the framework of an ethic of response is open to decisions involving the active termination of life but only after the most careful and comprehensive assessment centred on a respect for life which places the highest value on persons. Our contemporary cosmological, biological, technological and environmental knowledge requires a revision, but not the abandonment of the sanctity of life doctrine, as Singer proposes. Calculations about the quality of life must be tempered by a profound reverence for the life that resides in individuals. Such an approach is consistent with the ethic of response. There is no reason why these bioethical dilemmas cannot be judged within a dialectic between sanctity and quality of life considerations, which results in respect for life. Indeed, the failure to do this may invite grave social errors, such as a careless depersonalising of the elderly, the deformed, or the disabled, which will, in turn, erode the bonds of covenantal integrity upon which the moral community depends.

In an important contribution to this debate Jennifer Fitzgerald has observed:

> It is through society's growing willingness to make quality of life judgments that the lives of people with disability become endangered. It is through this willingness that people with disability lose protections, basic protections to their lives, which other members of society enjoy.[13]

One significant dimension of her argument, which is designed to challenge those who promote the legalisation of euthanasia, is that attitudes and social practices relating to illness, dying and disability are a product of social influences. This social construction view claims "that disability arises not so much from one's physical or intellectual incapacity, but from society's attitude to that incapacity".[14] She reports the case of Kenneth Bergstedt, a 31-year-old American quadriplegic who had lived with the assistance of a respirator for 20 years. He successfully pursued legal channels to exercise the right to be assisted to die. Fitzgerald questions whether or not it was the social circumstances confronting Bergstedt which shaped his request to die. He was cared for by an ageing father and lived an isolated existence with little outside stimulation or support. According to Fitzgerald, "All these things override the intrinsic will of a person with disability to live".[15] Her discussion brings to mind the suicide of Ricky Brooks: perhaps, his sense of hopelessness was, in part, socially defined. More available care and counselling for HIV patients may have made his suicide unnecessary.

Of course, it can be replied that this line of argument is all very well but it is hardly just or fair to suspend the rights of an individual to deal with their own suffering just because society is slow to repair its lack of compassion or its inadequate allocation of supportive resources. Nonetheless, it is undeniable that our discussion of these matters of life and death must take account of the social values which legitimate certain approaches to these questions, approaches which in turn further shape the values of society.

As we noted earlier, quality of life judgments have a distinctly utilitarian character. They fit with a broader cultural ethos which is largely driven by pragmatism underpinned by the principle of utility (or usefulness) and interpreted in terms of physical prowess or economic productivity; material and financial reward is often the measure by which we value these attributes. In such an environment it is likely that, in practice, principles of respect for life or justice for vulnerable minorities, as well as obligations to extend a duty of care to all members of society are modified and diluted.

Levels of violence in our communities are another troublesome indicator of social values. Occasionally, episodes such as the horrific Australian massacre in April 1996 at Port Arthur, Tasmania, (ironically, the site of nineteenth century prison violence) cause communities to realise how the violence endemic to contemporary culture has been systematically promoted. In addition, it can be argued that the way society gives priority to individual rights contributes to social fragmentation and, consequently, the devaluing of vulnerable members of society, whose ongoing support generally requires a greater sense of communal responsibility and care. The rhetoric of self-determination and autonomy may so elevate our sense of individuality that we lose touch with our need for each other, and we cease to care for each other.

Over all, the mixture of individualism, pragmatism and violence is a dangerously potent one in which to pursue the ethical debate about abortion, euthanasia, suicide, capital punishment and war.

In appropriating the ethic of response to the life and death decisions under review in this chapter, our judgments need to consider the impact of, and on, social values. Furthermore, the cultivation of a social environment which fosters empathy, compassion and care based on the intrinsic worth of other beings is the necessary counterpoint to scientific research or social legislation which furthers our capacity to decide who lives and who dies.

Euthanasia

Euthanasia (literally, "a good death") refers to cases where death is brought about or allowed because death is thought to be in that individual's interest, normally because the patient is suffering from an incurable and terminal illness. In these cases the ethical justification may be summarised colloquially as "he (or she) is better off dead". It is therefore inaccurate to associate the term "euthanasia" with the extermination camps of Nazi Germany or with ideas of killing off the so-called useless or undesirable members of society. For instance, to kill someone merely because some other person decided they were too old could not count as euthanasia. Therefore, there is little virtue in the argument against euthanasia on alarmist "slippery slope" grounds; nonetheless, as our previous discussion about values illustrated, and as our later analysis in this section will indicate, caution over the social consequences of instituting euthanasia as a medical practice may be justified.

"Euthanasia, in the strict sense, is understood to be an action or omission which of itself and by intention causes death, with the purpose of eliminating all suffering".[16] There are several distinctions which help categorise different instances of euthanasia.

The first distinction is between *voluntary* and *involuntary* euthanasia. Voluntary euthanasia involves the informed consent of the one who is to die, whereas involuntary euthanasia proceeds without that consent, when the individual is incapable of informed consent (for instance, a comatose adult).

These categories can be combined with another distinction, that between *active* and *passive* euthanasia. In the active cases there is direct intervention to cause death, whereas in the passive case there is no direct intervention though the patient is allowed to die, and procedures which might prevent death are withdrawn. Now, let us summarise, illustrate and combine these categories:

(i) *active voluntary*, covers cases of assisted suicide or so-called mercy death, for example, the deliberate administration of a lethal injection with the patient's previous consent (even perhaps via a previously declared "living will").

(ii) *passive voluntary*, covers cases where someone is allowed to die and where they have expressed a wish so to do, for example, meeting the request of a patient not to treat a secondary illness, like pneumonia, when that patient is already dying of cancer.

(iii) *passive involuntary*, covers cases where someone is allowed to die even though they have not clearly expressed a wish, for example, turning off life-support machines for a comatose accident victim whose brain function will never return, according to best medical opinion.

(iv) *active involuntary*, covers cases of so-called mercy killing, where someone is caused to die even though they are incapable of expressing a wish on the matter, for example, promoting the death soon after birth of severely impaired anencephalic babies.

Though not all cases of euthanasia fit neatly into these categories, it is instances of active intervention that are most problematic ethically as well as legally. Despite ambiguities in the law, there is a wide community consensus supporting passive voluntary euthanasia, and possibly passive involuntary euthanasia.[17] Even amongst Christian moral theologians opposed to euthanasia and to changes in the law especially, there is an openness to considering the morality of certain cases based on further distinctions. They may call on a distinction between the use of *extraordinary and ordinary means* of treatment. Some[18] prefer to use terms such as "proportionate" and "disproportionate" or "reasonable" and "unreasonable" rather than "ordinary" and "extraordinary". Extraordinary means could include the continued use of life support machinery when it is believed that the patient will never recover consciousness, whereas ordinary means are those that keep the patient comfortable and pain-free but may not prolong life. As it is usually employed, the distinction may be clinically useful because it allows for quality of life factors (such as cost and psychological stress) as judged by the patient. It is sometimes difficult to be precise about this distinction and, in an ethical sense, its significance is debatable.

Similarly, to cover the fact that moral choices often include subsequent consequences which may be unavoidable, some ethical commentators invoke the *doctrine of double effect.*[19] Suppose a doctor gives a terminal cancer patient an overdose of morphine, sufficient to kill a patient. If the doctor intends only to reduce the patient's pain or suffering, and not to kill the patient, then according to the doctrine of double effect, the doctor's action is not wrong, even though he or she can foresee that the patient will die presumably from the overdose. Critics complain that this distinction is unclear and therefore untenable. What is more, they say, it may open up a line of argument which can be used to defend any evil act provided it is merely foreseen but not intended.

A further distinction is that made between actions which *allow someone to die* and those which *cause someone to die*. Here attention and significance is given to the moral intent of an action, not simply its mode or outcome. Some say that if a physician allows someone to die by withdrawing a respirator but does not intend them to die, that should not count as a (morally reprehensible) case of euthanasia. But how, we might ask, is there any practical or moral difference between allowing someone to die when it is known that they will die, and actively promoting their death? This is the issue taken up in a debate between James Rachels and Thomas Sullivan.[20] Rachels defends a liberal approach to euthanasia invoking utilitarian/humanitarian arguments supplemented by a Kantian-like appeal to the Golden Rule. Sullivan defends a conservative approach by invoking a deontological style "sanctity of life" principle augmented by a rule-utilitarian argument that the systematic acceptance of active euthanasia will lead to a damaging lessening of respect for life in society.

It is interesting to note how various normative theories can be used to support similar and opposing positions on euthanasia. One may be in favour of, or opposed to, euthanasia on either or both utilitarian and deontological grounds. Once again, the ethic of response provides a framework for assessing and deciding among the competing factors in a decision about euthanasia. Of course, it is a useful tool only to those who acknowledge that quality of life considerations are to be put alongside a profound respect for life including the dignity of the person, within a principled framework guided by our obligations to keep faith with each other.

Overall, it is not inconsistent with an ethic of response to argue that, in certain cases, euthanasia, even "active involuntary situations", is justifiable as morally fitting. However, should, or how can, that conclusion be translated into law and social policy? There are certainly major objections to the legalisation or decriminalisation of euthanasia to be considered:

- is there not a danger that legalised euthanasia will put undue pressures on medical practitioners and nurses, subtly altering their duty to care?
- is it possible to devise a law which is not open to abuse?
- is it not conceivable that carefully framed laws might later be amended or extended by regulation, bypassing public debate?
- might not legalised euthanasia open the door for elderly people to be quietly disposed of against their will?
- if euthanasia is legal, might not an old person feel pressured to die because they are a burden to their relatives?

The ethic of response with its concern for social justice, universality, accountability and social solidarity also infers that a major consideration for particular, individual cases of euthanasia is the broader social impact of the ethical decision. For this reason the judgment of Baroness Warnock, in the 1994 *Report of the Select Committee on Medical Ethics of the House of Lords* opposing a law change on euthanasia, expresses a perspective which should weigh heavily in any responsible decision:

> Ultimately, however we do not believe that these arguments are sufficient reason to weaken society's prohibition of intentional killing. That prohibition is the cornerstone of law and of social

> relationships. It protects each one of us impartially, embodying the belief that all are equal. We do not wish that protection to be diminished and we therefore recommend that there should be no change in the law to permit euthanasia. We acknowledge that there are individual cases in which euthanasia may be seen by some to be appropriate. But individual cases cannot reasonably establish the foundation of a policy which would have such serious and wide-spread repercussions. Moreover dying is not only a personal or individual affair. The death of a person affects the lives of others, often in ways and to an extent which cannot be foreseen. We believe that the issue of euthanasia is one in which the interest of the individual cannot be separated from the interest of society as a whole.[21]

Warnock's views speak to the debate about euthanasia. This debate has been promoted recently in various countries, including the Netherlands, but notably in Australia with the passage of the Northern Territory *Rights of the Terminally Ill Act* 1995 which (though it was later overturned by Australia's Federal Parliament) legalised euthanasia.[22] In other Australian jurisdictions where euthanasia is still illegal, a minority of medical practitioners admit to practising active voluntary euthanasia and most of them feel they have "done the right thing".[23]

Euthanasia policy is also likely to be influenced by two contemporary developments. The first, developments in palliative care, represents part of the case that there are positive alternatives to euthanasia in a "bad dying" process. The claim is that through more sophisticated pain relief measures and the caring of the hospice movement support for a "good death", without active termination of life, is possible.[24]

The other development is what is claimed to be the complex social cost of an ageing population. Can societies afford the escalating costs of keeping people alive to an advanced age especially when a large proportion of limited resources are devoted to the terminally ill? This utilitarian consideration is arguably unfair and disrespectful of persons, and needs further factual substantiation. However, it is on the community agenda and rightly or wrongly, may subtly influence social policy with respect to euthanasia.

In the community debate over euthanasia, religious believers represented by Christian churches are officially cautious, even hostile, though it must be added that many individual Christians have another view and are even active in groups such as the Voluntary Euthanasia Society.[25] The major churches in Australia have expressed concern about the moves to legalise euthanasia. Representative of these views is a resolution passed unanimously by the national body of the Anglican church in 1995. The General Synod resolved *inter alia*:

> affirms that life is a gift from God not to be taken, and is therefore not subject to matters such as freedom of individual choice.
>
> ... questions whether a practice of voluntary euthanasia can easily be prevented from sliding into a practice of involuntary euthanasia.
>
> ... affirms the right of patients to decline treatment but not to expect the active intervention by medical staff to end their lives ...[26]

Undoubtedly, one's beliefs influence how one approaches life and death dilemmas, especially euthanasia. Some simply claim that only God can take an individual's life. Other critical questions relate to one's beliefs about suffering: might not suffering be redemptive and purposeful? Does it make any difference that it is the suffering of dying? Might we not cheat ourselves of something life has to offer when we terminate life prematurely? On these questions, Elizabeth Hepburn offers a fitting observation with which to conclude this brief discussion:

> A philosophy which sees suffering as absurd will lead us to seek relief in the form of euthanasia. We must decide whether we will interpret the dispossession we experience in the face of suffering as absurdity or mystery. If we opt for mystery we will be committed to living life to the full in both ecstasy and sorrow.[27]

Life, Death and the State

Liberalism, the law and bioethics

The state (essentially, the apparatus of government) has a legitimate interest in both the fact, and the manner, of the birth and death of its citizens. This interest arises from a duty to safeguard respect for human life in the public interest. How that interest should be enacted in law within a liberal democratic society (as opposed to a totalitarian one) is our concern here.

Already in this chapter we have alluded to the community uncertainty about laws on bioethical issues. Yet these are matters of such importance to the community and future generations that it is unsatisfactory if the law is silent or ambivalent about them. At the same time, as we have pointed out earlier in this book, what is legal is not necessarily what is right, good or fitting in an ethical sense.

Consider abortion as a matter of public policy for the state. According to the National Medical Health and Research Council, more than 80,000 abortions are carried out each year in Australia. Regardless of the various reasons for these abortions, it is safe to say that abortion is a traumatic experience which touches the lives of a great many Australian women and their families. It is also a procedure technically subject to criminal law sanctions in several Australian jurisdictions. Abortion is therefore a major social policy question combining considerations of law and public policy. There is plenty of evidence that criminalising abortion produces great social harm: making abortion illegal is likely to create a further toll of human suffering through backyard and self-inflicted abortions, more unwanted children and a further burden on disadvantaged women.

Because abortion is such a contentious issue and because there are a variety of circumstances in which abortion seems the best choice to families and their doctors, it is futile and even unjust to legislate against personal choice in this matter, although the moral choice remains even when the legal impediments are removed. To reduce the number of abortions in society, a desirable and responsible goal, social policy measures such as ethics counselling and education along with better support services for women and families are needed rather than legislating to enforce morality. At least this would seem to be the preferred option in a liberal democratic society.

In *Bioethics in a Liberal Society,* Australian ethicist Max Charlesworth argues that in passing laws relating to new procreative technologies, genetic intervention in human life, the limits of medical treatment and so on, priority should be given to the promotion of personal autonomy and choice. For Charlesworth,

> What is of the essence of liberalism is the moral conviction that, because they are autonomous moral agents or persons, people must as far as possible be free to choose for themselves, even if their choices are, objectively speaking, mistaken; and further that the state may not impose one moral or religious position on the whole community but, so long as they do not violate or harm the personal autonomy of others, must treat all such positions equally.[28]

As indicated by our earlier outline of the relationship between social values and bioethics, critics of Charlesworth might assert that he overemphasises autonomy and takes inadequate account of socially destructive values and practices in so-called liberal democratic societies.

In fact, Charlesworth goes on to defend liberalism against the charge of ethical relativism just as he distinguishes it from libertarianism which promotes the idea of limited or minimal government intervention especially on economic matters. He points out that government in a liberal society is obliged "not merely to prevent, in a negative way, restrictions on the exercise of personal autonomy, but actively and positively to promote the socio-economic conditions within which personal freedom and autonomy can flourish".[29]

From this viewpoint, the criminal law has no place in matters of abortion, suicide, euthanasia, and reproductive technology except to prevent exploitation of the individual. On such questions, according to the liberal view, the state cannot legislate for morality, though, by the same token, it must protect the rights of those who have a moral objection to abortion, euthanasia, or certain procreative technologies. To say this is not to claim that there is no need for the state to regulate some procedures in the interests of good medical practice and social health; similarly, in the uncertain area of genetic intervention it is likely that law must be developed to serve the common good and to protect the individual as well as future generations. Also, as Charlesworth stresses, if choice in these bioethical issues is to be preserved and to be meaningful to disadvantaged members of society, the state and its institutions have a particular responsibility to create conditions of economic well-being through education, health-care, employment and community support.

There are other ethical questions involving life and death which are in the province of the state and toward which liberal democracy is likely to take a different stance from totalitarianism. Let us briefly consider two instances in which the state might claim the right and responsibility to take human life.

Capital punishment

Some democratic societies have delegated to the state the right to kill criminals, chiefly murderers; most totalitarian states have taken to themselves this right, and have generally defined criminality so widely that capital punishment becomes an instrument to purge political enemies. Even in democratic states, the debate about capital punishment has often manipulated people's irrational fears and been used cynically as a vote-winning tactic. When capital punishment is combined with the power of the state it can become a potent mixture which invites abuse.

Certain relatively democratic states such as Australia have removed the death penalty from the statutes. That does not mean that violence resulting in death has been removed from the criminal justice system. One measure of this is the escalating number of deaths in custody (generally, as reported, by suicide). Years after the final report of the Royal Commission into Aboriginal Deaths in Custody, Aborigines and non-Aborigines alike continue to die in increasing numbers in Australia's jails.[30] With or without capital punishment, prisoners suffer premature death in jail.

The death penalty is presented as "punishment", capital punishment. As such it should be subject to a critique about the theories of punishment which underpin it. Major theories of punishment may be grouped as:

(1) *Retributive* theories, which propose punishment only when and in a manner that it is deserved. Capital punishment may be proposed on retributional grounds. Indeed, Kant supported this theory and insisted that death is the proper punishment for murder.[31]

(2) *Results* theories propose that punishments should produce good results for society, and usually for the criminal who is to be rehabilitated. This is a utilitarian approach and could be appropriated to support or reject capital punishment depending on how the consequences of capital punishment in certain cases are calculated.

(3) *Restitution* theories propose that justice requires that the victim(s) of crime be given restitution or compensation for harm done. Though it would appear that restitution requires that the criminal be kept alive to work for the victim(s)' benefit, in cases of murder it could also be maintained that to satisfy and compensate the victim, capital punishment is necessary.

Those who argue in favour of capital punishment generally make some of the following claims: (a) it is an effective deterrent; (b) it is more economic; (c) killers forfeit their right to life; (d) society is entitled to revenge. Much of the debate centres on whether capital punishment actually is a deterrent. White cites several authorities that put considerable doubt on this claim.[32] If it is no deterrent, then capital punishment may be presented, by utilitarians especially, as pointless suffering serving no social good. A potent argument against capital punishment derives from the *respect for life principle*; though we may not need to go to the extent of absolute pacifists who insist that the state should be totally non-violent and never take a life, it can be plausibly claimed that official vengeful killing by the state devalues life for all its citizens, and is cruel and inhumane. Considerations of *justice and fairness* invite us to note how capital punishment may lead to the irrevocable mistake of killing an innocent person and that, in societies like the United States, where the death penalty remains, it is racial minorities, the poor and uneducated whose lives are most likely to be officially terminated.

Within the framework and ethos of a liberal democratic state, an ethical analysis of this issue from a deontological or consequentialist approach, as well as from the virtue viewpoint (that is, considering "the character of the state"), suggest that there is no justification for laws which permit capital punishment. Such a conclusion is arguably consistent with how the ethic of response would decide these cases. However, because of its comprehensive consideration of all the factors involved, the ethic of response might be willing to consider some over-riding, extreme circumstances where anarchic criminality threatened the very existence of a society as a justification for capital punishment. In such a case however, it is likely that the state would be changing its moral character to such an extent that it would be taking on totalitarian characteristics.

War[33]

War inevitably involves killing, state sanctioned killing, through the military means amassed by warring states usually in the name of national security. Though war is often allegedly waged for political and ethical ideals like freedom and democracy, war-making generally involves totalitarian measures which leave their mark on a warring society. We know that "truth is the first casualty of war",[34] that powers of coercion and the suspension of normal liberties are assumed by the state at war, that there are countless innocent victims in modern war, that in the "war effort" everything (all citizens, the economy, political activity) is harnessed towards the objectives of the war. In the twentieth century, repeated war horrors have seen tens of millions killed and maimed. If ever there is a social ethical question for humanity it is about the morality of war: what justifies putting at risk a civilised, relatively harmonious society? What can justify killing in war? Are there limits to the means used in any justifiable war? How should a citizen be able to protest or conscientiously object to participating in national war policy?

Though the only war waged within Australia since European settlement has been the "undeclared war" against the indigenous inhabitants, the national self-identity via the ANZAC tradition has been largely linked to efforts of war alongside great and powerful friends in other parts of the world. While the contemporary Australian defence forces are seen as part of international peace-keeping efforts, Australia supplies armaments to potential belligerents in its near region.

An ethical analysis of war is generally classified in three positions. One view attempts to justify war as a *righteous cause*, a crusade or holy war. This position is exemplified by those like the American Cardinal who told troops bound for Vietnam, "You are the soldiers of Jesus Christ" [engaged in a sacred cause against the spread of Communism] or who like the Islamic Imam declare a *jihad* promising those who wage war a life in eternal paradise. A second view is the *pacifist* approach which elevates non-violence to an absolute principle and refuses to participate in any war, though there are varieties of pacifism. Both these extremes tend to come from a non-consequentialist form of reasoning, presenting what is right or wrong in relation to war in terms of an ethical duty.

The third ethical approach to war is known as *the just war theory*. Developed first by Augustine to justify a transformation in the Christian ethic from a pacifist position to one in which Christianity could co-operate with the Roman state, the just war theory provides a mode of calculating what war-making is ethically justifiable. It is therefore a consequentialist theory compatible with the ethic of response. The theory has two components: *jus ad bellum* (the end or goal of war must be just and result in more justice than would have resulted otherwise) and *jus in bello* (the means of engaging in the war must also be just). *Jus in bello* has several requirements: (1) violence must be limited to what is necessary to achieve one's aim, (2) bad consequences of the act of war must not outweigh good consequences, and (3) force must be directed only against legitimate targets. So "rules of war" may be derived. The theory has been refined to meet changing contexts over the centuries but its inadequacies for modern warfare are apparent: for instance, no modern war could be waged without affecting non-combatants; the weapons of mass destruction (nuclear, chemical, biological) available in modern war are unlikely to meet the criteria of the just war; the revolutionary, guerilla, or terrorist warfare characteristic of modern conflicts does not easily fit the just war model (because traditionally a just war can only be waged by a legitimate government). Other specific questions need to be asked such as: Is the preparation for war as a defence legitimate? What if that preparation includes nuclear weapons? What of the global arms trade, is it an act of war, is it an ethically justifiable business?

The conclusion may be drawn that the usefulness of just war theory as an ethical guide is limited, although it remains a framework for all who cannot adopt the absolutist approaches to war of pacifism or the crusade. Only a war that could be justified as just will be ethically acceptable to those who recognise that the ambiguities of the global human condition require at times a calculated response which may include the ultimate form of politics, war. Indeed our consideration of war leads us to a major concern of the next chapter, namely, the ethics of politics.

This section has presented only a rudimentary discussion of the morality of killing by the state. However, there is arguably more ethical significance in the violence of the modern nation-state toward its citizens and enemies than there is in the termination of life by individuals in the bioethical topics considered earlier in this chapter. There is also a sad irony in the fact that leaders of state are appalled at mass murders by a crazed lone gunman, while they may promote the use and manufacture of weapons of mass destruction. As Amnesty International Reports record, the violence of the state in many parts of the world, ranging from police harassment to torture and unlawful detention, is part of a systemic culture which violates the value of life, the integrity of human relationships and any sense of justice or fairness.

A final note: On biotechnology

> "Biotechnology" is a broad term given to a wide range of technologies which use living organisms, biochemistries or synthetic DNA to make or modify products, improve plants or animals, or develop micro-organisms for specific uses. Biotechnologies have a wide range of applications in medicine, agriculture and food production, horticulture, industry and the environment. A frequent misconception is that biotechnology is of recent origin ... Traditional plant and animal breeding techniques also form part of biotechnology. However, "biotechnology" is usually applied to new techniques associated with the contemporary "Biotechnology Revolution." [35]

Biotechnology is an ethically complex area of scientific and commercial development. Arguably, the uncertain consequences of many of the discoveries and inventions of the so-called "Biotechnology Revolution" require regulation of the biotech industry by the State. However, precisely how or whether the law can restrain developments which are both hazardous and promising, is one aspect of the ethical debate about technology. For a start, so transnational are biotechnology ventures and their promoters that it is difficult to see how the nation-state alone can control these developments. Across the world for instance, there is widespread concern about genetically engineered crops[36] developed in conjunction with the emergence of transnational agribusiness conglomerates.

Some of these ethical questions include matters of conflict of interest (an issue discussed in the next chapter). For instance, how should we manage the conflicts which arise for researchers who may also be financial beneficiaries of their discoveries? Should all biotech organisations be obliged to inform people about their products, the technologies employed and any potential risks or side effects? Then there are matters of confidentiality, which have ethical ramifications. For example, should the results of genetic testing be kept confidential? Should insurers or employers be able to make decisions about an individual's insurance risk or employability on the basis of DNA tests?

Then, how do we proceed as pluralistic societies in ways that respect the views of those who disagree on those questions and how do we consider the rights of future generations? The ethical issues raised by the new biotechnologies need also to be examined in a context of social justice, around the question of who is actually benefiting from new discoveries? Is this scientific endeavour a just use of precious resources? Are these inventions accessible to the poor of the world? For instance, is the exploitation of resources for scientific purposes, as in the removal of, and experimentation with, exotic species of flora and fauna in the Brazilian rainforests, accompanied by just compensation to the poor indigenous population of the Brazilian forests?

Medical science provides some of the most dramatic ethical dilemmas especially on the frontier of new genetic futures. Consider the following list which is by no means exhaustive, and which contains within it the promise of reducing disease and extending human life: molecular genetics, human genome research, organ transplantation (sometimes across species), and cryo-preservation of human tissue. "Cloning" is one technique, now a reality, which quite properly provokes ethical debate. Nations like the United Kingdom and Australia have legislated to forbid the cloning of an entire human being. A more debatable matter is whether it is ethically permissible to undertake more limited cloning, for therapeutic purposes, eg cloning nerve cells to treat spinal cord injuries, or pancreatic cells to treat diabetes? What if this type of cloning requires the use of stem cells from human embryos?

Embryonic stem cells possess the unique ability to develop into different types of tissue in the body – nerves, muscles, organs and bones – depending on the chemical cues given. Grown in a laboratory, they could be used to make replacement tissue for such degenerative diseases as Parkinson's and Alzheimer's, bone cells for osteoporosis, eye cells for macular degeneration, blood cells for cancer, insulin-providing cells for diabetes, nerve cells for spinal cord injury and so on. It is difficult to see what bioethical argument could be made to oppose such discoveries and treatments – except, of course, and it is, in the minds of some, a big exception that it is always morally unacceptable to employ therapies that involve experimentation on embryos, the basic form of human life. The resolution of this ethical question depends on an argument that gives greater weight to the interests of more fully developed human beings; it also stresses "quality of life" considerations rather than an absolute "sanctity of human life". Such an argument may be made within an ethic of response by calling on the openness of that approach to utilitarian judgments. Ultimately it affirms that the lives of people with cancer, diseases like Parkinson's and organ failure, who could be saved by the development of stem cells, deserve to be given a higher value than that attributed to early-stage human embryos.

These are matters not simply of life and death, but of reshaping and redefining life. Not only do they illustrate how imperative it is that the professions and the community generally need to become more ethically aware to engage this brave new world, but also, they indicate that previous approaches to ethics, and the metaphysical assumptions that go with them, may be under challenge. Not surprisingly, our discussion on environmental ethics in Chapter Nine, a field not unrelated to bioethics, will also demonstrate this.

CHAPTER REVIEW

1. Initially, this chapter raised ethical dilemmas about terminating the life of an individual human being via several case studies.

2. Three key issues which are complex but pertinent to the agenda of this chapter were analysed: the concept of a person; the quality v sanctity of life argument; the influence of social attitudes on the value of (human) life.
3. Euthanasia was examined as a particular matter:
   (a) The term, euthanasia, applies to cases "where death is brought about or allowed because it is thought to be in that individual's interest".
   (b) Four categories of euthanasia were defined: *active voluntary, passive voluntary, passive involuntary* and *active voluntary.*
   (c) Distinctions between *ordinary* and *extraordinary* means, and *allowing to die* and *causing to die,* were canvassed.
   (d) The implications for society in legislating for euthanasia were explored, and the relevance of religious belief in some cases noted.
4. The next section of the chapter examined how the state in a liberal democratic society should approach matters of life and death. In this context the discussion was extended to include capital punishment and war.
5. Finally, we noted a range of ethical questions raised by recent biotechnology developments.

AN EXERCISE

- Analyse the topics of this chapter (abortion, suicide, euthanasia, biotechnology, capital punishment, war) in relation to the substantial values endorsed by the ethic of response;
- Identify implications of the chapter's discussion for legislation and social policy;
- Finally, consider how the poor and most disadvantaged may be affected in terms of the topics of this chapter.

FURTHER READING

Beauchamp, TL (ed) (1996) *Intending Death: The Ethics of Assisted Suicide and Euthaniasia,* Upper Saddle River: Prentice Hall.
Feinberg, J (ed) (1984) *The Problem of Abortion,* Belmont, Cal: Wadsworth Publishing Co.
Glover, J (1987) *Causing Death and Saving Lives,* Harmondsworth: Penguin.
Hepburn, E (1996) *Of Life and Death: An Australian Guide to Catholic Bioethics,* Melbourne: Harper Collins.
Hood, RG (1996) *The Death Penalty: A Worldwide Perspective,* Oxford: Clarendon.
Kleinig, J (1991) *Valuing Life,* Princeton, NJ: Princeton University Press.
Kuhse H and Singer, P (eds) (1999) *Bioethics: An Anthology,* Oxford: Blackwell.
Teichman, J (1986) *Pacifism and the Just War,* Oxford: Basil Blackwell.

CASE STUDIES

Examine each of these cases in terms of the decision-making model of the ethic of response.

CASE 1
BONHOEFFER AND HILL – RIGHTEOUS KILLING

In 1944, the Reverend Dietrich Bonhoeffer, a Lutheran theologian, was hanged by the Gestapo in Nazi Germany because he had been implicated in a plot to assassinate Hitler. Bonhoeffer had become part of the German Resistance as the horrors of Hitler's Germany became clear. In an attempt to end the war, Bonhoeffer and several others plotted to assassinate Hitler. A bomb exploded in a briefcase near Hitler at a meeting but failed to kill him though others were injured. Bonhoeffer was arrested for his part in the plot. Since his death, and because of his writings, Bonhoeffer has become a revered and influential figure.

In 1995, the Reverend Paul Hill, a former Presbyterian minister, was sentenced to death in a Florida (United States) court for shooting a doctor who performed abortions. Hill's defence was that he killed Dr Britton to save the lives of the unborn. During his trial he protested, "You may mix my blood with the blood of the unborn - may God help you to protect the unborn as you would want to be protected".

- Do you see any difference in the actions and intentions of Bonhoeffer and Hill? Were they ethically justifiable? Why or why not?
- What do these scenarios suggest about the ethics of (i) capital punishment and (ii) killing to prevent further evil?

CASE 2 – DR SHANN'S BABY

In February 1991, Melbourne's Royal Children's Hospital hosted a conference entitled "Anencephalics, Infants and Brain Death: Treatment Options and the Issue of Organ Donation".

The practical issue that had led the Royal Children's Hospital to support the conference was dramatically presented to us by Dr Frank Shann, director of the hospital's intensive care unit. He began by describing how, a couple of years previously, a baby boy had been brought into the hospital with severe heart disease. After suffering repeated heart failure, he needed to be put on a ventilator and given drugs continuously in order to keep him alive. Apart from his heart disease, the baby was quite normal; but because the disease itself was so serious, the outlook was, Shann said, "hopeless". Tragic as this situation is, it is not a rare occurrence in a major children's hospital. But what was to come was more unusual. I shall let Shann continue the story:

At the same time in the adjacent bed in the Intensive Care Unit, was another baby who had been well until a sudden and catastrophic collapse occurred. He had some abnormal blood vessels in his brain and these suddenly burst; there was massive bleeding into his brain causing destruction of the whole of his cerebral cortex. However, his brain stem was partially functioning, and he made irregular gasping movements. These were not enough to enable him to survive off the ventilator but they were evidence that he did not have death of his whole brain, so he was not legally dead.

There was therefore one child who was completely normal except for a dying heart in one bed, and in the next bed, a child with a dead brain cortex but a normal heart. As it happened, the two children had the same blood group, so the heart of the child with no cerebral cortex could have been transplanted into the child with cardiomyopathy (heart disease).

Under Australian law – and the legal situation would have been the same everywhere in the world – there was nothing that Shann could do. The child whose cortex had been destroyed was not legally brain dead, so he could not be considered as a heart donor. No other heart could be found for the child with heart disease. Within a short time, both children were dead.

(This is an extract from Peter Singer's (1994) *Rethinking Life and Death* Melbourne: Text Publishing Co, pp 38, 41-2.) Note: On the question of so-called "brain death" see footnote 6 to this chapter.

- Is the law applicable here ethically sound? Would it be unethical to terminate the life of one baby so that another might live?
- What are the considerations in this case? What would you do? Analyse your decision. What type of moral reasoning supports that decision?
- Do cases like this provide an ethical justification for ante-natal screening? Are there ethical problems in ante-natal screening?

CASE 3 – THE TROUBLE WITH JACK

Jack, a 65-year-old man who was a widower, father of two daughters and grandfather of an 18-month-old grandson, was involved in a car accident which left him in a coma. He had willed his body to the Medical School for research. Jack was clearly brain-damaged but his respiratory and cardiac functions were stabilised by machines. After one week the medical staff were unsure how long he would need the support of machines, though they had estimated that 60 per cent of his brain was irretrievably damaged, and that his best prospects were that he would be bed-ridden and severely intellectually handicapped. However, he showed reaction to pain and his EEG revealed some brain activity. Doctors said the coma could lift at any time. Because he could not be pronounced dead in any medical or legal sense, the hospital and doctors refused to take him off the respirator or stop other treatments, though there was anxiety in some quarters that the equipment might be needed in other emergencies.

One other aspect of Jack's situation was that he was in the early stages of Alzheimer's disease (which results in a debilitating mental disorientation and degeneration of any capacity to care for himself). This had been diagnosed two years earlier though it was still anticipated that it would be 5-7 years before he would be in an advanced stage of the disease.

Jack's brother recalled a conversation with Jack soon after the diagnosis in which he said, "I hope I die before the Alzheimer's takes over". Sitting in the hospital room alone with Jack, the brother was tempted to disconnect the respirator and cause Jack's death.

- What ought to be done?
- What reasons can you offer for your view?
- Evaluate those reasons ethically. Have you employed an ethic of response approach? If not, what ethical approach justifies your decision?

CHAPTER SEVEN NOTES

1 Steven Morris, "Siamese twins must have fatal surgery" in *Guardian Weekly*, 31 August – 6 September 2000, p 9.

2 This case is taken from Roy Eccleston's report, "Death before Deformity" in *The Australian Magazine*, 20-21 January 1996, p 10.

3 *Bioethics* literally means "the ethics of life". It is the term used for a major area of applied ethics: the attempt to develop ethical reasoning, guidance and reflection on matters associated with medical science and technology, the care of the ill and dying, and the health care industry generally. One of the seminal texts in bioethics is Beauchamp, TL and Childress, JF (1994) *Principles of Biomedical Ethics* (4th ed), Oxford: Oxford University Press. The authors nominate four ethical principles which have been widely employed in bioethics: autonomy, beneficence, non-maleficence and justice. Many major topics which are dominating contemporary discussions in bioethics are not analysed at length in this chapter. They include:

- *Reproductive technology* - a range of excellent discussions on these topics can be found in Mappes T and Zembaty, J (eds) (1992) *Social Ethics: Morality and Social Policy*, New York: McGraw Hill Inc, Chapter Two "Surrogate Motherhood and Reproductive Technology", pp 56-104.
- *Genetics* – See, for example, Thompson, L (1994) *Correcting the Code: Inventing the Genetic Cure for the Human Body*, New York: Simon and Shuster. For up to date discussions of this topic it is necessary to monitor journals such as *Journal of Medical Ethics.*
- *Resource allocation in health care* – A discussion of this question is to be found in Chapter Five of Charlesworth, M (1993) *Bioethics in a Liberal Society*, Cambridge: Cambridge University Press. See also Chapter Fourteen in Hepburn, E (1996) *Of Life and Death*, Melbourne: Dove.

4 Singer, P op cit. The Linares case is reported on pp 114-115.

5 One traditional way of defining personhood is linked to dualistic, religious and metaphysical approaches that maintain certain beings (human beings at least) have a soul or spirit. This approach claims that this is the characteristic which determines personhood, and as long as the soul is present in the body, the life of that body is inviolable. The idea of "ensoulment", which defies empirical verification, could be critical on decisions about abortion or euthanasia. For instance, Thomas Aquinas, the medieval Catholic theologian, maintained that the souls of girls were implanted at 90 days and of boys at 40 days. This of course led to the idea that abortion was not a problem provided it was carried out before the soul was implanted, although it is unclear how the sex difference could be allowed for in an era without ultra-sound technology. It is dubious indeed for contemporary ethics to link the idea of personhood to ensoulment, although the notion of the dignity of human beings, which attaches to "soul" is of ongoing ethical importance.

6 The following definitional distinctions are provided by Dr Ronald Cranford: (a) Brain death = irreversible loss of all brain functions, both cerebral hemisphere and brain stem. (b) Persistent vegetative state = irreversible loss of all neocortical functions: brain stem functions in-tact. The patient is still breathing. Most jurisdictions which use brain death as a criterion mean whole brain death, that is, cortex and brain stem activity have ceased. Some medical ethicists argue that death of the cortex should be regarded as death. Such an interpretation facilitates organ transplants. It is also noteworthy in the context of this paragraph that while anencephalic babies have no cortex, many have a functioning brain stem. See also Peter Singer's chapter, "How Death was Redefined" in op cit.

7 This discussion presumes some overlapping, between "life", "sentience" and "personhood" as distinct criteria of moral status.

8 The "viability" of a foetus is another complex matter. Although it is an imprecise point (let us say around the twentieth week of pregnancy), viability is morally significant in the debate about abortion, because prior to viability the foetus could not be anywhere other than in the womb (even if it were artificial) and can not possess a sense or awareness of being a separate individual.

9 Singer, P op cit, Chapter Six.

10 Hepburn, E (1996) *Of Life and Death*, Melbourne: Dove, p 46.

11 McCormick, R (1978) "The quality of life, the sanctity of life", *Hastings Center Report*, 8 (1), p 35.

12 Reiskin, J (1992) "Suicide - Political or Personal", *Quad Wrangle*, Autumn, 7.

13 Fitzgerald, J (1996) "Legalised Euthanasia: its Implication for People with Disability", unpublished paper presented to Rights, Ethics and Justice for People with Disability Conference, Brisbane, 11 April 1996, p 9.

14 Ibid, p 5.

15 Ibid, pp 5-6.

16 John Paul II (1995) in *Evangelica Vitae*, Vatican City, note 65.

17 See Baume, P (1995) "Voluntary Euthanasia - Mercy or Sin", *New Doctor*, Winter, pp 13-14.

18 McCormick, R op cit.

19 Hepburn, E op cit, pp 19-20, provides a fuller account of the doctrine. In a note to me, Elizabeth Hepburn says that, in practice, according to many specialists this Doctrine of Double Effect does not apply because it is not the overdose of narcotic analgesics which kill the patient but the underlying illness.

20 The Rachels and Sullivan papers are reproduced in Chapter Three of Mappes, T and Zembaty, J (eds) (1992), *Social Ethics*, New York: McGraw-Hill.

21 Reproduced in *National Outlook*, September 1995, p 21.

22 Hepburn, E op cit, pp 48 ff for a summary of international legislative developments. This text also includes the Northern Territory *Rights of the Terminally Ill Act* 1995 in full as an appendix.

23 See Kuhse, H and Singer P "Doctors' practices and attitudes regarding voluntary euthanasia", *Medical Journal Australia* 1988; 148:623-627 and Baume, P and O'Malley, E "Euthanasia: attitudes and practices of medical practitioners", *Medical Journal Australia*, 1994; 161: 137-144.

24 It is claimed by palliative care authorities that fewer than five per cent of terminally ill cancer patients are not able to benefit from pain relief techniques.

25 See Kenneth Ralph's contribution to Kuhse, H (ed) (1994) *Willing to Listen, Wanting to Die*, Penguin, pp 187-200.

26 Reproduced in "Euthanasia and Palliative Care", a paper of the Social Responsibilities Office, Anglican Diocese of Brisbane, Australia.

27 Hepburn, E (1995) "Moral dilemma of euthanasia", *Courier Mail*, 23 June 1995, p 17.

28 Charlesworth, M (1993) *Bioethics in a Liberal Society*, Cambridge: Cambridge University Press, p 4.

29 Ibid, p 5. For another piece by Charlesworth on the law and bioethics in a liberal state see "Dying and the Law", *Res Publica*, vol 4, no 2, 1995, pp 12-16.

30 "More deaths in custody than before probe", report by J Walker in *The Weekend Australian*, 27-28 April 1996, p 3. Walker reports a 50 per cent increase in annual rates of death in custody over a five-year period.

31 See an extract from Kant's, *The Philosophy of Law*, in J White (ed) (1991) *Contemporary Moral Problems*, St Paul, MN: West Publishing Co, pp 198-199.

32 White J (ed), op cit, p 187.

33 Ibid, Chapter Nine for some excellent readings on the themes raised in this brief account. Also, for a fascinating and insightful account into the politics, psychology and ethics of modern ethnic warfare see: Ignatieff, M (1998) *The Warrior's Honour: Ethnic War and the Modern Conscience*, New York: Henry Holt.

34 Knightly, P (2000) The First Casualty: The War Correspondent as Hero and Myth-Maker from the Crimea to Kosovo (revised edition) London: Prion Books.

35 This definition is contained in the Code of Ethical Practice for Biotechnology in Queensland issued by the Queensland government. The literature on the topic of biotechnology, both scientific and ethical, is immense and growing daily. One comprehensive listing of resources on Bioethics is provided by the Georgetown University's National Reference Center for Bioethics. This literature may be accessed at email:medethx@gunet.georgetown.edu, <http://www.georgetown.edu

/research/nrebl/>. The Australian discussion of biotechnology is Hindmarsh R (et al) (1998) *Altered Genes: Reconstructing Nature,* Sydney: Allen and Unwin.

36 For an excellent discussion of the advantages and disadvantages of the genetic modification of food see, J Madeleine Nash, "Grains of hope", *Time,* 7 August 2000, pp 60–67.

CHAPTER EIGHT

PUBLIC RESPONSIBILITY, POLITICS AND THE PROFESSIONS

I have dirty hands right up to the elbows. I've plunged them in filth and blood. Do you think you can govern innocently?

Hoerderer, the political leader in Jean Paul Sartre's play, *Dirty Hands*

People who follow a one-dimensional perception of moral values in foreign relations pursue a misleading caricature of reality. They confront no complexities, experience no difficulties arising from a range of considerations of the sort which often restrict action to second best, or even lesser order, solutions. For such individuals the issues always embody universal, absolute, and straightforward principles. They enjoy another advantage: They are free to denounce and criticise publicly without having to worry about the consequences of their actions on the foreign political and external commercial relations of their country. The working foreign minister is denied that luxury, being required to balance a number of considerations before initiating action. Temporising on an issue of principle is a matter of great and binding common sense if an alternative hasty act or assertion of abstract principle provides a net result much worse than a temporised outcome. To do this is not necessarily to discard moral objectives. It is far more difficult to be consistently moral in the superintendence of a country's foreign relations than to be a moralising commentator.

Bill Hayden, *Into Exile - The Reason Why*, Angus & Robertson (1996)

Only they deserve power who justify its use daily.

Dag Hammarsjold
Former Secretary-General
United Nations Organisation

Defining the Public Good

Sometimes we discriminate between ethical responsibilities which are "private" and those that are "public".[1] Family matters might be regarded as private, while political or commercial activity is in the public sphere, although the private and public necessarily interact. Indeed, it is not uncommon to encounter conflicts of loyalty between responsibilities in the external, public world and commitments of our interpersonal or intrapersonal private lives. The world of public affairs is often experienced as supra-personal or impersonal, and as a powerful, formative influence on our life chances as individuals. Our community life also is fashioned through public institutions, such as the law, education, government and business.

It follows that if we are to live the good life we must discover how to be ethical in the public domain. In other words, how are we to achieve *the public good*? The public good may be conceived in various ways. In this chapter, however, it will be explored through two allied terms, the *public interest* and the *common good*.

The common good and social solidarity are companion concepts, nurtured by the conviction that the interests of others deserve equal consideration with anyone's personal interests. Though the common good may flourish better in conditions of social democracy, it need not be equated with collectivism. Indeed it is not inconsistent with the common good to respect the autonomy of individuals or to foster cultural diversity.

Decisions taken for the common good require a comprehensive ethical evaluation similar to that prescribed by the ethic of response. That approach (outlined in Chapter Four) enshrines three principles which are integral to the public good: the first endorses respect for life, including persons and the environment, while the third, the principle of covenantal integrity, enjoins us to be honest and faithful in our private and public agreements. The second principle, of justice and fairness, is essential to the public good. As an expression of *social justice*, understood in terms of the Rawlsian analysis outlined in Chapter Three, the common good requires policies which give priority to the needs of the disadvantaged or disempowered, giving all in a community access to social goods. While social equity suggests an end to all discrimination in society, social justice sharpens that by establishing special measures for particularly disadvantaged groups and individuals. It invokes the adage, "there is nothing so unequal as the equal treatment of unequals", thereby endorsing positive discrimination in certain instances. In sheer political terms, social justice may be something of a visionary ideal, the achievement of which requires social struggle, especially because it implies sacrifice by the most advantaged in the development of a more inclusive society. Nevertheless, without the vision and the struggle, attempts to embody social justice in public policy are likely to degenerate into something less than social justice.

The link between "common good" and this approach to "justice as fairness" modifies the tendency for the common good to be interpreted in simplistic utilitarian or majoritarian terms which equate the common good with "the greatest good for the greatest number", overlooking the needs of minorities. Consideration of the common good may function as a beacon in public life assisting policy-makers to search out ethical policies which are both desirable and feasible.[2]

Another term used in the discourse about "the public good" is *the public interest*.[3] Public officials are exhorted to act in the public interest and to declare conflicts of loyalty between public and private duties. Policies of government or particular commercial activities like newspapers are criticised in terms of how they serve the public interest. Yet it is an elusive, value-laden term, not easily defined and open to various interpretations. Who is to define "the public interest" and who are "the public" anyway? Should elected governments define it, or is there some more objective cost-benefit analysis which can identify what will benefit the public? Is it only the constituents within a particular jurisdiction whose interests are relevant, or should we take a more global view of public interests? Despite the difficulty in being precise about what we mean by the public interest, and despite the need to resist the tendency for it to be defined in terms of particular, dominant social interests, the concept enshrines two assumptions which, arguably, are essential to the public good: first, in the public sphere, considerations of a wider, public interest take precedence over private, personal or sectional interests, that is, conflicts of interest are to be resolved in favour of the public interest; and secondly, public practices and policies should be subject to a process of open and public justification.[4]

Understood in these terms, the concept, public good, provides a cornerstone for the discussions of this chapter. Though I will argue later that it is also pertinent to the commercial domain, its relevance to the political sphere is self-evident. As Michael Walzer expresses it, public officials are "citizens in lieu of the rest of us. The common good is, so to speak, their speciality".[5]

Political Ethics

Politics is a noble art because it is a key practice through which the common good may be attained.[6] In Western thought and practice, the relationship between ethics and politics has been acknowledged since Aristotle. Unfortunately however, many citizens and a few politicians regard the term "political ethics" if not an oxymoron, then at least an uneasy conjunction. Of course this would be the case if politics were understood as a realm of pure power, unremittingly pragmatic, and ethics as a realm of pure principle, unceasingly idealistic. So described, it becomes easy for politicians to question the relevance ethics has to political practice, or for moralists to despair that ethics seems irrelevant to the pursuit of power. Neither view of politics or ethics is accurate or acceptable.

Unfortunately, the view that politics and ethics diverge rather than converge is reflected in opinion polls which give a low rating to the behaviour of politicians.[7] Social commentator Hugh Mackay concludes from his research that "a significant shift in the character of Australian politics has left voters confused and cynical ..."[8]

While some of this denigration results from the action of a few politicians, much of it is the consequence of misinformed attitudes about the nature of political responsibility and the role of parliamentarians. In any case, the revelation of ethical shortcomings in politics is no cause for self-righteousness in the rest of the community. We are all actors on the political stage, and, if we fail to participate politically as citizens we limit our right to criticise. We all share some responsibility for whatever dirty linen is lying around the political household. Sometimes it is relevant to consider how the private behaviour of an elected official impinges on their capacity to serve the public, but as a matter of political ethics the relevance of private "misbehaviour" extends no further than this. Certainly, preoccupation with the personal ethical behaviour of politicians may achieve nothing for the wider public good.

The substantial concern of political ethics is not whether individual politicians are unethical. That is a much over-stated proposition. The core issue we need to address is how ethical judgment can proceed along with political practice. To deal with that issue we need a clearer picture of the differentiating characteristics of political practice as a public activity.

For a start, parliamentarians and unelected public officials are entrusted with public money. Corresponding with that trust is power over people's lives. They assume responsibility in a significant way, for protecting the rights and interests of the public. Much of the work of public officers - elected or appointed - involves choices amongst values; indeed, it is this characteristic of their role in a liberal democracy that often makes their decisions contestable, debatable and requiring public justification. Elected and unelected officials have to make choices in an environment where they have limited resources and options, choices which will benefit some and disadvantage others. The political environment is a highly competitive and adversarial one, which by necessity is fuelled by the quest for power. Before becoming an elected official, deals of dubious kinds may be done to win pre-selections. Politicians are constantly faced with the demands of interest groups, factions, institutions, powerful individuals as well as ordinary constituents. The conduct of parliamentarians is potentially under constant scrutiny by journalists whose integrity can often impinge on political practice. As the managers of the state, public officials are able to sanction the use of violence, for instance through war, capital punishment, or the police force; similarly, they may be put under pressure to make alliances with those they find distasteful or to conceal information from those seemingly entitled to it. Though it may not be the only human endeavour confronted with this constellation of pressures, politics is "an area where conscience and power meet, where the ethical and coercive factors of human life will interpenetrate and work out their tentative and uneasy compromises".[9]

Even though a case may be made that behaviour which is unacceptable in other spheres is unavoidable in politics, the demands and characteristics of political life do not make ethics irrelevant to politics. In fact, ethical decision-making is part and parcel of the political realm. At the same time, it is fitting to take account of the special characteristics of politics as we construct a framework for political ethics.

As Bernard Williams concludes:

> It is a predictable and probable hazard of public life that there will be those situations in which something morally disagreeable is clearly required. To refuse on moral grounds even to do anything of that

> sort is more than likely to mean that one cannot seriously pursue even the moral ends of politics.[10]

Williams is suggesting that ethical political action involves "something morally disagreeable", a paradoxical state of affairs which is often referred to in the literature of political philosophy by the term, *the dirty hands dilemma*.

The descriptor, "machiavellian", is also associated with the view that getting one's hands "dirty" is inevitable in politics. Machiavelli, a Renaissance bureaucrat, challenges the notion that canons of personal morality can be simplistically employed in political decision-making, thereby lending support to the view that one's role shapes ethical standards (role morality) and that in politics, consequentialist ways of moral reasoning must dominate. In *The Prince* he argues that: "a man who wishes to profess goodness at all times will come to ruin among so many who are not so good. Hence it is necessary for a prince who wishes to maintain his position to learn how not to be good, and to use this knowledge or not to use it according to necessity".[11] If that implies that a politician whose politics are good for the people need not necessarily himself be a good person, then we must agree with Machiavelli. Actions and outcomes in politics are arguably more important than motivations.[12]

However, we should not be too persuaded by Machiavelli, especially for the pursuit of political ethics in twentieth century democracies which rely on responsive and accountable government. The suggestion that ordinary politicians in societies such as Australia have blood dripping from their dirty hands is a gross exaggeration, (although it may have been that which many members of the national Parliament feared when they were forced to comply with a cabinet decision for Australia to enter the Gulf War in 1991). In policy terms, the clearest illustrations of the dirty hands dilemma are generally derived from foreign affairs: the Vietnam War or recognition of the Indonesian takeover of East Timor for instance.[13] Not all matters of political policy or process need to be decided on consequentialist grounds however. There are moral rules which can be applied in politics. Corruption[14] in political office ought never be sanctioned; the deliberate use of misleading information to damage a political opponent is unjustifiable; the public declaration of conflicts of interest is a moral duty. In other words, we need to be careful about accepting too easily the notion that political ethics is irredeemably devoid of clear ethical standards.

In his analysis of the dirty hands dilemma, Peter French[15] alerts readers to the danger of becoming too comfortable with the moral ambiguity of political practice. He draws on Michael Walzer's[16] analogy between the morality of civil disobedience and the immorality of certain necessary political actions. Civil disobedience as a moral act usually involves breaking a law for a greater ethical cause, but also includes taking the penalty under the law for that defiance. In cases where politics requires some defiance of a moral norm there should also be a penalty, says Walzer. The argument is that the ethically problematic nature of dirty hands needs to be recognised. In line with this approach, French quotes the senior government official who said, "If the moment came when I saw an overwhelming need to lie in the nation's interest, I would lie ... Of course, I would resign immediately afterward". For Walzer, therefore, the resolution of the dirty hands dilemma includes "honouring the man who did bad in order to do good, and at the same time we would punish him". That is, the moral justification of political actions which are ethically dubious but "necessary", may include bearing a penalty, such as resignation from office.

Politics is sometimes described as "the art of compromise". Certainly, if compromise results in the abandonment of sound principles or a violation of the moral agent's character, it becomes morally suspect, and in politics, such compromise warrants personal and public justification. Nonetheless, there is nothing intrinsically immoral about employing compromise in ethical decision-making. Indeed, if that is all we mean by the dirty hands dilemma then, as Tony Coady[17] maintains, "it is an issue which can arise in any area of life. It is not special to politics, though there are some aspects of politics which perhaps raise the issue more acutely or dramatically".

Given the morally difficult context in which politics is practised, what models of ethical reasoning, justification and decision-making can best serve the political endeavour? The limitations of deontological rules in politics are obvious, though some sense of duty to office and reliance on a fundamental respect for persons in the Kantian mould, are vital to political ethics. In *Politics as a Vocation*, Max Weber argued against the relevance of Kantianism, which he described as "an ethic of ultimate ends". Instead he proposed an "ethic of responsibility" to be pursued by persons "with a trained relentlessness in viewing the realities of life and the ability to face such realities and to measure up to them inwardly."[18] Weber's ethic of responsibility (which overlaps with, but is not to be confused with, this text's "ethic of response") has been accused (perhaps unjustifiably) of being too amenable to the utilitarian calculus which is widespread in political practice. Agnes Heller and Ferenc Feher make the salient point that we need to retain principles and values in political ethical decision-making. They suggest that the weakness of Weber's ethic of responsibility is that it "cannot answer the crucial question concerning which consequences are good (desirable) and which are bad (undesirable)".[19] Others have claimed that despite the inevitable attractiveness of utilitarianism for public officials seeking to resolve conflicts among policies, utilitarianism is too inclined to reduce competing social goods to one measure (chiefly money in capitalist societies) and also, that the maximisation of social welfare does not necessarily ensure justice especially for minorities.

A more commendable framework for those seeking an ethical judgment fitting to the political context is the comprehensive model of ethical decision-making in the ethic of response. Politicians do well to take on board the range of interests, elements, and factors suggested in this model, which also provides them with a process amenable to public explanation. Of course, the peculiarities of the political context will influence the weighing up of considerations and the assessment leading to a responsible decision: significant factors include the need to seek and maintain power in government, or to be a representative of particular constituencies, as well as the need to decide and act in the public interest (interpreted, in the light of our earlier discussion with a focus on social justice and the common good). Indeed, Weber's rhetoric appears to endorse the integrated and comprehensive approach of the ethic of response when in *Politics as a Vocation* he makes the following appeal:

> it is immensely moving when a mature person … is aware of a responsibility for the consequences of his [sic] conduct and really feels such responsibility with heart and soul. He [sic] then acts by following an ethic of responsibility and somewhere he [sic] reaches that point where he [sic] says: "Here I stand; I can do no other". That is something genuinely human and moving … *In so far as this is true, an ethic of ultimate ends and an ethic of responsibility are not absolute contrasts but rather supplements, which only in unison constitute a genuine person – a person who can have the "calling" for politics.*[20]

Conflict of Interest[21]

A recurring issue in public and professional life is that of conflicts of interest. A conflict of interest arises when there is a conflict between the private interests of a public official and public duty. We may distinguish between an *apparent* conflict of interest (when it appears that an official's private interests may have the potential to interfere with the proper performance of that official's duties) and an *actual* conflict of interest (when a reasonable person, in possession of the relevant facts, would conclude that the official's private interests are likely to interfere with the proper performance of that official's duties). Such conflicts may take many forms: the receipt of gifts and entertainments, employment outside one's job as a public official, information peddling and dealings with relatives. Clearly, conflicts of interest extend beyond pecuniary or financial matters; they may extend to the temptation to give favoured treatment to private organisations which may be future sources of employment for the official. Indeed, in recent years interest has shifted from a limited application to the dilemma of public officials enriching themselves to a wide-ranging concern about the integrity of officials and the public sector.

Conflicts of interest are not in themselves unethical. The ethical challenge resides in the recognition and management of them. Professionals other than public officials are likely to encounter conflicts of interest. An academic who sets a text book from which he receives royalties or a doctor who refers patients to a clinic she owns, both face conflicts of interest.

However, the stakes are much higher when elected or unelected public officials mismanage conflicts of interest. The appearance of a conflict between public duty and private benefit is unacceptable because a potential conflict can damage the public confidence which is essential to good government.

One trend creating confusion about these conflicts is the blurring of the line between the private and the public, as governments corporatise and enjoin their employees to adopt private sector practices, even to the point of seeing the goal of their activity as profit rather than service. Another reason conflicts of interest matter is that, when ignored, they violate a key principle of the rule of law, that every citizen is equal before the law and deserves unbiased treatment. Finally, conflicts of interest are significant because the failure to declare, avoid or manage them can lead to corruption. For instance, the Suharto family eventually corrupted the Indonesian economy because they consistently ignored the conflict between the public good and their private interest.

Nonetheless, "conflict of interest" remains a term which is not always simply applicable; it is not always precisely clear when public officials are acting officially or in a private capacity, or when a government Minister is acting in that role or is merely acting as a servant of his or her political party. Because of the ambiguity sometimes surrounding the term, and because human beings are prone to self-deception when their own interests are at stake, prudent public officials will be wary of relying solely on their own judgment (or that of mates) to identify and resolve conflicts of interest.

The fundamental and essential course of action in the ethical management of conflicts of interest is the *recognition* and *disclosure* of the conflict. At this point it is wise for the official to seek *advice* or an independent appraisal of the issues at stake in the conflict, and step aside from all the decision-making associated with the conflict. (Some public sector ethics systems have instituted the position of ethics counsellor to encourage this practice.) *Other procedures* for managing conflicts of interest can include (i) withdrawal from the conflicting situation or divestment in the case of pecuniary interests, (ii) appeal to laws, rules or procedures that accommodate clashing interests, (iii) changes to institutional procedures or policies, and (iv) negotiating revised expectations of involved parties.

Public Sector Ethics and an Ethic of Role

Central to the exercise of public office is the expectation that officials are responsible and accountable. Responsible for what? Accountable to whom? Here the debate begins – and it is an ethical debate because it involves value-laden decision-making, just as it involves choices, choices shaped by the requirements of a democratic ethos and its institutions. Responsibility may be to the public and/or to an elected official (the mayor or minister). Accountability may be for policy advice and/or for carrying out orders. Guidelines are needed if there is to be appropriate responsibility and accountability.

Fundamental to the design of ethical guidelines is an understanding of the role of a public official. A major theme in our discussion of political ethics is that the justification for a distinctive approach to ethics in politics resides in the unique responsibilities and circumstances inherent to the role of parliamentarian or public official.

The idea of role morality or an ethic of agency is helpful in professional ethics generally, for it reminds us that the ethical obligations of professionals stem from the role they are performing or the institution they are serving. According to role ethics, the test of professional or public ethics is not that of satisfying one's personal conscience, but of acting in ways that are consistent with the duties entrusted to one in a public or professional role.[22] The development of an ethic of agency is compatible with virtue theory in the sense that its core consideration is the virtues/characteristics/excellences which support the role.[23] In Chapter Four we noted how the ethic of response responds to the matter of role understanding.

However, there are problems in the employment of a role morality. This is especially the case for public officials, when the ethic of role is interpreted to mean that a public official has only one line of moral obligation, that is, to the government of the day alone, regardless of matters of personal morality, social responsibility or duties to her profession (as with a social worker committed to clients, for instance). After all, the Nuremberg Trials were about this matter: public officials who abandoned moral responsibility, and blindly carried out the immoral, if lawful, orders of their Nazi superiors. Nuremberg remains a constant reminder that in certain cases of professional behaviour, role morality alone is an inadequate guide.

On the other hand, it is also untenable to the good order of government and society to have public officials who, in the normal course of events, disregard their loyalty to government whenever their personal convictions, professional obligation or vision of society is at variance with their public duty. What is required is a more profound understanding of the role or profession for which the public official is agent. That understanding needs to take account of the institutional obligations a public official has. So, while a public official clearly has an obligation to act lawfully, that obligation derives from a more profound obligation: to support the system of government and its democratic purposes. Consequently, the ethic of role may at times require, in the public interest and in the interest of the democratic institutions of government, the exposure of a minister of the government (even though technically that official's employer) who is deceiving the parliament and the people. Such an action is not subversive but stems from the professional obligation of the public officials and their ethic of agency. The case of Clive Ponting,[24] a British public servant who passed on secret government information regarding the sinking of the Argentine warship, *The Belgrano,* during the Falklands War, is instructive for this point. A jury accepted Ponting's defence that he had a duty ultimately to the Parliament, the institution representing the public, rather than to the government of the day. It is a defence which rests on a particular interpretation of the ethic of agency.

In response to the perceived need for more explicit ethical guidance for public officials in the exercise of their role, governments across many jurisdictions in numerous nations have recently instituted ethics programs usually centring on the development of codes, designed around a role ethic. For example, in 1995 a British Report by a Committee headed by Lord Nolan[25] recommended a range of measures to enhance the focus on ethics in public and political life. The Report nominated "Seven Principles of Public Life": selflessness, integrity, objectivity, accountability, openness, honesty, leadership.

So significant has this concern for public ethics become in the last decade of the twentieth century that the Organisation for Economic Cooperation and Development (OECD) has taken a direct interest in it, emphasising that a fourth "E", *ethics,* should be added to the public sector reform triumvirate of *economy, efficiency* and *effectiveness.* In fact, the OECD has declared:

> OECD countries are concerned about declining confidence in government. This so-called "confidence deficit" has been fuelled by well-publicised "scandals" ranging from inappropriate actions on the part of public officials, to full-scale corruption. Few, if any, member countries have escaped the taint, if not the reality of wrongdoing. As a result, ethics or standards in public life have become an important public and political issues.[26]

Often ethics reforms are taken after scandals or corruption inquiries, though the capacity of public sector ethics regimes to prevent such incidents or to develop more ethically autonomous public servants is open to question. In Australia,[27] most governments are now instituting ethics codes and training for public officials; initiatives in the parliaments themselves are less advanced, though several Australian parliaments have codes and are establishing parliamentary ethics committees. The efficacy of these moves is unproven but they are a recognition of the possibility and desirability of a more explicit discourse about ethics in politics. At the same time, it has been suggested that ethics impedes the processes of good government, especially when ethics is presented prescriptively as a set of regulations. It is often asserted that legislatures in the United States have gone too far in this respect so that ethics has been politicised and the political process frustrated, against the public interest. The *Wall Street Journal* once editorialised under the caption, ETHICSGATE: "We are going to have to kill ethics before ethics kills us ..."[28] Maybe such disquiet is inevitable in the political process. Regardless of it, there is an overwhelming case requiring governments to pursue these programs because public confidence in government demands accountability measures. Furthermore, they are necessary if public office is to be regarded as a profession, given that clarification of a coherent set of ethical responsibilities is one defining characteristic of a profession.

Professional Ethics

Of course, it is a matter of debate as to what precisely constitutes a profession. Bernard Shaw's quip that professions are conspiracies against the laity suggests that specialist knowledge allied to structures of institutional collegiality such as we find in medicine, the law or theology, is a key defining characteristic for professions. However, this may lead to a definition of professions based on technical competencies alone. According to William May,[29] technical competence and special knowledge are only partial requirements of "the professions". He reminds us that the word "profession" etymologically means to "testify on behalf of" or "to stand for something", to profess something that defines one's fundamental commitment. "Profession" then is more akin to the term "vocation" (a calling) than it is to the term "career". As vocations, the professions may be said to have an intrinsic commitment to the public good, including a willingness to provide services gratuitously beyond the call of duty. The professions are to foster a disposition among their members characterised by civil responsibility. In these terms professional ethics will place a strong emphasis on community service informed by the idea of responsibility which was outlined in Chapter Four.

As it transpires, in practice the qualification for the label "profession" usually relies on other criteria: a certain status in the community, a university level professional preparation, a professional association and code of ethics; recognition of a trust on behalf of clients seeking specific services is another qualification for the label "professional". On these standards the range of occupations which are termed "professional" can be expanded to include, for instance, social workers, teachers, engineers or even law enforcement officers.

Likewise, I maintain that the occupations we discuss in this chapter, public servants, parliamentarians and business persons should be so regarded, and the ethical requirements for people in those occupations are to be regarded as a sub-set of professional ethics. Business and politics may not require the specialist knowledge which is normally unavailable to the laity to the extent that the professions of medicine or the law require that knowledge. However, it is increasingly evident that given the complexity of contemporary societies, the practices of public administration, legislation and commerce demand education and training in certain skills and knowledge, together with structured opportunities to reflect on the principles which underpin those practices. Furthermore, these roles, which impinge so directly on the public interest and the common good, are best performed when they are approached with a sense of responsibility to the community, in other words, as "a vocation".

We move now to extend our discussion of professional ethics to the commercial domain.

Business Ethics

Though it may be an expression of private enterprise, business is not an activity of isolated individuals. Business owes its existence to society. Whether we are talking about the cornerstore or a gigantic transnational corporation, business is a social practice with implications for the public good. The social responsibility of business is therefore a fundamental element in business ethics; at least this is what this discussion will attempt to demonstrate.

Though moral questions have always been debated throughout the evolution of commercial activity,[30] business ethics is a recent but fairly vigorous business. Since the 1980s, this branch of applied and professional ethics has developed a significant literature along with education and training programs. At the level of business practice, however, it is arguable that the treatment of business ethics requires a more critical perspective. Ethics in business is often presented as part of a marketing technique or a human resource management concern, an adjunct of quality management. In other words ethics becomes another tool in a totally pragmatic and instrumentalist domain as is typified by the slogan: "The Bottom Line = Business + Ethics = Survival in the 90s".

At the same time, fundamental questions are being raised by business ethicists:

- what ought to be the purpose of business? is "profit" a morally legitimate goal? who are its stakeholders?
- is a corporation a moral agent? in what sense then does it have moral obligations?
- what sort of economic system will cultivate ethical business best? is a co-operative approach to the production of goods and services more ethically justified than a competitive one?

An examination of the topics discussed in business ethics texts[31] reveals the following:

- the ethics of marketing and advertising;
- responsibilities to employees;
- consumer protection;
- ethical investment;
- business and the environment;
- bribery/corruption/insider trading;
- whistleblowing;
- matters of economic justice (fair price; international obligations);

The subject matter of business ethics is multi-faceted. We may distinguish between *micro* and *macro* concerns. The rules for fair exchange between individuals are the focus of the micro concerns, whereas the institutional or cultural rules of commerce reaching to the wider society are the macro concerns. At the micro level we may be concerned to identify virtues which make a good business person, for example, diligence and service; this level also includes the ethics of intra-organisational relationships, matters of employee well-being for instance, or respectful treatment of customers. The macro level refers to the moral duties of a company with respect to the rest of society. It implies leadership in business characterised by the virtue of civic responsibility. It includes an obligation to be lawful, but understands business ethics more broadly than that. Macro business ethics analyses the ethics of business itself, including the values which define democratic capitalism in a global environment.

The remainder of this discussion is devoted to the macro question of business' *social responsibility*. Three recent examples illustrate this dilemma:

- Some Australian banks impose charges on small savings accounts adversely affecting low income earners. Their defence is that governments should look after social welfare policy not financial institutions, whose core business is to make money.
- The chief executive of a trans-national company received a salary increase taking his annual personal income to US$31 million in a year when the combined income of 25,000 of his company's employees in a Third World country totalled only half that amount.
- In the eighties, investment support was withdrawn from South African companies by private and public commercial bodies in a successful attempt to persuade South African business to disengage from apartheid and to urge them to put pressure on the South African government to change the national constitution.

The view that business has no social responsibility beyond that of making profits for its stockholders has been vigorously proposed by Chicago economist, Milton Friedman. For him, "there is one and only one social responsibility of business – to use its resources and engage in activities designed to increase its profits so long as it stays within the rules of the game, which is to say, engages in open and free competition without deception or fraud".[32] Friedman is even opposed to businesses contributing to charity or other social causes (unless those actions contribute to the business and its profitability). The basis of his view is that company directors have a fiduciary responsibility to stockholders to maximise profits and to act otherwise is, in effect, stealing which moves away from the free market approach toward socialism. He endorses William Vanderbilt: "The public be damned. I'm working for my stockholders".[33] In effect, he is also summoning a narrow role morality to buttress his position: the role of the business person is to develop a profitable business, not to be a legislator or a social reformer, or even a good corporate citizen.

The argument against this view is that, even within the parameters of a capitalist economy, a much wider understanding of the nature of business is required. The proposal is that business sometimes has social responsibilities which conflict with, and override, the responsibility to maximise profits. Arguably, companies that withdrew from the South African economy as an action against apartheid were exercising social responsibility in spite of its effect on profits. On the other hand, an international satellite television service withdrew news on human rights abuses because it offended a government on which the company depended for televising rights to about a billion people.[34] In that case it would seem that consideration of profits overrode social responsibility.

While Friedman's view rests on several half-truths, it overstates the capacity of the free market to correct itself and to work for the wider public good. It is a nonsense to suggest, as he implies, that all steps which maximise profits are socially beneficial. In fact to focus narrowly on profits as the aim of business is misleading. Though a business aims to be profitable, it does so only by supplying quality goods and services, while providing employment and relating to its community. Business both lives off, and impacts upon, the society in which it operates (and for some corporations that society is global). Because business interacts with society,[35] questions of job creation and fair pricing for example are matters of integrity for business. Of course, no issue exemplifies the need for social responsibility by business better than the environment, because, as we know, some business activities have an enormous capacity to damage the life support systems of Earth. There is no acceptable justification for business, as moral agents, to respond to the environmental crisis in a minimal way and only under the duress of legal sanction. Business, like the rest of the community, is not exempt from the injunction to value life. Proactively sustaining the environment, as an ethical imperative regardless of the law, is a new bottom line for commerce.

Solomon invokes the term "stakeholder" to dismiss Friedman's argument that the ethical responsibilities of business stop with stockholders:

> The stakeholders in a company are all of those who are affected and have legitimate expectations and rights regarding the actions of the company, and these include the employees, the consumers and the suppliers as well as the surrounding community and the society at large. The virtue of the concept is that it greatly expands the focus of corporate concern, without losing sight of the particular virtues and capacities of the corporation itself. Social responsibility, so considered, is not an additional burden on the corporation but part and parcel of its essential concerns ...[36]

Fitting, ethical business decisions based on the comprehensive range of concerns indicated by Solomon require an approach consistent with the ethic of response; that approach endorses the need to respect life, act fairly and be true to obligations with the wider community. While an ethic of response applied to business includes the so-called micro concerns, it will also introduce a critical perspective which incorporates a broad social responsibility. Social responsibility is arguably a constituent of business best practice. An approach to business ethics which fails to serve the common good and the public interest is unethical, chiefly because it fails to understand that business, like all human activity, is dependent on life's interconnectedness.

CHAPTER REVIEW

1. The chapter identified two important descriptors of *"the public good"*:
   - *the common good* is a term used in conjunction with social justice and social solidarity to refer to public policies which serve the interests of all those affected by a public decision;
   - *the public interest* is a term used to contrast with private interest. In the public sphere, public interests over-ride private or sectarian interests.
2. *Political Ethics* is concerned with how ethical judgment can affect political practice. We outlined the pressures of the political environment which make ethics unavoidable and essential in that sphere. The ethical dilemmas of politics are sometimes characterised as *dirty hands dilemmas.* This section claimed that while consequentialism remains crucial in political ethics (as Machiavelli and Weber show), there is a place for ethical rules and guidelines. Furthermore, the ethic of response provides a procedure which can take account of the realities of political decision-making eg the quest for power, the representative function and the public interest.
3. *The Ethic of Role* (or agency ethics) asserts that the ethical obligations of professionals stem from the role they perform or the institution they serve. We noted public sector ethics developments based on an ethic of role, and some of their problems, including the resolution of *conflicts of interest.* We explained that *Professional Ethics* is

supported best by a view of the professions which refers not only to the special expertise of various professions but to the view of professions as "vocations" committed to community service.

4. *Business Ethics.* A distinction can be made between *micro* concerns in business ethics which focus on the relationship within a business and *macro* concerns which focus on business relationships with the wider society. A macro issue is whether businesses have a responsibility to society as a whole. Rebutting Milton Friedman, we argued that there is a social responsibility for business, based on the view that business operates within a social environment from which it benefits and to which, as a moral agent, it is obliged to contribute.

FURTHER READING

Charlesworth, M (1991) *Ethics in Public Life,* Occasional Papers in Applied Ethics, No 1, Queensland University of Technology.

Cohen, S and Grace D (1995) *Business Ethics,* Sydney: Oxford University Press.

Koehn, D (1994) *The Ground of Professional Ethics,* London: Routledge.

Preston, N and Sampford, C with Bois, C-A (1998) *Ethics and Political Practice,* The Federation Press and Routledge.

Sampford, C and Preston, N with Bois, C-A (1998) *Public Sector Ethics: Finding and Implementing Values,* The Federation Press and Routledge.

Thomson, DF (1987) *Political Ethics and Public Office,* Cambridge, Ma: Harvard University Press.

QUESTIONS FOR DISCUSSION

1. What are the dangers of basing public sector ethics on an ethic of role? What do you think of those dangers? What place should personal morality play in public judgment? What value do you place on codes of conduct in professional ethics?

2. Politicians often get into public trouble for their private sexual indiscretions. Is this justified? Why or why not? Under what conditions is the personal behaviour of parliamentarians relevant to their public role? For instance, is an affair between an MP and a member of the Parliamentary Press Gallery acceptable?

3. "The Minister for Tourism conducts a dinner for the tourist industry charging $500 a head to raise money for party funds". Is this corrupt? Is it unethical? Is there a conflict of interest or a dirty hands dilemma involved?
4. What responsibilities do ordinary citizens have to contribute to the ethical health of political life in a democracy?
5. Is ethics good for business profits? What are the virtues which characterise sound ethical business practice? Do they conflict? How would you rate them? By what criteria?
6. Is the following statement by Fox a fair challenge to our economic system? Can business ethics within our current economic system respond to such a view? What is his view of the common good?

> Do not tell us whether our economy is growing in Gross National Product yearly: rather, tell us whether our world-wide economics are accomplishing the following: housing for the homeless, feeding the hungry, educating the ignorant, caring for the sick, humanising the prisons, creating good work for the unemployed, encouraging technology with a human face, passing on nature's energies to other generations.(Fox, M (1979) *A Spirituality Named Compassion*, Minneapolis: Winston Press, p 220)

CASE STUDIES

CASE 1 – EAST TIMOR AND POLITICAL DIRTY HANDS

Australia knew in advance of the 1975 Indonesian invasion of East Timor and stood by for three days as Jakarta's troops prepared for the attack. The release of government documents has now confirmed this.

It is claimed, by human rights groups, that up to 200,000 people died during the invasion and the subsequent fighting and famine in East Timor, which was sparked by the Portuguese withdrawal in 1975.

Successive Australian governments in an apparent manoeuvre to appease the Indonesian government offered no assistance to the East Timorese struggle for independence and covered up the truth on many occasions over more than twenty years. Finally in 1999, but at great cost to the East Timorese, they achieved their liberation and received direct assistance from Australia.

- What does this case reveal about political dirty hands, international ethical responsibility and truth telling in politics? What alternatives did Australia have?
- In these matters, do international realities over-ride normal ethical considerations?
- Is your reasoning in line with the ethic of response?

CASE 2 – PROFITS AND COMMUNITY RESPONSIBILITY

A thriving town grew up around a textile factory; for the past 100 years the community has relied on the factory for jobs and its general economic viability. Factory profits have declined, and the company is planning to move off-shore to a country where labour is cheaper. This will save the company, and its profits will increase significantly, providing some jobs elsewhere.

- Does the company have a social and ethical responsibility to remain and settle for lower profits?
- Consider the question in the light of Friedman's view of business ethics or Niebuhr's notion of responsibility and social solidarity. What do you think?

CASE 3 – ORGAN TRANSPLANTS, POLITICS AND JUSTICE

Faced with the need to control an expanding health budget in 1987 the Arizona State legislature voted to eliminate funding for most organ transplants from the State's health care program for the public system. At the same time they increased funding for several health measures such as providing basic health services to pregnant women and children between the ages of six and 13 years, in a group that were below the federal poverty level but previously had no assistance. Within months, the first case came to light of a 43-year-old woman, Diana Brown, who died of a liver disease because she was ineligible for support to receive a transplanted liver.

(See "Defunding Organ Transplants in Arizona" in Gutmann, A and Thompson, D (eds) (1991), *Ethics and Politics: Cases and Comments* (2nd ed), Chicago: Nelson Hall Publishers, p 178).

- Can this policy be defended on grounds of the public interest or the common good?
- What approach to social justice might support it?
- What approach would challenge it?
- Should public money be used to fund expensive organ transplants assisting certain individuals or to extend basic health care to the poor and young, or both?
- Did the politicians who passed this measure end up with dirty hands?
- Try to employ an ethic of response in your judgment.

CHAPTER EIGHT NOTES

1 As feminists properly assert, for women whose roles have been historically developed around the so-called private sphere, it can be a disempowering distinction.

2 *Common Wealth for the Common Good*, Melbourne: Collins Dove (1992). This statement (198 pp) by the Australian Catholic Bishops' Conference provides an analysis of the distribution of wealth in Australia with a clear perspective on social justice and the common good. Also Goodin, RE (1995) "Political Ideals and Political Practice" in *British Journal of Political Science*, vol 25, pp 37–56.

3 See Chapter Two of Kerneghan, K and Langford, J (1990) *The Responsible Public Servant*, Halifax, NS: Institute for Research on Public Policy.

4 For one extensive discussion of the criteria for public justification see Gaus, GE (1996) *Justificatory Liberalism*, New York: Oxford University Press.

5 Quoted by Cooper, TL (1991) *An Ethic of Citizenship for Public Administration*, Englewood Cliffs, NJ: Prentice-Hall, p 139.

6 When we speak of politics in this section we are referring to that activity which pertains to the exercise of government. Other spheres of life are political. So "politicians" in this case refers essentially to parliamentarians. On the link between politics and the common good, the Queensland *Public Sector Ethics Act* 1994 specifically enjoins public officials "to advance the common good of the community the official serves", s 9 (1) (b).

7 For a report on opinion polls see "Politicians: how low can they go?" *Bulletin*, 12 September 1995, pp 14-17. Since that date, polls in the Australian context consistently report the low rating of MPs.

8 Mackay, H (1993) *Reinventing Australia: The Mind And Mood Of Australia In The 90s*, Sydney: Angus and Robertson, p 23.

9 Niebuhr, R (1963) *Moral Man and Immoral Society*, London: SCM Press, p 4. For an excellent discussion of an empirical study into ethical questions arising in politics, see Manusco, M et al (1998) *A Question of Ethics: Canadians Speak Out*, Toronto: Oxford University Press.

10 Williams, B "Politics and Moral Character" in Hampshire, S (ed) (1978) *Public and Private Morality*, Cambridge: Cambridge University Press, p 62.

11 Machiavelli, N (1513) *The Prince* ed Bondanella, P, Oxford: Oxford University Press, 1984, p 52.

12 Goodin, RE (1992) *Motivating Political Morality*, Oxford: Blackwell.

13 For an illuminating account of the ethical tensions in the conduct of foreign affairs, see the reflections of former Australian foreign minister Bill Hayden. Hayden, B (1996) *Hayden: an Autobiography*, Sydney: Angus and Robertson, especially pp 410-423.

14 Corruption includes bribery, influence peddling, abuse of office, manipulation of public service appointments and so on.

15 French, PA (1983) "Dirty Hands" in Madsen, P and Shafritz, JM (1992) (eds) *Essentials of Government Ethics*, Meridian Books, pp 243-257.

16 Walzer, M (1973) "Political Action: the Problem of Dirty Hands", *Philosophy and Public Affairs*, vol 2, no 2, pp 160-180.

17 Coady, CAJ (1991) "Politics and the Problem of Dirty Hands" in Singer, P (ed), *Companion to Ethics*, Oxford: Basil Blackwell, pp 373-383.

18 Weber, M "Politics as a Vocation", *From Max Weber: Essays in Sociology,* Gerth, HH and C Wright Mills (trans, ed), New York: Oxford University Press, 1958, pp 115-128. The use of Weber may be problematic for, especially in "Politics as a Vocation", his argument may not be in harmony with a hard-nosed ethic of role.

19 Heller, A and Feher, F (1987) *The Postmodern Political Condition,* Oxford: Polity Press, p 62.

20 Weber, M, op cit, p 128. The italics are my emphasis.

21 Readers who wish to explore this topic much further than this short essay might consult the following: Carney, G (2000) *Members of Parliament: Law and Ethics,* Sydney, Prospect Media, chapter 10; Carson, T (1994) "Conflicts of Interest", *Journal of Business Ethics,* vol 13, pp 387–404; Langford, J (1991–92) "Conflict of Interest: What the Hell is it?" *Optimum,* vol 22, no 1, pp 28-33; May, L (1994) "Conflict of Interest" in Wueste, D (ed) *Professional Ethics and Social Responsibility,* Maryland: Rowman and Littlefield; Stark, A (2000) *Conflict in Public Life,* Cambridge: Harvard University Press; Williams, S (1995) *Conflict of Interest: The Ethical Dilemma in Politics,* Aldershot: Gower.

22 Uhr, J (1994) "Managing the Process of Ethics Training" in Preston, N (ed) *Ethics for the Public Sector,* Sydney: Federation Press, pp 165ff.

23 See Cooper, TL (1992) "Hierarchy, Virtue and the Practice of Public Administration", Madsen P and Shafritz JM (eds), op cit, and May, W (1994) "The Virtues in a Professional Setting", in Fulford, K (et al) (eds), *Medicine and Moral Reasoning,* Cambridge: Cambridge University Press, p 75-90.

24 Ponting, C (1985) *The Right to Know,* London: Sphere.

25 *First Report of the Committee on Standards in Public Life,* (Nolan Report), United Kingdom, 1995. For another British study illustrative of issues pertinent to this chapter, see Mancuso, M (1995) *The Ethical World of British MPs,* London: McGill-Queen's University Press.

26 PUMA/OECD (1996) *Ethics in the Public Service: Current Issues and Practice,* Puma (96) 13, OECD, p 5. See <http://oecd.org/puma/> for more details on international developments.

27 See Preston, N (1994) (ed) *Ethics for the Public Sector: Education and Training,* Sydney: Federation Press. Also, Preston N (1995) "Public Sector Ethics in Australia: a Review", *Australian Journal of Public Administration,* 54 (4), 462-470 and Preston, N (2000) "Pubic sector ethics: What are we talking about?", in Bishop, P and Preston, N (eds) *Local Government, Public Enterprise and Ethics,* Sydney: The Federation Press.

28 Cited in Jennings B and Callahan, D (1985) (eds) *Representation and Responsibility,* New York: Plenum Publishing Corporation, p 154. For an Australian example of this concern some might quote the termination of Nick Greiner's Premiership of NSW after an adverse finding by the Independent Commission Against Corruption.

29 May, W (1989) *Vocation, Career and Profession*, Australian Institute of Ethics and the Professions Monograph Services, vol 1, no 1.

30 Until the seventeenth century in Europe there was widespread opposition to usury, the charging of interest. For a short account of business ethics including its history see Solomon, R (1991) "Business Ethics" in Singer, P (ed) *A Companion to Ethics*, Oxford: Basil Blackwell, pp 354-365.

31 Students of business ethics have a growing, excellent literature to consult. A recent Australian text which shows the extent of this vast topic is Harrison, J et al (eds) *Ethics for Australian Business*, Sydney: Prentice Hall.

32 Friedman, M (1982) "The Social Responsibility of Business is to Increase its Profits" in Abelson, R and Friquegnon, M-L (eds) *Ethics for Modern Life*, (2nd edn) New York: St Martin's Press, p 324.

33 Cited by Solomon, R, op cit, p 354.

34 ABC-TV *Four Corners*, 8 April 1996, referred to Foxtel's relationship with the People's Republic of China.

35 Margaret Thatcher, Prime Minister of the United Kingdom and disciple of Friedman reportedly said: "There is no such thing as society, only families".

36 Solomon, R, op cit, pp 360-1.

CHAPTER NINE

GLOBAL RESPONSIBILITY AND THE ENVIRONMENT

My first step from the old white man was trees, then air. Then birds. Then other people. But one day when I was sitting quiet and feeling like a motherless child, which I was, it come to me: that feeling of being part of everything, not separate at all. I know that if I cut a tree, my arm would bleed. And I laughed and I cried and I run all around the house. I knew just what it was.

Alice Walker, *The Colour Purple* (New York: Pocket Books, 1982) p 178.

We stand at a critical moment in Earth's history, a time when humanity must choose its future. As the world becomes increasingly interdependent and fragile, the future at once holds great peril and great promise. To move forward we must recognize that in the midst of a magnificent diversity of cultures and life forms we are one human family and one Earth community with a common destiny.

The Earth Charter (2000)

The Challenge

Undeniably, the most important issues of applied ethics have been left to this, the penultimate chapter. I believe there is no higher ethical calling than to protect the well-being of life-systems on planet Earth and to speak on behalf of future generations of human and non-human beings. If we were to focus our attention on the ethical matters of earlier chapters only, while neglecting the ethical challenges posed by threats to Earth's environment and the suffering of people and other species because of those threats, we would be guilty of moral myopia.

As citizens of this global village in the late twentieth century we can reflect more accurately than our predecessors on the magnificence of spaceship Earth and the wondrous story of the universe.[1] The planet itself is thought to be about 4,600 million years old, though the ancestors of our ancestors, a group called *Homo erectus*, probably appeared relatively late in this story, a mere million or two million years ago. Until recently, life on Earth flourished, but in our generation the level of damage done to a system that has been almost five billion years in the making gives us cause to re-consider the basic ethical question: *how ought we to live with the Earth?*

Environmental scientists tell us that the quality of our air, soil and water has diminished to worrying levels in some regions while the rapacious depletion of Earth's rainforests, the nurturing cradle of the planet's biodiversity, may be beyond repair. Driven by narrow economic imperatives, we continue to pump toxins into the atmosphere and waterways as environmental crises proliferate. The names of the more notorious of these crises sound like warning sirens that cannot be ignored: the Chernobyl nuclear fire, the Aral Sea dries up, worldwide floods and global warming.

Governments, industry and communities have heard the warning and some have made a response. Generally, however, it is a limited response. In the world's affluent democracies, the environment is now a top political priority but there is little will to surrender economic growth for environmental conservation; this dubious approach to the environment is evidenced by the focus on ecotourism, which emphasises the preservation of natural values for the sake of human exploitation and as a profitable resource in an economy driven by financial gain.

We still struggle to establish an appropriate relationship between technology and nature. According to former American Vice-President, Al Gore,[2] "the transformation of the way we relate to the earth will of course involve new technologies, but the key changes will involve new ways of thinking about the relationship itself". There is a correlation between the environmental degradation of recent decades and the technological "advances" of that period. Yet some still cling to the naive and ethically suspect belief that if technology causes problems we will be able to fix them with a further technological development. Still others defend the unbridled use of technology to exploit natural resources and regard the environmental movement as an insidious force undermining civilisation itself.[3]

In earlier chapters we have observed how technology is both a threat and a promise. Its double character - illustrated well by nuclear technology - generates ethical dilemmas. By and large, we now recognise that the ethical challenge of technology resides in the choices facing us over how we are to employ technology. The issues are complex and any environmental ethical position which seeks to abandon the technological society altogether is not feasible. Paradoxically, it is relevant to observe that modern technology has enabled us to be more conscious of our common global environment and its problems. Yet global solidarity is not realised. Poverty, starvation and malnutrition afflict a major proportion of Earth's human population. Technological development, care for the environment and justice for human communities cannot be divorced. The development and deployment of technology require an ethical analysis which poses the prior questions of social analysis: who owns and who benefits from the use of technology? and what sacrifices are justified in its use and who should be expected to make them?

Given this introductory overview, we shall now outline how ethicists have approached the question: *what is the basis for our ethical obligations for the environment*?

Environmental Ethics: Various Approaches

Attempts to articulate an environmental ethic necessarily assume that human beings have ethical responsibilities toward the natural world. The different attempts reflect various views about the nature of those responsibilities. For instance, one view might argue broadly and instrumentally that this responsibility arises from our rights and needs as human beings: "the environment is necessary to human survival, therefore we ought to protect it". Another view rests on the belief that the natural world has intrinsic worth: "the environment is to be valued, and therefore protected, for its own sake".

Before outlining particular theories, we need to examine these broad assumptions. They represent the parameters of the debate and are generally defined as *anthropocentrism* (the view that *Homo sapiens* is the central moral concern) and *ecocentrism* (the view that the whole of nature should be given moral consideration).

Anthropocentrism has been the dominant emphasis in western worldviews for centuries. The Renaissance thinker, Descartes, is identified with the insight which provided a philosophical basis for setting *Homo sapiens* apart from the rest of the world. Dualism is the term given to this worldview. Its effect was to sanction the human endeavour to explore, dissect and master natural forces, the endeavour which gave momentum for scientific discovery and invention. The Judaeo-Christian teaching that man [*sic*] is made in the image of God to have dominion over nature, which has been the orthodox interpretation of the biblical account of creation, reinforced anthropocentrism and provided a theological cornerstone for philosophical dualism.[4]

The contemporary realisation that human domination of nature has also been destructive, has been accompanied by new scientific and theological paradigms which reject anthropocentrism.[5] However, the question persists for environmental ethics as to what value the human has with respect to the non-human. Is there a hierarchy of beings when it comes to moral concern? Is a distinction to be drawn between the welfare of human beings and the preservation of non-human species?

We shall take up the question of animal rights later in this chapter. However, it is appropriate at this point to note the argument that anthropocentrism leads to discrimination against other species. That discrimination is known as *speciesism*. Just as it is generally regarded as ethically unjustifiable and sexist to discriminate against women because of their sex, or racist to discriminate against Aboriginal peoples because of their race, so it is speciesist to be prejudiced for one's species against other species. Of course, the argument must be extended beyond this consideration if we are to be persuaded by a theory which makes no moral distinction between humans and non-humans. Many animals share with human beings characteristics that imply moral worth – for instance a common interest to avoid suffering and a sense of individual being and relatedness. Nonetheless, the level of consciousness and comprehension of the human mind about the natural world, and indeed the universe, suggests a responsibility for nature and other beings which, as far as we know, is unique to human beings. If this is granted, then it is arguable that, at least for the sake of the natural world, the special status of the human species must be acknowledged. However, by virtue of such a justification, that status ought not to be used to exploit nature and other species. In effect, this argument is a version of the view that humans are "custodians" for Earth and its life.

Subsequently, we will insist that animals' ethical rights should be respected; however, at this point, we consider the view that to suggest that non-human animals have superior rights to human persons is counter-intuitive. That is, to suggest that it could be fair to feed starving dogs before starving children is unacceptable. As Bonnie Steinbeck claims, it is intuitively obvious that the interests of humans have a higher moral status than animals because humans have certain morally relevant capacities that animals do not have: to be altruistic on moral grounds or to be morally responsible for actions.[6]

It is one question to consider the value of human life with respect to non-human life, but further examination of the value of non-human life is warranted: is nature valuable in itself? is a wilderness more valuable than a restored piece of nature? when it comes to rights, what distinctions should be drawn between rocks, planets, trees, rivers, viruses, dead ancestors, individual animals, whole species of animals, generations yet unborn? One way of making the distinctions is to consider whether these beings have interests which make a claim on others; so, it might be said that future generations of humans have interests which make a claim on the present generation or that a domestic animal clearly has an interest in being treated affectionately; however, a river does not so obviously have an interest, though others with interests (fish, perhaps) might want the river's interests defended. Bernard Williams[7] tries to sort through this maze by making the distinction that though non-animal entities can have "interests" they cannot have "experiences". For Williams, trees and plants have interests (for example, to be fed and watered) but not experiences, even though we speak of them as growing, ageing and dying. It is not clear that Williams' distinction assists us with more definitive answers. It may be that in attempting to determine what is to be included as having moral standing or what duties are owed to the natural world, we should consider again the nature of life in the environment.

Throughout this text – and it is vital to this chapter – we have stressed the interconnectedness of life. Humans may claim a special moral responsibility for, and moral standing in, processes which give expression to that interconnectedness, but it may be that in the long run the significance of human reflection and moral action is overtaken by another force which cannot be said to be rational or ethical. I have in mind James Lovelock's Gaia[8] hypothesis which suggests that the Life or Nature of planet Earth (the Gaia "spirit") is so committed to its own survival that the future of the human race is of no significance to it in the long run. If this is the case, then human ethical reasoning about the environment must incorporate an over-riding consideration, namely, that which is good, right or fitting must be in harmony, as far as can be determined, with the Earth's survival (the Gaia spirit). The rights of particular species must be seen in that light, and, furthermore, we should evaluate the theoretical approaches which follow in terms of this perspective.

In its evolution over the past 20 or 30 years, environmental ethics has taken seriously the contention that the traditional approach of Western moral philosophy as reflected in the major normative theories discussed in Chapter Three is inadequate for its purposes. After all, so the argument runs, Western moral philosophy was part of that worldview which provided the ideology of development and human mastery over nature resulting in environmental crises. Whether it is feasible or desirable for environmental ethicists to dispense with the sort of critique which mainstream normative theory provides is disputable. Nonetheless, partly reflecting this disenchantment, the discourse of environmental ethics takes place in unique frameworks, as the following outline shows.

We may distinguish three different types[9] of approach to environmental ethics: (1) anthropocentric, (2) extensionist, and (3) biocentric or ecocentric.

1 *Anthropocentric*

Anthropocentric approaches determine the right, the good or the fitting for environmental questions in terms of their impact on human beings. On an anthropocentric approach, the claim that pollution of the environment is to be avoided could be justified by invoking the human right to clean air and water. The current focus on ecotourism is generally dependent on anthropocentric grounds: wilderness should be preserved for human recreation. Similarly, the ethical argument often advanced by the supporters of controversial biotechnological strategies which may have environmental impacts is that they are necessary for human well-being. As already indicated, anthropocentrism may lead to distortions which overlook the interconnectedness of life as it bonds human welfare to the welfare of other life forms. Beyond that shortcoming, there is the practical problem that reliance on human interests for resolving environmental ethical dilemmas is likely to lead into an impasse of conflicting interests. For instance, it is not unusual to find that one set of human interests, say for jobs or economic well-being, clashes with another, say for a pollution free environment. If we stay within an anthropocentric framework, we probably have to resolve such clashes in terms of a utilitarian cost-benefit calculation. The question then becomes whether the interests to be calculated should all have an anthropocentric reference.

2 *Extensionist*

Extensionist approaches extend moral rights beyond human beings to other individual non-human entities, even to non-animal forms in some instances. However, the most prominent form of this view is known as *sentientism.* Sentientism extends the community of moral consideration to include all beings who have the quality of sentience or feeling. On this approach the interests of sentient beings determine our obligations regarding the environment. The interests of human beings clearly fall within this category, but extensionism modifies anthropocentrism by the requirement to consider the interests of other animals. Obviously this approach raises the status of animal rights within environmental ethics and suggests that, at times, the interests of human beings need not determine an environmental question. On an extensionist argument, we might maintain that the interests of humans to build a road through a rare koala habitat do not over-ride the interests of the koalas, where it is unlikely that the koalas can coexist with the road as many individual koalas will die cruel deaths, and the species itself will be put under further stress and threat.

3 *Biocentric or ecocentric*

Biocentric or ecocentric views are the most radical form of environmental ethics because they interpret environmental matters in a more holistic way. These views encourage us to see the whole environment as a living organism. Where extensionism focuses on individual entities, ecocentrism looks at the whole system. Human interests or even sentient interests are subsumed in obligations to the whole of nature which has intrinsic value (rocks included, according to ecocentrism). A certain deontological obligation to nature can operate here, in the apparent fundamentalism of those described as "deep ecologists". On the ecocentric view, anthropocentism and extensionism are barely distinguishable. They are "zoocentrist", ignoring the rights of non-animal forms. The attempt to extend moral consideration to all of nature was articulated by Aldo Leopold earlier in this century. Known as "The Land Ethic", it "enlarges the boundaries of the community to include soils, waters, plants and animals, or collectively the land ..."[10] The biocentric/ecocentric theories provide the greatest challenge to policies which develop human growth economies alongside natural conservationist policies, such as mining in the Kakadu Heritage Park. In so doing, they provide the most complete protection for species biodiversity. Their strength is that they move beyond instrumentalist or consequentialist considerations. The arguments against these approaches tend to emphasise their impracticability, or even their injustice. Also, they question whether there is a sound philosophical basis for moral consideration to include inanimate natural features.

Criticisms of these approaches, particularly of deep ecology, have come from an *ecojustice* perspective. Murray Bookchin and certain spokespersons for the so-called Third World have argued that the domination of nature is a sub-set of the human domination of other humans. Some feminists have supported this argument as is exemplified by Rosemary Radford Reuther:

> Women must see that there can be no liberation for them and no solution to the ecological crisis within a society whose fundamental model of relationships continues to be one of domination. They must unite the demands of the women's movement with those of the ecological movement to envision a radical reshaping of the basic socioeconomic relations and the underlying values of this society.[11]

The ecojustice critique from the poorer nations takes the argument further. Ecojustice seeks to integrate the call for environmental responsibility with the demand for social justice. To the poor, preoccupation with the long-term survival of the environment may be a luxury, just another imposition from the rich of the world whose consumption patterns are a major reason for the problem anyway.

Justice in terms of global poverty is the priority. Consequently, the so-called developing nations are often resistant to the call to preserve their natural resources, because exploiting those resources is their only hope of staying viable in the global economy.[12]

This brief survey indicates the range of approaches in environmental ethics debate. While not explicitly articulating them, the discourse remains reliant on utilitarian and deontological considerations at points; indeed, it is arguable that the popular debate about environmental ethics would profit from a rigorous examination based on traditional ethical concerns. For instance, there is a distinct danger that the biocentric or ecocentric demand that "the natural or biotic" should determine what is right or wrong will lead down pathways which result in injustice and sabotage of human ethical responsibility. Indeed, this argument is reminiscent of the fallacious or simplistic view that "what is natural is what *ought* to be"; for a start, it overlooks the destructive potential of nature. By contrast, a fitting approach to environmental ethics could be informed by the comprehensive processes of the ethic of response. It should incorporate interpretations of the substantial principles (of respect for life, justice and covenantal integrity), thereby taking account of environmental realities, together with an appropriate sense of accountability and social solidarity which recognises the Gaia principle and the place of future generations. An ethic framed on this idea of responsibility challenges environmentalists and community decision-makers to avoid the excesses of anthropocentrism and see through the blindspots of ecocentrism.

Animal Rights

Billions of animals suffer every year to meet human requirements – for food, clothing, medical experimentation, sport and recreation. Transplantation of genes and organs across species is now practised in laboratories. Chickens, pigs, and calves are denied any life appropriate to their species except confinement and sustenance until they are ready to be slaughtered for the escalating human demand to eat flesh. Then there is the silent, barely observable suffering: the disappearance of whole species of animals, many of which are sacrificed by direct destruction of their habitat by humans. In a previous age, it was opposition to cruelty to slaves or leprous outcasts within our own species which defined the cutting edge of moral sensitivity. Now, it would seem the touchstone of moral sensitivity is our treatment of animals. Indeed, some ethicists argue that animals should be regarded as full members of the moral community.

It is likely that many people would agree that there are anthropocentric reasons why we have ethical duties to animals: the owners of domestic animals and those of us who take pleasure in the magnificence of animals in the wild, would ourselves be affronted or adversely affected if they were hurt. But invoking an extensionist perspective, can we say that we owe any moral considerations to the animals themselves? Do they have any moral standing?

Of course, many pet owners and observers of native animals testify that these non-humans have a capacity to express emotions and even values like love and self-sacrifice. Those who take the line of sentientists defend the moral standing of animals. Peter Singer is one of the outspoken proponents of this view. Indeed, for him, some non-human animals qualify as moral persons:

> There are other persons on this planet. The evidence for personhood is at present most conclusive for the great apes, but whales, dolphins, elephants, monkeys, dogs, pigs and other animals may eventually also be shown to be aware of their own existence over time and capable of reasoning. Then they too will have to be considered as persons.[13]

But what does this mean about the moral rights of animals and do humans have superior rights? Singer replies[14] that "animal liberationists do not minimise the obvious differences between most members of our species and members of other species ..." To advance his argument Singer invites us to consider the performance of lethal scientific experiments on normal adult humans, kidnapped at random from the public parks for this purpose. Under these conditions, it would be a terrifying experience for humans to even anticipate entering a park, and that anticipation would become a "form of additional suffering". By contrast he suggests that the same experiment on many non-human animals "would cause less suffering overall, for the non-human animals would not have the same anticipatory dread". He concludes,

> This does not mean ... that it is all right to experiment on animals as we please, but only that if the experiment is to be done at all, there is some reason, compatible with the equal consideration of interests, for preferring to use non-human animals rather than normal adult humans.

Singer goes on to explain that, in his view, brain-damaged humans could be used in preference to animals "at a similar mental level" for some experiments, but his overall point is that sentientism and the cause of animal liberation do not mean human interests are devalued. The principle of equal consideration of interests allows for a moral hierarchy between animals.

Singer's views have been criticised and challenged. In Chapter Seven it was claimed that Singer has too narrowly defined his view of moral personhood by linking it to mental states. As Mary Anne Warren[15] argues, though sentience is the basis for some rights, moral autonomy along with other differences between animals and humans is a basis for attributing stronger rights to humans. This is not to disagree with the conclusion that experimentation on animals should be severely restricted nor that the killing of animals for meat is a process that requires a much fuller ethical justification than is presently provided.

Tom Regan is another prominent animal rights ethicist who disagrees with Singer's utilitarian presuppositions. He[16] provides a deontological defence of animal rights asserting that, like humans, non-human animals have inherent value. Animals have inherent value because they are conscious creatures who value their own welfare, which is in no way dependent on their usefulness to others. Indeed, Regan has a stronger view than sentientists about animals' rights because he sees no place for calculations on the basis of intelligence. All beings that have inherent value have it equally.

Such a view challenges us to extend our interpretation of the three substantial values associated with the ethic of response. It suggests that on the question of animal rights: *respect for life* involves a total end to commercial animal agriculture; *justice and fairness* means an end to using animals for experiments we are not prepared to do on ourselves; *covenantal integrity* implies that animals cannot be used as means for sport, hunting and trapping.

Overpopulation and Global Poverty

The debate about the environment is related to matters of global justice, particularly to questions of poverty and overpopulation. As some critics of population control rightly point out, poverty and overpopulation are not necessarily linked; however, it is naive to believe that, providing we get the mechanisms of resource distribution right, Earth can support any number of human beings, just as it is folly to ignore the fact that levels of poverty are greatest in those regions of the earth where population density is also greatest.

Are there too many people on Earth? In late 1999, Earth's population reached the alarming milestone of six billion people. There are signs of a deceleration in the rate of population growth. If deceleration continues, it is estimated that global population may stabilise at 10 billion after 2200.[17] An informed prognosis based on these forecasts indicates that if poor countries develop their economies in the same wasteful way rich nations have, these population levels will put an intolerable burden on food and water supplies and the habitat of endangered species. Also, given the population numbers at this level, the standards of living enjoyed by the affluent minority can only be maintained through a massive escalation of injustice employing military oppression and what is, effectively, forced starvation.

The adverse impact of human population on the natural environment is undeniable. It is *Homo sapiens* who pollute and exploit natural resources. Even if we are ecologically sensitive, the more of us there are, the more likely it is that the environment will suffer. For those concerned for justice and the well-being of the Earth, the conclusion is clear: there are too many of us.

Such a conclusion impacts on how we might assess the importance of human life, even in terms of issues like abortion, euthanasia and war. Certainly, there is an overwhelming onus on those who espouse philosophical, theological and ethical positions which declare contraception, sterilisation and other population control measures to be intrinsically evil, to re-evaluate the relevance of their theories and conclusions.[18]

If, as we have argued, there are too many people, it is also the case that too many are too poor. World Health Organisation (WHO) Annual Reports consistently claim one fifth of the world's population live in extreme poverty characterised by malnutrition, illiteracy, disease, squalid surroundings, high infant mortality and low life expectancy. Such poverty is "the world's deadliest disease", according to Hiroshi Nakajima, a former WHO Director-General.[19] Perhaps it is also the most salient performance indicator of the global economy! By contrast, one fifth of the world's population live in extreme affluence because they control four-fifths of the world's resources. The statistics of poverty underline the indecency of military budgets and the arms trade, to say nothing of the mega-salaries paid to international executives, sports heroes, entertainers and the like.[20] The question is unavoidable: what ethical justification is there for such global inequities? More pertinently, we might ask: what is the responsibility of the rich toward the poor? This question presumes a more fundamental inquiry: *what is the moral basis for alleviating poverty anyway?*

Kantians regard the alleviation of poverty as a duty based on their concern that people have intrinsic worth, while utilitarians might argue that it is in everybody's interests that we alleviate the suffering caused by poverty. The principles of valuing life, promoting justice and fairness and keeping faith with our fellows (covenantal integrity) all support the view that it is fitting to alleviate the poverty of others. Another principle which should find support from various ethical discourses has been suggested: "if it is in our power to prevent something very bad from happening, without sacrificing anything of comparable moral significance, we ought to do it".[21] Given the context of global poverty, such a principle suggests that individuals, business corporations, national governments and multinational organisations all ought to take measures which alleviate poverty.

However, it is the means which will achieve this that seem elusive and debatable. What kind of assistance is likely to be effective? Personal charity and community welfare are not likely to be sufficient. A major structural realignment of socio-economic forces and objectives internationally, seems required. The question about alleviating poverty becomes an even more challenging social ethical question: *what are the requirements of a just world order?*

A Global Ethic for a Global Society

The question of a just world order has taken on even sharper urgency in recent decades with the developing phenomenon sometimes labelled "globalisation". Globalisation has become the overarching international system shaping the economy, domestic politics and foreign relations of virtually every nation on earth. Thomas Friedman outlines its impact as follows:

> Globalisation involves the inexorable integration of markets, nation states and technologies to a degree never witnessed before ... and in a way that is also producing a powerful backlash from those brutalised or left behind by this new system.
>
> The driving idea behind globalisations is free market capitalism ... (It) means the spread of free market capitalism to virtually every country in the world.[22]

Globalisation is demanding of global human society new institutions and new governance structures. The exploration for these new frameworks is led by bodies such as the World Bank, the International Monetary Fund, the World Economic Forum and the World Trade Organisation. However, this is a very controversial area, for globalisation and these international bodies threaten to ignore the welfare of the majority of global citizens, and to embark on policies which are not environmentally sustainable.

Consequently, in 2000 there emerged a global movement of resistance to globalisation. At the same time there were those arguing that, given the reality of global communications and world trade, the major challenge is not to reject globalisation but to structure it more justly. A responsible global society with institutions that serve the interests of people and the environment requires an appropriate global ethic, they maintain. One recent, lucid Australian account which advocates the democratisation of globalisation is provided by Duncan Kerr.[23]

The search for global values has been prompted in a growing dialogue between applied ethicists, religious leaders and environmentalists. One documented attempt at a global ethic launched in 2000 is the Earth Charter.[24] Its core values are grouped in four categories:

- Respect and Care for the Community of Life;
- Ecological Integrity;
- Social and Economic Justice;
- Democracy, Non-Violence and Peace.

In fact, the genesis of the Earth Charter was the Rio Earth Summit of 1992. Those who drafted it hope it will become as significant in the twenty-first century as the United Nations Universal Declaration of Human Rights became in the twentieth century.

A major difficulty for such attempts at statements of universal principles – as ethicists will appreciate – is that their very universality may make the terms of these declarations so general that they have little practical meaning, or so universal that these claims are unacceptable in many local communities. If a global ethic is to respect the deep plurality of our human society, and indeed the diversity of the natural environment, universality cannot be based on a particular culture's perspective imposed as the norm for the rest. Global ethics which respect contextual difference are arguably in harmony with the approach of an ethic of response. The Earth Charter, which was carefully and consultatively developed for nearly a decade, is a promising attempt at respecting the need to be "thinking globally" while "acting locally". It is a mandate for both sustainable development and ecojustice.

In an important work on the question of global justice the Australian philosopher, Janna Thompson[25] adopts what she labels a cosmopolitan and communitarian view. Echoing the themes of ecojustice, she argues that this includes the following: promoting individual liberty, respect for the communities valued by individuals, a distribution of resources which enables the maintenance of individual liberty and communal life, together with peaceful relations among communities based on principles and procedures which all agree are fair. Translating this into a program for justice is a complex political task. As such, it is not merely a matter of redistributing resources, but of a realignment of power, all at a cost to the powerful and affluent, especially if we are careful for the natural environment. The ethical response to poverty and overpopulation involves a commitment to struggle with the conflict of interests which constitute and constrain political choice. Those choices are, of course, ethical choices. They cannot be resolved impartially. The underlying challenge becomes: *are we prepared to take the side of the poor?*

Conclusion

This chapter illustrates the perspective signalled in Chapter One: the quest for a socially transformative ethic. At the heart of this ethic is the need to both care for nature and respect our fellow human beings. Anthropocentrism is no longer adequate as a basis for global morality. Responsibility, with its focus on social solidarity and comprehensive accountability, points to the claims of *ecojustice,* and its vision of a just, participatory (non-hierarchical) and sustainable society. This vision maintains that care for the environment and the liberation of oppressed peoples are linked. Furthermore, it reminds us that those most oppressed – the Aboriginal peoples across various societies – may possess clues for living in harmony with each other and Earth. They teach us that, in the long run, self-interest and other-regarding interest converge because all life is interconnected. We will spoil the world irrevocably for our own children's children if we continue to be careless with the world and with others' children.

CHAPTER REVIEW

1. Check that you understand new terms introduced in this chapter: speciesism, sentientism, ecocentrism, anthropocentrism, ecojustice, extensionism, the Gaia principle, zoocentrism, the land ethic.
2. Three differing approaches to environmental ethics were presented:
   (i) anthropocentrism
   (ii) extensionism and
   (iii) biocentrism or ecocentrism.

   We noted how these frameworks differ from traditional ethical theories.
3. Our discussion rejected anthropocentrism as a contemporary world view, and promoted the case for animal rights.
4. We noted the challenge of ecojustice which seeks to relate the claims of social justice and environmental concern. In particular, the connection between global poverty, overpopulation and environmental degradation was examined, and the development of global ethics was canvassed.

FURTHER READING

Des Jardins, JR (1993) *Environmental Ethics: an introduction to environmental philosophy*, Belmont, Ca: Wadsworth Publishing Company.

Dower, N (1983) *World Poverty: Challenge and Response*, York: Ebor Press.

Elliott, R (ed) (1995) *Environmental Ethics*, New York: Oxford University Press.

Isaak, R (1998) *Green Logic: Ecopreneurship, Theory and Ethics*, Sheffield: Greenleaf.

Singer, P (1993) "Rich and Poor", Briefing Paper, no 33, Australian Development Studies Network, Canberra, ANU. (This piece is adapted from a chapter in Singer's *Practical Ethics*, Cambridge University Press, 1993.)

Sterba, JP (ed) (2000) *Earth Ethics: Introductory Readings on Animal Rights and Environmental Ethics*, Upper Saddle River: Prentice Hall.

QUESTIONS FOR DISCUSSION

1. The Seventh Generation.

   The Seventh Generation

   "Will it benefit the seventh generation?"
   Is the question that the Hopi dwell upon.
   "Will it help the future people who will walk upon this earth
   Long after you and I are dead and gone?"
   And if the Hopi saw that the answer was "no"
   They would drop that new idea, they would simply let it go
   For the Hopi's ethic meant they thought not only of themselves
   But of future generations as well.

   I speak now for that seventh generation:
   For the seventh generation from now on.
   I speak for the people who will walk upon this Earth
   Long after you and I are dead and gone.
   Will they reap a bitter harvest from the things that we have done?
   Will they thank us for the healing that in our time has begun?
   Will there even still be people seven generations on?
   For I fear for the seventh generation.

   (Used with permission of the songwriter, Sue Doessel.)

   Find out about the Hopi and their religious culture. Do future generations have rights as the Hopi believe? What ethical difference does it make to believe that?

2. Michael Smith wrote an article called "Letting in the Jungle", *Journal of Applied Philosophy*, 1991, vol 8, no 2, and on p 153 says:

   > Perhaps the only long-term chance for the survival of the jungle lies in our coming to see it as a being of intrinsic value on its own terms. The jungle offers us a chance to escape a world where all we see reflects "humanity" back at us.

   - What environmental ethics perspective does this reflect – anthropocentrism, extensionism or biocentrism?
   - Do you agree with Smith's statement? What does it imply about technology?

- Does it imply anything about the rights of future generations? Explain.

3. Do you think we should use animals for medical experiments to benefit humans? Is it preferable to use severely brain-damaged humans if possible? What are your reasons in either case?
4. Do you believe Singer or Regan has the more defensible position on animal rights? Why?
5. Should an endangered species be protected even if it means the loss of jobs and economic disadvantage to humans? Why? Does it make any difference if the species is not endangered?
6. Should we try to alleviate poverty or disease if the effect of that is to support human populations and their growth? Isn't it more ethically justified to allow the "law of the jungle" to apply, so that nature will sort out the imbalances which affect the biological wealth of the planet. This is sometimes known as the "ethic of triage".
   - Why is it called this?
   - What are the alternatives to this strategy?
7. Does this chapter raise issues which are a personal ethical challenge to you? If so, what do you propose to do about them?

CASE STUDIES

Case 1 – The Burning of Amazon Rain Forests

Farmers and cattle ranchers in Brazil are burning the rain forests of the Amazon river to clear the land for crops and livestock. According to the article in *Time*, an estimated 12,350 square miles have been destroyed so far, and the burning continues. Conservationists and leaders of rich industrial nations have asked Brazil to stop the destruction. They claim that if the Amazon rain forests are destroyed more than one million species will vanish. This would be a significant loss of the earth's genetic and biological heritage. Furthermore, they are worried about changes in the climate. The Amazon system of forests plays an important role in the way the sun's heat is distributed around the earth because it stores more than 75 billion tons of carbon in its trees. Burning the trees of the Amazon forests will produce a dramatic increase in the amount of carbon dioxide in the atmosphere. The trapping of heat by this atmospheric carbon dioxide – the green house effect – will significantly increase the global warming trend.

Brazilians reply that they have a sovereign right to use their land as they see fit. They complain that the rich industrial nations are just trying to maintain their economic supremacy. Brazilian President José Sarney argues that the burning is necessary for Brazilian economic development, particularly when Brazil is struggling under an $111 billion foreign debt load.

(This case is based on the cover story in *Time*, 18 September 1989. See White, JE (1991) *Contemporary Moral Problems*, St Paul, MN: West Publishing Co, p 455)

Note: A 1989 story should not be treated as current fact. Indeed, reports in January 2001 indicate that the Brazilian congress is now voting on a project that will reduce the Amazon forest to 50 per cent of its size.

- Should Brazil continue burning the Amazon rain forests? If not, then what should rich industrial nations do to help Brazil?
- What ethical arguments would you present to Brazil and/or to rich nations? Use the ethic of response as a framework for your submission, identifying the elements to which you give greatest weight.

CASE 2 – HUNTING FOR WHALES

The Guardian Weekly, 3 August to 9 August 2000, vol 163, no 6, p 3 reported that Japan has resumed hunting some of the world's largest and most endangered whales despite major opposition from within the International Whaling Commission. These expeditions are presented as having scientific purposes but as the New Zealand Prime Minister reportedly said: "It is well known that meat from the whales killed during the 'scientific' expeditions finishes up at Japanese dinner tables". *The Guardian Weekly* report continued:

Sperm whales – the giant toothed whales immortalised by Herman Melville in Moby Dick – have the largest brains of any mammal, and the most valuable flesh. The Japanese eat it raw – for $30 a slice. The fact that Japan has decided to kill Bryde's and sperm whales – which are much larger than the minkes that they have already hunted "scientifically" over the past few years – has provoked fury. These animals require processing in large factory ships that are banned under International Whaling Commission (IWC) rules.

- Should Japan resume such whaling? Would it be valid if it were for scientific purposes alone? Do other nations have a right to interfere in Japan's policy?
- Is it because we are talking about whales, or about an endangered species that there is international opposition to the Japanese action? Does this case differ from the killing of other animals for human consumption or scientific experimentation?
- Consider your reasons carefully. What values are you employing? What type of ethical reasons are you giving? Is your view anthropocentric, extensionist or biocentric? Is consistency an important moral quality, when engaging in such debates?

CHAPTER NINE NOTES

1 See Swimme, B and Berry, T (1992) *The Universe Story*, Penguin Books. There are some wonderful magazines which tell this story. One is *Living Planet* <http://www.livingplanetmagazine.ws>

2 Gore, A (1992) *Earth in the Balance*, Boston: Houghton McMillan Company, p 35.

3 For example, the Australian mining leader, Hugh Morgan, "A threat expert's view of the green movement", *Age*, 30 December 1992, p 11.

4 See White, L (Jnr) "The Historical Roots of our Ecological Crisis", *Science*, Vol 155, No 3767, March 1967, pp 1203-1207. For a discussion of the harmful impact of Christianity on the environment see Kinsley D, (1995) *Ecology and Religion*, Englewood Cliffs: Prentice Hall.

5 For example, F Capra (1990) *The Turning Point*, London: Fontana, and Paul Collins (1995) *God's Earth*, Melbourne: Harper Collins, Chapter One. Also, Berry, T (1999) *The Great Work*, New York: Bell Tower, and Wilson, EO (1998) *Consilience*, London: Little Brown & Co.

6 See Bonnie Steinbeck (1978) "Speciesism and the Idea of Equality" in *Philosophy* 53, No 204, April. In this argument the term "human persons" is used deliberately. As Chapter Seven noted, there may be reason to differentiate "person" and "human" if the member of the human species has no awareness or consciousness.

7 Williams B (1992) "Must a Concern for the Environment be Centred on Human Beings", in Taylor C (ed) *Ethics and the Environment*, Oxford: Corpus Christi College, pp 60-68.

8 Lovelock, J (1979) *Gaia: A New Look at Life on Earth*, Oxford: Oxford University Press.

9 The classification provided here is a simple one. Fuller accounts and more precise categorisations of types of environmental ethics may be found in Robert Elliott's article in Singer, P (1991) *A Companion to Ethics*, Oxford: Blackwell, Chapter 24, or J Baird Callicott's article in Regan, T (ed) (1986) *Matters of Life and Death: New Introductory Essays in Moral Philosophy*, New York: Random House, pp 381-424.

10 Leopold, Aldo (1966) "The Land Ethic" in *A Sand Country Almanac*, New York: Oxford University Press, p 219.

11 Quoted in des Jardins, JR (1993) *Environmental Ethics*, Belmont, Ca: Wadsworth Publishing, p 241.

12 In the Rio de Janeiro conference on the environment in 1992 and in subsequent conferences like that in Kyoto over global warning, the difficulties of the poorer nations with environmental policies have become clear. For one critical review of the western deep ecology movement see Ramachandra Guha, "Radical American Environmentalism and Wilderness Preservation: a Third World Critique", *Environmental Ethics*, vol 11 (Spring 1989), pp 71-83.

13 Singer P (1985) *Rethinking Life and Death*, Melbourne: Text Publishing Co, p 182.

14 Singer, P (ed) (1991) *In defence of Animals*, Oxford: Blackwell, pp 6-7.

15 Mary Anne Warren, "Human and Animal Rights Compared" (1983) in Elliott, R and Gare, A (eds) *Environmental Philosophy*, Brisbane: Queensland University Press.

16 Regan, T "The Case for Animal Rights", in Singer, P (1985) op cit, pp 13-26. For the case for animals having legal rights see Steven Wise (2000) *Rattling the Cage: Towards Legal Rights for Animals*, Profile Books. For a view as to why animals have no rights, see Carl Cohen, "The Case for the Use of Animals in Biomedical Research", reprinted in Mappes, T and Zembaty, J (eds) (1992) *Social Ethics*, McGraw-Hill Inc.

17 *Time*, 8 October 1999, p 58.

18 See Collins, P (1995) *God's Earth*, Melbourne: Harper Collins - Chapter Two discusses the population issue and gives an exhaustive critique of Roman Catholic moral teaching on population control.

19 For example, report in the *Guardian Weekly*, vol 152, no 19, 7 May 1995, p 1.

20 See BA Santamaria's column, "After the rationalists, the deluge", in *Weekend Australian*, 23 March 1996.

21 Singer, P (1972) "Famine, Affluence and Morality", *Philosophy and Public Affairs*, 1, 3 (Spring).

22 This quotation is cited by Bishop Michael Putney in *National Outlook*, October 2000, p 19. Thomas Friedman is author of *The Lexus and the Olive Tree*.

23 Kerr, D (2001) *Elect the Ambassador: Building Democracy in a Globalised World*, Annandale NSW: Pluto Press.

24 The full text of the Earth Charter may be found at <http://www.earthcharter.org>. For a short analysis of the dialogue between world faiths and environmentalists, see my article in *Living Planet*, March-May 2001.

25 Thompson, J (1992) *Justice And World Order: A Philosophical Inquiry*, London: Routledge.

CHAPTER TEN

CULTIVATING AN ETHICAL LIFE

From *Good Will Hunting*

SEAN: Do you have a soul mate?

WILL: Define that.

SEAN: Someone who challenges you in every way. Who takes you places, opens things up for you. A soul mate.

WILL: Yeah.

Sean waits.

WILL: Shakespeare, Nietzsche, Frost, O'Connor, Chaucer, Pope, Kant –

SEAN: They're all dead.

WILL: Not to me, they're not.

SEAN: But you can't give back to them, Will.

Damon, M, & Affleck, B, *Good Will Hunting*
Faber & Faber, London, 1998, pp 126-127.

I have tried not to falter; I have made missteps along the way. But I have discovered the secret that after climbing a great hill, one only finds that there are many more hills to climb. I have taken a moment here to rest, to steal a view of the glorious vista that surrounds me, to look back on the distance I have come. But I can rest only for a moment, for with freedom come responsibilities, and I dare not linger, for my long walk is not yet ended.

Nelson Mandela, *Long Walk to Freedom* (1994)

A Perspective

It is one thing to be able to participate in ethical discourse or to offer critical arguments about moral dilemmas, but it is another to translate that understanding into ethical practice. Ethical literacy involves deeds, not mere words; there is no automatic correlation between the articulation of ethical values and the actual living of a life characterised by respect for others, fairness and faithfulness. In this chapter we address the question of cultivating an ethical life, as individuals and in our communal associations.

Merely understanding ethics is not enough. The study of ethics - the subject matter of previous chapters - does not in itself sustain the hope for a better life or a better world to which the ethical person aspires. Nor is the study of ethics enough to enable us to cope with our inevitable failure to live out all our ethical ideals. Likewise, understanding ethics is no guarantee that we can live with the doubts often generated by difficult ethical decisions. In other words, the question is not simply how do we learn to put our ethics into practice, but rather, how do we journey through life with a maturing moral will and vision, despite the ambiguities and limitations of the human condition?

Traditionally religion has provided answers to this existential dilemma. Even those who do not embrace traditional religion but who wish to pursue the ethical life seriously need an answer to this question. The ethical life involves more than the exercise of rationality. It demands a profound and complex expression of the whole person responsive to other whole persons. This suggests a comprehensive life of integrity.

The Life of Integrity

Integrity is derived from the Latin *integritas*. Translated from Latin to English it means: unaffected, intact, upright, reliable. The same root word has given us "integer", the mathematical term for any whole number, one that is not fractionalised. When something is "integrated" its many parts have been brought together, unified. We hear of "maintaining the integrity of the eco-system" which implies protection of species diversity and our reliance on natural landscapes and vegetation. We do not find that usage of the term strange when it refers to ecological interconnectedness because the word, integrity, names a unifying, connecting, relating process in a system.

Indeed, the idea of integrity and the idea of responsibility, as described in Chapter Four above, have a lot in common. So we might expect that a life of integrity responds comprehensively and consistently to the need to integrate faithfully a respect for all life with a commitment to justice. "Integrity" also signifies that a person, a profession, an institution knows what it stands for, values that knowledge and acts on it. Not surprisingly, David Newton describes integrity as "the consummate virtue" noting that in the moral life it results from the "integration of separable aspects of the self – notably faculties, desires, roles, life-shaping choices – into a self-consistent whole".[1] It suggests a connection between the externalities of one's life, our conduct towards others, and an interior life, our private thoughts, our prayers and dreams and fears. To recall language not always invoked these days in ethics, integrity suggests living by one's conscience, having "a centre of values", even an awareness of one's god. The biblical injunction[2] "where your treasure is there your heart will be also" is really a statement about integrity.

No wonder that Erik Erikson, the seminal scholar renowned for stage development theory, describes the challenge for personal growth in the latter stage of life, as the achievement of integrity, which involves bringing together, with a certain wisdom and serenity, all the successes and failures of life's journey. Of course, few of us fully achieve this, and that is a reminder that those of us charged with promoting integrity should exercise moral judgment with grace and humility. A person of integrity is especially conscious of the ambiguities and limitations of the human condition. After all, integrity is compatible with responding to our creaturely needs, and does not deny what psychiatrist Carl Jung names as the "shadow side" of human personality.

Honesty is often used as a synonym for integrity. Politicians have integrity when they are honest, some say. But that is only a half-truth. Certainly, the person of integrity is truthful in the sense of being true to herself. The great moral exemplars of recent history, such as Martin Luther King and Nelson Mandela, exhibited integrity, not because they were morally perfect at all points (for they weren't). The subject of integrity is much more the sum of an entire life than the analysis of each act of it. The moral exemplars of history are characterised by integrity because, like countless unheralded persons, they were true to their beliefs, values, and convictions at the crunch-points in their lives.

Consistency or predictability is crucial to integrity. If persons act differently in similar circumstances the word integrity does not readily come to mind in describing them. And yet, in certain circumstances it is possible to act inconsistently and yet maintain an inner integrity. Integrity is indeed complex as Martin Benjamin reminds us in his excellent treatise on the topic. He presents an account of individual integrity that is "at once determinate enough to provide for a unified self and flexible enough to respond to new circumstances and the requirements of social as well as individual existence".[3]

So we need to be very discriminating in our analysis of the concept. As Stephen Carter observes: "To admire someone's integrity is not to say that he or she is right about the issue in question; we can hope to admire the virtue of integrity in people with whom we have sharp political and moral disagreements".[4] A person may be true to themselves and yet be misguided or even unjust; they are consistently and sincerely unethical as it were. The community conflict over abortion illustrates this state of affairs: integrity may be demonstrated by people on both sides of the moral argument over abortion.

Nonetheless, there are examples where this is surely not the case. What if we said: "John was a man of uncommon integrity. He let nothing – not friendship, not justice, not truth – stand in the away of his assessment of wealth." Obviously that is a nonsensical way of using the term "integrity",[5] just as it would be to say Adolf Hitler was a man of integrity simply because there was some coherence between his evil mind and his evil actions. In a sense he was true to himself but not a man of truth or truly human. That is, he was not true to the moral possibilities of humanity.

It is useful to recall how we often use the term. We may say people have personal integrity or moral integrity but we may also say they have intellectual integrity, artistic integrity or professional integrity. In one sense, the ethical content of integrity relates to particular practices, roles or spheres of human endeavour.

This is not to deny the desirability of extending integrity beyond particular domains. For instance, it may be the case that politicians may be ethical in their exercise of public office but in private life as a husband (or wife), or even in dealings within their own political party, ethical principles may count for little. While such a person may be a good politician, and worthy of election, we would be reluctant to describe that person as having integrity. This, of course, was the situation that confronted Bill Clinton, the American President (1992-2000). The debate around his sexual behaviour demonstrates that a life of integrity in one sphere may be undermined when it is not integrated with the coherent pursuit of a life of integrity.

So, cultivating the ethical life, a life of responsibility, wisdom and integrity, requires integration of multiple dimensions of the self: the intellect (the cognitive), the emotions (the affective), the will (the conative), and what Carl Jung[6] and others call "the inner life" or "the life of the spirit". In a way, these considerations are reminiscent of Aristotle's approach to ethics. The human *psyche* has an important role in his account of ethics. For Aristotle, the cultivation of the moral life involves developing a capacity for practical wisdom (*phronesis*). He believed that we are not spontaneously or naturally ethical, morally excellent or virtuous. *Phronesis* (and the virtues it endorses) are qualities acquired, if at all, by persons (and communities) as a result of habituation or commitment to practice and training. In other words, moral or ethics education is required.

Ethics Education[7]

As we have already indicated, our ethical beliefs and practices are learnt in a more complex way than we learn mathematical or certain technical skills. For instance, it is sometimes said that "ethics is caught not taught". The suggestion of "catching ethics", as if it were a virus, contains an important half-truth. When we consider how we learnt our ethical values and what interactions made such an impact on us that they affected our behaviour in an ethical sense, it is clear that *morality is learned essentially in communal relationships* like the family or the gang or a religious group or workplace sub-cultures. It follows that a vital factor in moral development is *modelling* or learning by example. At critical stages the models will be parents. The importance of parenting cannot be underestimated: when parents do not respect others or act unjustly or practice deception and infidelity, then children suffer a severe setback in their moral development. At other stages we will be influenced by other models: peers, or the culture's popular icons like sporting heroes, or some moral exemplar who inspires an idealistic response. Story-telling and powerful drama can have a parallel impact for good or ill.

As well as learning from *significant others,* we may learn from *significant encounters.* I vividly recall an early lesson I had about fairness and empathy. I was a six year old in my first grade, walking home from school. The entertainment for the afternoon was to tease a little migrant Scottish girl. We called her names and threw stones at her. My father found out about this incident. He was very angry with me, wrathful in fact. He did not hit me but he gave me a piece of his mind (and heart) and insisted on taking me around to the girl's house to apologise. This I did very tearfully. My father had opted to take the side of the aggrieved and ostracised migrant girl to correct the hurt and injustice we boys had perpetrated. The whole encounter made a profound impression on me, searing into my self (my emotions, my will, my mind, my spirit) a sense of injustice, righteous anger and empathy on behalf of the underdog.

The point is simple and elementary: we learn our moral behaviour *experientially,* albeit through a complex, ongoing process. This is not to say that rational or intellectual stimuli, along with learning the language of ethics, have no impact on moral development. Depending on how it is taught, the formal study of ethics can certainly help people learn how to address ethical decisions and how to critique their own ethical decision-making processes.

Studies of moral development[8] confirm that a critical factor is the development of *moral autonomy.* The essence of autonomy is the capacity to exercise choice in making independent decisions. It requires owning and acting on a value system that is internalised rather than merely adopted because it is prescribed by an external authority. Doing something just because you are commanded to do it, or just because others are doing it, or because you will be punished if you do not do it, are immature reasons for ethical action, though they are also quite prevalent.[9] Cultivating a mature ethical life involves the development of an internalised moral authority (*conscience*) or sense of inner direction which is obeyed autonomously, while taking into account the ethical views of others. The responsible moral self who decides and acts with reference to the idea of responsibility outlined in this book is clearly an autonomous agent. He or she is prepared to object in conscience (conscientious objection) to what is perceived as unjust, wrong or morally inappropriate. Though we cannot deny that autonomy is sometimes expressed in misguided or ethically destructive ways, the consistent practice of autonomy is one indication of a cultivated ethical life.

Indeed, the great exemplars of the ethical life, those who challenge us across the ages, those who appear to be acting selflessly for others, at great cost to themselves, who have inspired significant moral causes like the abolition of slavery, the suffragette struggle for women's rights, the preservation of the environment, exhibit moral courage and conviction which comes from an autonomous, inner self. Above all, it is to oneself that one must be true. This was the case for Thomas More whose conflict with the King of England over More's allegiance to the Pope put his life on the line. In Robert Bolt's play *A Man for All Seasons*, the Duke of Norfolk points out to More that he is jeopardising his life for an unverifiable belief (the theory of the apostolic succession of the Pope). More acknowledges this and then adds: "But what matters to me is not whether it's true or not but that I *believe* it to be true, or rather not that I *believe* it but that *I* believe it".[10]

Therefore, the cultivation of autonomy remains an important aim of ethics education, because while moral education acknowledges the need to introduce students to the value patterns of their community, it must also equip them to critique the arbitrary or conventional rules of society according to autonomously chosen ethical frameworks. This process occurs in a variety of settings but here we ask: what does all this mean for moral or ethics education in schools with pre-adult children, especially in a culturally pluralist environment where differing social backgrounds probably mean there is a lack of consensus on certain ethical issues?

For a start, we need to acknowledge that education is an inherently ethical enterprise; school life is a moral mosaic. Though this is now widely recognised in school communities, a diverse range of interests gathers under the banner of schooling ethics. To some, the restoration of ethics in the curriculum is seen as part of the "back to basics" movement; for those who define the task of education in instrumentalist, technicist or vocational terms, ethics might be narrowed to mean "the work ethic" or "workplace honesty and efficiency"; to others emphasising "character education", the aim sometimes becomes an individualistic one which is blind to social inequities. The approach advocated here opposes narrow moralising which degenerates into an authoritarian ethic. Rather, ethics is best dealt with through a pedagogy of critical inquiry. That approach dares to broach the controversial questions often avoided in other contexts. Consequently, ethics education will generally be appreciated by students for its relevance to their life circumstances.

This perspective will be informed by an ethic of care, an ethic of justice and what educationalist, Robert Starratt, terms an ethic of critique.[11] Ethics or moral education (in the style of transformative or socially-critical ethics) aims to build schools as models of "the just community" in which principles (or virtues) of sharing, caring, fairness, responsibility, truthfulness, cooperation, and democratic respect for the rights of others are cultivated in the whole school ethos. Such a community prefigures a better society and provides an environment in which ethics can be learnt and moral development practised. This vision is not to be dismissed as utopian; it may be essential and practical if schooling is to be redeemed as a justifiable social institution.

Any school which is serious about an ethics education program should consider implementing the following package:

1. An ethics audit to scrutinise current practices, documents and policies.
2. The development of statements of core, agreed values, a values charter, as a basis for ethics education.
3. Reviewing and updating the professional ethics of the staff, particularly asking, "What are the ethical responsibilities of teachers and where do they begin and end?"
4. Professional development in the teaching of ethics and teaching ethically.
5. Teaching ethics in all subjects across the whole curriculum; this is strengthened when it is linked with a futures perspective and environmental education.
6. Developing a discrete place for ethics in the curriculum; including in the secondary curriculum, teaching responsible ethical decision-making.
7. Community service programs.
8. Integrating ethics education and social justice strategies.
9. Involvement of parents and the home in the ethics curriculum.

While such a program begs numerous questions about detailed implementation,[12] it is critical for society because schools act as a bridge between the micro-moral world of the home and the macro-impersonal ethical systems of society. One important educational function for schools in this domain is to introduce students to the language or discourse of ethics. In this way they can be educated to recognise when they are encountering ethical issues, and to be aware of the principles or normative considerations at stake, and then to be able to relate this to decision-making in their own lives. This approach goes well beyond the clarification of values to a conversation about the justification of ethical decisions within a caring environment. Of course, this task is quite problematic and challenging but, without addressing it, our communities are likely to flounder in ethical confusion and illiteracy, struggling to converse about how and why we ought to live the ethical life.

Institutionalising Workplace Ethics

For many of us, life centres to a significant extent on our workplace (however broadly we understand that term). In turn these institutions and places of occupation combine to weave the social fabric. Therefore the ethical health of society and its members is determined to a significant extent by the ethical practices in the organisations where we are employed. In Chapter Eight we briefly considered the nature of professional ethics and role morality. Here we extend that discussion by considering how, as part of cultivating an ethical life, we might develop an ethical culture in our vocational and institutional environments.

The "institutionalisation of ethics" requires a multi-faceted process which mainstreams concerns about ethical issues and develops mechanisms for monitoring and encouraging discourse around ethical concerns in such a way that this process is integrated into management and organisation, and accepted by all stakeholders to such an extent that it has a continuing impact on the practices and policies of those organisations. Strategies for ethics education and training are critical elements of these processes.

Internationally, the field of health care and bioethics has been the subject of an institutional approach to ethics for many years: hospital ethics committees, national medical and research supervisory bodies, ethics training, ethics officers, and charters or codes of ethics are now widely established in the policy and practice of health care delivery. Some other institutions and professions are beginning to formalise an institutional approach to ethics. The package of ethics education measures for schools outlined above can be interpreted as an example of this trend. In the field of public administration (and even in legislatures) there are clear indications that jurisdictions are following up the era of administrative law reform and wider accountability measures with an institutionalised approach to ethics.

The private sector, as well as the public sector, has felt the impact of moves for quality assurance which have an ethics dimension.

The process we call "institutionalising ethics" rests on two basic assumptions. In the first place the most important ethical problems in organisations are related to institutional performance rather than individual conduct. It follows from this that to meet the organisational ethical challenge a combination of legal reform, ethical standard setting and institutional design are required. At the end of the day, the task is to address "the culture" of the organisation.

Critical in the cultivation of an ethical ethos in any agency is the nature of relationships and the distribution of power throughout the organisation. Many organisations tend to be dominated by rules and standard procedures, instilling fear about promotion, reinforcing "group think", limiting freedom of choice and promoting the idea of loyalty to the organisation to the point where it fosters attitudes which are blind to malpractices. On the other hand, the style of organisation which allows freedom, creativity and "bottom-up" decision-making is more likely to foster ethical behaviours which rest on autonomy and empowerment rather than compliance or control. So, a democratic work-culture is more likely to be an ethical one, even though some form of discipline or sanction needs to be built into the ethical contract governing members of an organisation.

The following framework[13] has been suggested as a process for developing an institution specific ethics regime:

1. *The preparatory phase* – involving an ethics audit, awareness raising sessions, forming an ethics steering group, and consulting with staff to develop a profile of relevant case studies.
2. Appoint a representative *ethics committee,* including an external adviser with ethics expertise, to monitor and guide the process.
3. Develop a draft, general aspirational *code of ethics,* based on the values which justify the organisation's existence.
4. Form *ethical circles* across the organisation to consider the implications of the code, ensuring that the process is not a tool of management.
5. Draft a *more detailed code of conduct* which addresses more specific agency issues.

6. Clarify *disciplinary elements* and develop clear *whistleblower protection* measures.
7. Seek *feedback* on the codes to ensure *ownership* by members of the organisation.
8. Implement *ethics education and training* to assist all members of the organisation to understand the codes and to handle ethical issues, as well as providing special ethics induction for new members.
9. Appoint *ethics advisers* for individuals needing assistance. The organisation may create the position of ethics officer in much the same way as there are equity officers.
10. *Review* the process and code regularly to ensure relevance and ownership by members; establish *communication* mechanisms, including advice to members about best and worst ethical practice.

A key aspect of this process is simply to inquire: "what is our organisation for? what is its mission and purpose?" By identifying "the justification of the relevant institution or professional activity, a justification that is based upon the values the institutions are supposed to serve",[14] a basis for institutionalising ethics is established. In approaching this task of justification from a critical perspective it is desirable to subject the organisation's own values to ethical standards wider than those of the organisation itself, standards such as the substantial values of respect for life, justice and covenantal integrity or even, say, the Universal Declaration of Human Rights.

The development of codes is often seen as the centre-piece of such regimes. It is important to clarify the nature and purpose of a code: is it to be a code of ethics which is likely to be aspirational or a code of conduct to define practical guidance on detailed matters? It is also necessary to appreciate the limitations of codes. Broadly, the concerns are:

- Sometimes codes are adopted for the wrong reasons. The code is seen as a status symbol, a public relations exercise designed to protect the profession or organisation and its monopoly of a certain practice or commerce.
- A serious case of misplaced expectations for codes emerges when it is assumed that they should, and can,

cover every contingency of misconduct, or that once declared they become immutable, almost holy writ.

- More fundamentally, it is sometimes asserted that codes have severe limitations as instruments of ethics, and that in their regulatory capacity, they undermine the possibility of a mature, open-ended, autonomous and reflective ethical response, diminishing personal responsibility.

These criticisms can be met by a careful approach to code development and use. They do not negate the value of codes altogether. Codes are useful declarations of common ethical standards and a valuable basis for teaching about those standards. These criticisms do, however, remind us that codes should be treated as a means to an end, one strategy in a comprehensive ethics program.

None of these measures designed to cultivate the ethical life of individuals and organisations can guarantee ethical performance. For a start, teaching ethics to those determined to be corrupt or unethical is unlikely to make a difference, just as teaching ethics to individuals when organisational cultures are unchallenged is likely to be fruitless. Not all ethics teaching will be effective; it will remain difficult to determine effectiveness in this field. Nonetheless, it is unthinkable that we should continue to pursue a general and professional education which equips us technically and intellectually, while ignoring the need to cultivate the ethical life and, with it, the capacity to make responsible ethical decisions, because this capacity is absolutely essential in contemporary workplaces and social relationships.

In this chapter our discussion has been directed toward the transmission of transformative ethical perspectives in an institutional setting. Though we will not address it now, there is a wider agenda to pursue and broader questions to ask, which are integral to an applied ethic. For instance, what are the social, cultural and economic conditions necessary for the individual and institutional cultivation of an ethical life? Or, does a "whole of society" approach to ethics require something beyond the formation of moral communities? In other words, cultivating ethics, a key objective of ethics education is a multifaceted task, and an ongoing one, to be redeveloped in every generation.

EPILOGUE: A Letter to My Grandchildren[15]

I write to you as you are at the threshold of adulthood. As you know, this letter is an epilogue to a book about ethics, so there is a wider audience listening. I hope you get to read the whole book, even if you find parts of it quaint. The ethical issues of your time may be somewhat different. For a start, I suspect that the advances of biotechnology and genetic manipulation are creating ethical opportunities and problems of enormous significance to you and future generations. Still, I expect that the matters which underpin our ethical life – the need to care for each other, the inevitability of moral choice, and life's interconnectedness – remain the same. If you will, listen to your grandfather, and be ready to challenge him. What I want to share with you is one version of the story about living a good life!

It makes sense that we start by examining ourselves: *what* is your life *for*? *who* do you want to *be*? Of course, our answers relate to the work we do and the family responsibilities we have, but it is a deeper question than that. It invites you to look into the core of yourself (some call it "conscience") and identify what are your most important concerns, the options that are most fundamental to you, the matters you would attend to if you were given a few last wishes before you died.

I wonder whether you have heard the story of the eagle that grew up with chooks.

> An eagle egg was placed in a chicken coop to see if it would hatch. It did and the young eagle learnt to behave like a chicken living with the poultry fowls. One day he was spotted by a fellow eagle who flew down to speak to him, "What are you doing with your beak in the mud? You were made for greater things: to soar about the heavens, to hunt for prey and to contemplate the earth from a mighty height". Finally, the young eaglet was persuaded to imitate the other eagle and test the capacity of his wings. He became an eagle instead of acting like a chicken. He soared to the heavens.

The moral of this tale is clear: we should not be content merely imitating those around us. Being human means being ethical. To live a good life we need to set ideals that are consistent with our potential as human beings, and to live by a vision that things can be better.

I take it that the good life for human beings includes trying to make the world a better place, enhancing the well-being of others, human and non-human. The central virtue for such a life is *compassion* (literally, feeling with others). I have another short story to tell:

> There was a little boy whose mother sent him on an errand and it took him a long time to come home. When he finally got back, his mother said: "Hey, where were you? I was worried about you." The boy said, "Oh, there was a child down the street who was crying because his tricycle was broken and I felt so bad I stopped to help him." Then the mother says, "You don't know anything about fixing tricycles", and the boy replies, "No, of course not. I stopped and I helped him cry".[16]

That's compassion. It is the well-spring of love and those substantial values which I have emphasised in this book: respect for life, justice and fairness, and integrity in our covenants. Compassion produces sharing, the quality which is necessary to maintain a feeling of belonging in a community. In fact, it is compassion which sustains obedience to that time-honoured ethical injunction, which some people call the Golden Rule ("Do to others as you would have them do to you").

Compassion's companion is empathy. Empathy for others in their suffering or oppression often makes us angry, righteously angry. This passion can fuel commitment to great ethical causes, producing moral courage for the struggle to remove injustice or support the vulnerable. Let me be clear. There is more than one way to work for justice, and we each have to make a personal response appropriate to our situation. Nonetheless, let me encourage you to become familiar with the great ethical causes of history in which our predecessors overcame tyranny and established our basic human rights. For instance, there was a time not so long ago when men could vote but women could not. When some men and women publicly opposed that injustice they were ridiculed; some were even put in jail. But they persisted till eventually that undemocratic discrimination was removed.

You might choose, in some shape or form, to get involved in politics because it is through political action that we may restructure the world to improve it. At the same time, I need to point out two dangers: (i) be wary of self-righteous zeal which sometimes blindly drives people who take up good political causes; compassion requires us always to temper our judgmentalism with mercy, and (ii) do not become so obsessed with the "big picture" that you lose sight of the "little things" close at hand, perhaps your own children's needs. As someone said, "Injustice anywhere [right in your own backyard perhaps] is a threat to justice everywhere".

Now, it is not always good enough to act with good (or ethical) intentions. We need to act accurately, effectively, and fittingly. This requires carefully researched insight. When I wrote about the ethic of response in this book, I had that in mind: a comprehensive discernment of all the relevant factors leading to a fitting decision. For questions of social justice, this implies that an ethical protest without a competent social analysis may miss the point. If you commit yourself to working for social justice, you will need the resources of groups who do thorough social research.

Does this all sound too overwhelming? Perhaps it is. Might not these exhortations amount to a recipe for guilt and depression for instance? Being guilt-ridden or chronically depressed would hardly be characteristic of the good life, although we should not dismiss the good that can come from guilt or depression. They may be the prompts from our inner life to take up new priorities for the good of others and ourselves. At another level, ethical decision-making can be overwhelming. For instance, some of the choices we may be forced to make about life and death seem to take us into a realm of mystery where the categories of right and wrong have little meaning. At times you might ask: is it enough to be ethical, or is the ethical life too difficult and how is it sustained amidst the ambiguities of human existence?

I have had to face those questions personally, and while I do not have answers which are beyond rational dispute, let me offer some advice. First of all, be ready to forgive yourself for your mistakes. Then, do not expect good results from every moral decision. Do not expect that all the good causes to which you are committed will come to fruition in your life-time. History is a long-time, and life is a complex web of interconnectedness. Cultivate a carefree attitude to caring. The prayer used by Alcoholics Anonymous is a statement of practical wisdom for the ethical life: "God grant me the serenity to accept the things I cannot change, the courage to change the things I can, and the wisdom to know the difference".[17]

In the end, the ethical life requires a certain optimism and staying power which is nurtured more by faith than cold reason. I believe there are various sources of faith, but one is the recurring capacity of the human spirit to hope and work for a better world. That spirit has given expression to many reform movements and faith traditions (theistic and non-theistic). From them we may glean resources to sustain the moral life.

I acknowledge that I came to understand the good life through the Christian story - though the beliefs of my youth have changed in my adult years. Christianity taught me something about grace, hope, trust and redemption and above all, that love and goodness have eternal significance. I surmise that these insights are necessary to maintain the ethical life. Be encouraged to explore the Gospel accounts of Jesus of Nazareth. More than a moral teacher, he prophetically engaged unethical practices of his time and has inspired many to work for a better world. Other spiritual leaders, from various religious traditions, share this in common with him.

If I have a motto for the ethical life, it is borrowed from the ancient Hebrew prophet, Micah. Interpret it in your own way: "Act justly, Love tenderly, and Walk humbly with your God".[18]

I must conclude because I should not over-indulge my grandfatherly prerogatives. I once saw an advertising billboard which exhorted: "Live life to the limit". What an irony that this sign was promoting a casino, for this slogan fits the human quest to transcend and improve our present circumstances - a basic motivation of the ethical life. Perhaps the casino's advertising agents understand the inner desires of human beings, even if their product does not satisfy those desires. By all means, live life to the limit; go beyond the limits of self-centredness or narrow interests; exercise your freedom with responsibility. Life is a gift to enjoy with, and for, others. And remember the good life is a balanced life: give expression to urges of creativity, invigorate your body as well as nourish your mind, and above all else, care for the Earth for its own sake and also for the sake of your generation's grand-children!

Yours ever,
Grandfather.

AN EXERCISE

As a discussion or reflection point, *write your own letter to future generations* to recall and summarise the moral wisdom you have gathered and wish to share. Though no texts for further reading are listed in this chapter, the reader could scan references in the notes to this chapter to find helpful follow-up reading.

CHAPTER TEN NOTES

1 Newton, D is quoted by Hart, D and Cooper TL (eds) (1994) *Handbook of Administrative Ethics*, New York: Mareel Decker Inc, p 113.

2 Matthew 6 v 21, *The Bible.*

3 Benjamin, M (1990) *Splitting the Difference: Compromise and Integrity in Ethics and Politics*, University of Kansas, p 46.

4 Carter, S (1996) *Integrity*, Basic books, p 25.

5 McFall, L (1987) "Integrity" in *Ethics 98*, October 1987, p 5.

6 For example in Jung, CG (1990) *Memories, Dreams, Reflections*, London: Fontana Paperbacks. For a challenging Jungian comment on the ambiguity of the ethical life see *Memories, Dreams, Reflections*, pp 361-2.

7 I prefer the term ethics education to moral education (though they are virtually synonyms). Ethics education is a more generic term than moral or values education and does not so easily evoke associations with moralising or values clarification. There is a wide literature on this topic, but the following are a few of the texts which I have found especially helpful:

Hill, BV (1991) *Values Education in Australian Schools*, Hawthorn, Vic: ACER.

Noddings, N (1992) *The Challenge to Care in Schools: an alternative approach to education*, New York: Teachers College Press.

Purpel, DE (1989) *The Moral and Spiritual Crisis in Education: A Curriculum for Justice and Compassion in Education*, Boston: Bergin and Garvey Publishers.

Resources for the Study of Ethics (Primary), Health and Personal Development Unit, Department of Education, Queensland.

8 This discussion of autonomy as indicative of the highest stages of moral development reflects the work of Lawrence Kohlberg. For a pithy, accurate version of his theories and their revision by Carol Gilligan, see Martin, MW (1989) *Everyday Morality*, Belmont, CA: Wadsworth Publishing Co, pp 24-32.

9 As was shown in the experiments of Stanley Milgram. For a brief account of this see Straughan, R (1982) *Can We Teach Children to be Good?*, London: Geo Allen and Unwin, pp 6-7.

10 Bolt, R (1970) *A Man for All Seasons*, London: Heinemann, p 3.

11 Starratt, RJ (1994) *Building an Ethical School: a Practical Response to the Moral Crisis in Schools*, New York: Falmer Press.

12 I have written of this detail in other places: "Ethics Education: a Comprehensive Approach", *New Horizons*, December, 1994. See also, Preston, N and Symes, C (1992) *Schools and Classrooms: a Cultural Studies Analysis of Education*, Melbourne: Longman Cheshire.

13 One place in which this approach is discussed is: Sampford, C (1994) "Institutionalising Public Sector Ethics", in Preston, N (ed) *Ethics for the Public Sector: Education and Training*, Sydney: The Federation Press.

14 Ibid, p 21.

15 One of the inspirations for this task is a small book about ethics by a Spanish philosopher written to his fifteen-year-old son. I commend it to all readers. Savater, Fernando (1995) *Amador: A Father talks to his son about happiness, freedom and love* , Melbourne: Text Publishing.

16 This story comes from Rabbi Harold Kushner and is recorded in Trenoweth, S (1995) *The Future of God*, Sydney: Millennium Books.

17 This prayer is attributed to Reinhold Niebuhr but has been widely adopted by the Alcoholics Anonymous Movement.

18 Micah 6 v 8, *The Bible*.

Glossary

Communitarianism: an umbrella term referring to any approach to ethics which determines the "good", the "right" or the "virtuous" in relation to particular traditions or social contexts. Communitarians stand in opposition to the view that ethical obligations are universal and therefore argue that principles such as justice must be understood and interpreted in relation to certain traditions or social spheres.

Consequentialism: ethical decisions are based primarily on calculating the possible outcomes or consequences of an action. These theories are based on realising a particular end or goal *(telos),* and are therefore one form of *teleological* ethics. Examples include: *utilitarianism* where the goal is to maximise utility or happiness; in *situation ethics* the end, according to Fletcher, is to maximise loving consequences; the *ethical egoist* seeks to maximise self-interest.

Egoism: that theory which is concerned with self-interest. Psychological egoism is a theory which describes how people are thought to behave. In contrast, ethical egoism is a prescriptive theory about how people ought to act. There are two broad types: An *individual ethical egoist* believes that "everyone ought to act in my self interest"; a *universal ethical egoist* maintains "everyone ought to act in his or her own self-interest".

Epistemology: the philosophical inquiry into knowledge or any theory of knowledge. For the study of ethics it is important to examine epistemological questions such as: what constitutes moral knowledge?; how do we determine moral objectivity, if at all?; how do people learn what they know (or value)?

Essentialism: a term which asserts that morality properly involves some *essential* or basic moral principles and values or that there are certain basic elements of human culture which ought to be preserved and endorsed across time and space. Proponents stress the importance of promoting a structured and orderly view of reality and human society.

Ethic of Care: a theory proposed in particular by feminist writers which focuses on care, compassion and relationships. In contrast to traditional ethical approaches which emphasise rights, autonomy and abstract reasoning, proponents seek to maintain human-connectedness, stress the importance of context and situational demands and responses that emphasise the moral sentiments of nurture and care.

Ethic of Response: grounded in an integrated framework of consequentialist and non-consequentialist theories, as well as acknowledging the importance of a virtuous character or disposition, this approach to ethical decision-making emphasises that action which is the most "fitting" or most responsible. What is fitting should be guided by four elements: (1) a responsiveness to all factors and parties concerned; (2) an appropriate interpretation of the situation; (3) a framework of social solidarity, and (4) accountability for the action decided. In addition, three procedural values are specified in this book to help guide decisions on normative issues: the respect for life principle; the justice principle; and, the covenantal integrity principle.

Ethics: ethics is fundamentally interested in character (from the Greek *ethos*, meaning "character"). It may sometimes refer to: (a) the actual values and rules of conduct by which we live, or (b) the study of our values and their justification (sometimes called moral philosophy). In this book the adjectives "ethical" and "moral" are used interchangeably.

Existentialism: according to Jean-Paul Sartre who coined the term, "existence precedes essence". This theory claims that we are not born pre-determined but we make ourselves into what we are. A person bears the sole responsibility for all his or her actions. Choices are directed by one's radical freedom of the will rather than by society, nature or God.

Justice: what is right, fair or just in any social arrangement. What is just or "due" to a person may be adjudicated in different ways. *Distributive justice* is concerned with who ought to get what goods; it may take a person's due to be based on merit or desert, need or ability. It is akin to *social justice.* In contrast, *retributive justice* takes a person's "due" to mean what he or she deserves with particular reference to retribution for wrongdoing – also known as an "*eye for an eye, tooth for a tooth*" philosophy.

Meta-ethics: "meta" is the Latin term meaning "beyond" or "prior to". Hence, metaethics (including analytic ethics) involves considerations beyond or prior to the making of any moral judgments or the prescribing of a preferred ethical system (as in normative ethics).

Metaphysics: the philosophical inquiry into reality as a whole, beyond the world of immediate experience. It includes questions about the nature and the existence of the physical world, human nature and God (or the gods).

Natural Law Theory: a theory which equates a moral life with the life of reason, as discerned from nature or God's eternal law. Natural law theorists argue that whether one believes in God or not, moral agents share the same rational human nature and therefore the same human concept of morality (or what is right or good). "Law" in the term natural law is used to mean laws that apply to everything in nature as opposed to humanly constructed or government law.

Nihilism: literally, "belief in nothing". In the prescriptive sense, the nihilist might claim that there *ought* not be any cultural values and that nothing ought be seen as a "good". Some philosophers such as Nietzsche and the existentialists have been accused of descriptive nihilism because of their emphasis on the belief that people *make* the world everything that it is – denying any appeal to non-human or "other-worldly" factors such as God.

Non-consequentialism: an approach to ethics where decisions are based on some clear intrinsic view of the right or one's duty rather than according to consequences. Traditionally known as *deontological* – from the Greek *deon* meaning "duty". Examples include: *Kantian* ethics where one's duty is absolute, gleaned through powers of rationality and autonomy; *WD Ross' theory* of *prima facie* duties where obligations are viewed as hierarchical and able to be overridden by higher duties; and *divine command theory* which claims one's duty is informed by adherence to principles of divine teaching.

Normative Ethics: provides frameworks or theories to help in the making of moral judgments. It is prescriptive in the sense that it involves deciding what we ought to do, how we ought to live and why.

Person/Personhood: its origins are from the Latin term for a mask worn by an actor (playing a role). The word person has come to mean one who plays a role in life or one who is an agent. While human being denotes biology, the term person emphasises the public, social and hence *moral* aspects to being. Many modern philosophers emphasise characteristics of self-consciousness or rationality. Thus entering personhood is contingent upon being autonomous and rational, carrying with it the responsibilities of full moral agency and moral accountability.

Philosophy: literally means "love of wisdom". The broad, overall purpose of what philosophers do is engage in a critical, rational appraisal of significant social beliefs. *Moral philosophers* study *moral* beliefs and values and their justification (ie ethics).

Rationalism: takes reason as the ultimate authority in all matters of knowledge, belief or behaviour.

Rawlsian Social Contract Theory: For Rawls, the ideal social contract would be a situation governed by justice as fairness where justice is built on: (i) *the freedom principle* – an equal right to basic liberties and; (ii) *the equality and social difference principle* – where any inequalities could only be justified if they are to the greatest benefit of the least advantaged. The assumption is that rational persons would choose such principles impartially if they did not know their position in society (the original position).

Relativism: a theory which claims that what is right or good is always relative to the particular circumstances and beliefs of a person or group of persons. There are no objective or absolute standards to appeal to when trying to decide what is right.

Universalism: refers to an ethical approach which claims a particular principle always applies across cultures and generations (such as *Kantianism)* or that a particular method is always the best means to producing the most ethical outcome (some forms of *utilitarianism).* The assumption is that ethics goes beyond local interests or cultural constraints to a standpoint that is eternal or universally valid.

Utilitarianism: a normative ethical theory originally established by Jeremy Bentham and John Stuart Mill that seeks to bring about good consequences to all concerned – that is the "greatest good for the greatest number" principle, calculating the interests of all concerned in terms of pleasure, happiness or utility.

Virtue Theory: (Greek *arete,* virtue) another form of teleological theory. Originally presented by Aristotle, this ethic centres on character or the moral qualities of a person. The aim is to foster living well so that good and right behaviour becomes a habit. Moral virtues (or excellences) tend to be practice or tradition specific.

A note on the history of ethics and moral traditions

It is futile to try to convey the development of ethical thought in the Western tradition in one page. Nonetheless, something might be said to convey a sense of timelines and perspective. Two broad approaches have influenced common ethical thought into the twentieth century. On the one hand, via Jewish and Christian religious influences, moral views subject to inspiration or revelation, were preserved in ecclesiastic teachings and The Bible. *St Augustine* (354-430) and *St Thomas Aquinas* (c. 1225-1274) were the most significant Christian thinkers on ethics in pre-modern times.

On the other hand, the most influential approach in terms of philosophical ethics, may be termed rationalistic, relying on human reason. It finds its origins in ancient Greece especially through the writings of *Plato* (427-346 BCE) and *Aristotle* (384-322 BCE) though Plato and Aristotle developed significantly different philosophical systems and ethical teaching. In the English tradition, the works of *Thomas Hobbes* (1588-1679) and *John Locke* (1632-1704) are significant to social ethics because they argued that society and ethics rest upon an implicit social contract. The German, *Immanuel Kant* (1721-1804) was a giant of moral philosophy who argued for a universal law of morality based on practical reason. In the nineteenth century with the rise of modern European societies and the emergence of democratic sentiments, the views of *John Stuart Mill* on liberalism and utilitarianism marked a major development in ethical systems. We encountered other figures in the pages of this book, especially twentieth century ethical thinkers, but one who requires mention in this briefest of surveys is *Jean-Paul Sartre*, the French spokesperson for existentialism which radically challenged previous moral traditions.

Serious students of ethics need to consult other texts to familiarise themselves with not only the history of ethics but the original works of some of these well-renowned moral philosophers as well. The following would make a good start:

Alasdair MacIntyre, (1998) *A Short History of Ethics*, (second edition) London: Routledge and Kegan Paul, and his other works, *After Virtue* (London:Duckworth, 1981) and *Whose Justice? Which*

Rationality? (London: Duckworth,1988), Peter Vardy and Paul Grosch, (1994) *The Puzzle of Ethics* London: Harper Collins, and Peter Singer (ed) (1991) *A Companion to Ethics,* Oxford: Blackwell, have good readable sections outlining the history of ethics.

We have said nothing of ethics in the *eastern world* (Indian, Buddhist, Chinese) or Islamic ethics, but these are major moral traditions impacting on the ethical practice of many millions of people. Again it would be oversimplifying and insulting to attempt a brief outline of these traditions. However, their contribution to a global ethic should not be underestimated for they emerge in cultures of rich human experience. Furthermore, as East and West extend their cultural exchange, and as societies such as Australia develop pluralistically and multi-culturally, it is essential that students of ethics dialogue across the divides of traditions. There is a growing body of semi-popular literature by Western authors trying to interpret Eastern religions and ethical teachings which may interest some readers. For example, one volume which explores Zen Buddhist ethics is *The Mind of Clover* by Robert Aitken (San Francisco, North Point Press, 1984).

An exhaustive bibliographical collection of ethics from the Eastern traditions is to be found in Carman, J and Juergensmeyer, M (eds) (1993), *A Bibliographic Guide to the Comparative Study of Ethics,* Melbourne: Cambridge University Press. Articles in Part II of Singer, P (ed) (1991), *A Companion to Ethics,* Oxford: Blackwell and in Becker, LC and Becker, CB (eds) (1992), *Encyclopaedia of Ethics,* Vols I and II, London: St James Press; survey relevant topics. Comprehensive reading lists accompany these articles.

Index

Aboriginal Australians, 10, 54, 96
    and Mabo case, 96, 103
Abortion, 24, 43, 50, 126, 127, 133, 138-140, 147
Absolutism,
    and relativism, 34-37
    and universalism, 36
Accident (case of, the), 84-86
Accountability, 73
Aesthetics, 21
Alcoholics Anonymous, 222
Almond, B and Hill, D, 39
Altruism, 28-30
Amazon rainforest, (case of), 204
Amnesty International, 149
Anglican church, 143
Animal rights, 194-196
    and interests, 190
Ante-natal screening, 131
Anthropocentricism, 71, 189, 191, 201
Apartheid, 9, 23
Applied ethics, 19-21, 92
Aquinas, St Thomas, 60, 120, 157, 230
Aristotle, 58-62, 164, 212, 230
Augustine, St, 148, 230
Autonomy, 32, 34, 36, 163, 213
Baron, M, 64
Baumann, Z, 16
Baume, P, 158, 159
Beauchamp, TL and Childress, JF, 153, 157
Becker, E, 5, 15
Becker, LC and Becker, CB, 87, 231
Belliotti, R, 123
Benjamin, M, 211, 224
Bentham, J, 43-44
Berg, J, 39
Bible, The, 1, 5, 22, 94, 223, 230
Biocentricism, 71, 189, 192-194
Biodiversity, 5, 188, 193
Bioethics, 130-143
    defined, 157
Biotechnology, 149-151
Birch, C, 40
Bok, S, 99, 100, 101
Bonhoeffer and Hill, (case of), 153
Bonhoeffer, D, 97, 103
Brain death, 133-134, 158
Brooks, R (case of), 126, 131
Buber, M, 87
Business ethics, 174-178
    micro and macro concerns of, 175
Callicott, JB, 206
Capital punishment, 145-147
Capra, F, 206
Care - (see also Ethic of Care)
Carmen, J and Juergensmeyer, M, 231
Casuistry, 19, 77
Categorical Imperative (see Kant)
Censorship, 121-122, 122
Character education, 214
Charlesworth, M, 77, 144-145, 159, 179
Chinese earthquake, (case of), 66
Chomsky, N, 104
Civil disobedience, 167
Clinton, Bill, 89, 212
Cloning, 150-151
Coody, CAC, 157
    Codes of Conduct and Code of Ethics, 218-219
Cohen, S and Grace, D, 179
Collins, P, 206,207
Common good, 5, 75, 162-164, 178
Communitarianism,
    defined, 226
    and universalism, 62-3, 68
Compassion, 221
Conflict of interest, 150, 169-170
Conscience, 213, 220

Conscientious objection, 147, 213
Consequentialism, 42-47, 85 166, 193
  defined, 226
Contraception, 107, 197
Contractarianism, 51-55
Cooper, TL, 86, 88, 183
Corruption, 166
Covenantal integrity principle, 75, 109, 114
  (see also Ethic of response, substantive values)
Crime and punishment, 70, 146
Critical morality, 23
Declaration of Independence, 53
Deontology, 43, 47-51, 62-63, 97, 141, 147, 228
Des Jardins, JR, 201
Descartes, 189
Determinism and freedom, 31-34
Difference principle, (Rawls), 54, 228
Dirty hands dilemma, 166-167, 183
Disinterestedness, 20, 44
Divine Command Theory, 48, 288
Doctrine of double effect, 140
Doestoevsky, F, 103
Domestic Violence, 113
Dower, N, 201
Dualism, 189
Dworkin, R, 67
Earth Charter, 186, 199-200
Eastern world ethics, 231
Eckhart, M, 129
Ecocentricism (see Biocentricism)
Ecojustice, 193, 200
Egoism,
  defined, 226
  ethical, 28, 47
  psychological, 28
  and altruism, 28-30
  universal ethical, 28, 47
Elliott, R, 201
Empathy, 221
Environment, 10, 187-188, 193, 198-200
Environmental ethics, 188-194
Epistemology, 2-22, 26
  defined, 226
Equality,
  and inequality, 54
  and social difference principle, 54, 288
Essentialism, 48
  defined, 226
Ethic of care, 55-58, 100, 205
  defined, 226
Ethic of response, 13, 46, 71-76, 85, 141, 147, 167-168, 194
  defined, 227
  as fitting response, 72, 116, 194
  procedural values, 75
Ethic of responsibility, Weber's, 167-168
Ethic of role, (see Role morality)
Ethical decision-making, 13, 69, 167-168
  justification of, 20, 38, 42
  model of, 76-80
Ethical life, 2-5, 209-222
Ethical theory, 41-63
  a preferred theory, 63-64
  (see also Normative ethical theory)
Ethics,
  audit, 215, 217
  committees, 217
  defined, 2, 15, 227
  distinction between ought and is, 18, 29
  in Eastern world, 231
  history of, 230-231
  (see also Applied Ethics)
Ethics and law, 23-25
Ethics and religion, 25-28
  and faith, 27, 222
Ethics education, 8, 212-216, 224
  program, 215
  and virtue theory, 62
Eudaimonia, 60
Euthanasia, 60, 137-143
  active and passive, 139
  voluntary and involuntary, 139

Existentialism, 33
    defined, 227
    and liberalism, 33
Extensionist approach, 192
Extraordinary and ordinary means of treatment, 1139-140
Feinberg, J, 153
Feminism, 11, 63
    and ethics, 55-58
Fitzgerald, J, 136-137, 158
Fletcher, J, 15, 46-47, 66, 97, 103, 126
Foucault, M, 16
Fox, M, 128, 180
Freedom, 70
    and determinism, 31-34
    principle of, 54, 222
French, P, 167, 183
Friedman, M, 176, 177, 179, 181, 185
Fromm, E, 110, 127
Fundamentalism, 8, 193
Gaia, 194, 201, 206
Gandhi, M, 3, 23
Genetic testing, 131
Genetics, 150
Genital mutilation, 34
Gilligan, C, 56, 224
Global ethics, 198-200
Globalisation, 198-199
Global poverty, (see Poverty)
Global responsibility, 186-201
Glover, J, 15, 44, 86, 153
Golden Rule, the, 49, 74, 221
Goodin, RE, 182
Gore, A, 188, 206
Habermas, J, 16
Hard case, (case of), 81
Harm, 128
Hayden, W, 183
Heinz's dilemma, 65
Held, V, 58, 68
Heller, A and Feher, F, 168, 184
Hepburn, E, 135, 143, 153, 157, 159
Hindmarsh, R, 160
Hiroshima, bomb on, 81-83
History of ethics, 11, 230-231
Hobbes, T, 52, 230
Homosexuality, 48, 117-119
Human rights, 51
Incest, 106, 113, 127
Interconnectedness, 6, 10, 25, 36, 191, 210
    and responsibility, 72, 74
Injustice, 9, 10, 26
Integrity, 90, 209-212
Interpretation, 73-74
Isak, R, 201
Jagger, AM, 57, 68
Jennings, B, and Callahan, D, 184
Jesus Christ, 3, 223
Jonsen, AR and Toulmin, S, 40
Jordan, T, 103
Judaeo-Christian tradition, 11, 26, 189
Jung, C, 212, 224
Just society, 25, 47, 200
Just war theory, 148-149
Justice, 13, 47, 51-57, 75
    defined, 227
    as fairness, 145, 162
    as social justice, 54, 162, 215
    (see also Contractarianism)
Justice and fairness principle, 75, 90, 147
Justification, (see Ethics decision-making, justification of)
Kant, I, 17, 27, 49-52, 57, 103, 108, 159, 230
    categorical imperative, 49, 63, 74
    on lying, 97
    moral philosophy of, 49
Kantianism, 52, 53, 63, 85, 120, 167, 229
Kerneghan, K and Langford, J, 183
King, ML, 3, 23, 24, 210
Kleinig, J, 87, 153
Kohlberg, L, 56, 65, 224
Kushner, Rabbi H, 225
Land ethic, 193, 201, 206
Law and bio-ethics, 143-145
Law and ethics, 23-25
Leopold, A, 193, 206

Liberal democracy, 24, 119, 122, 143, 144
Liberalism, 33, 44, 52, 54, 230
Linares, S, (case of), 132
Locke, J, 57, 68, 230
Logic, 21
Love, 46, 57
agape, 46
and commitment, 109, 110, 114, 115
eros, 108, 109
and justice, 114, 119, 120
philia, 21, 109
and sex, 106-115
(see also Sex, love and morality)
Lovelock, J, 191
Loyalty, 162-163
Lying, 59, 90
the case against, 96
and cheating, 91, 92, 98, 102
definition of, 92
and slippery-slope effect, 98
Machiavelli, 166, 178, 183
MacIntyre, A, 60-61, 62, 68
Mackay, H, 164
Madsen, P and Shafritz, JM, 183
Mancuso, M, 184
Mandela, N, 3, 23, 24, 210
Manners, 20
Mappes, T and Zembaty, J, 128, 157, 158, 207
Mappes, T, 115, 128
Marriage, 45, 91, 98, 106, 107, 109, 113, 116, 118, 119, 120, 124
Martin, MW, 103, 128
Marx, K, 9, 16
May, W, 184, 185
McCormick, R, 135, 158
Meta-ethics, 19, 39
defined, 227
Meta-physics, 2, 22, 27, 39
defined, 227
Milgram, S, 224
Mill, JS, 33, 44, 119, 128, 230
Moral authoritarianism, 8, 33, 36, 213
Moral character, 9, 59-60, 62, 213
(see also Virtue ethics)
Moral community, 5, 15, 36, 134, 195
Moral decision-making, (see Ethical decision-making)
Moral development, 56, 212, 213, 215
and gender, 56
Pavlov, I, 32
Skinner, BF, 32
theories, 30
(see also Gilligan, C and Kohlberg, L)
Moral duty, 23
Moral education, (see Ethics education)
Moral law, 23, 34, 36
Moral philosophy, 19
Moral responsibility (see Responsibility)
Moral traditions, 13, 230-231
(see also Western moral tradition)
Morality, defined, 18
More, T, 214
Muelder, W, 67
Narrative ethics, 68
National Medical Health and Research Council, 8, 143
Natural law, 48, 63, 67, 107
defined, 227
Niebuhr, HR, 72-76, 83, 86, 87, 181
Niebuhr, R, 87, 183, 225
Nielsen, K, 16
Nihilism, 31
defined, 228
Noddings, N, 58, 68, 224
Non-consequentialism, 42, 47-51
act, 67
defined, 228
rule, 67
Ten Commandments, 48
Normative ethical theories, 38, 41-68, 71, 87
Normative ethics, 19, 21
defined, 228

Northern Territory, Rights of the Terminally Ill Act 1995, 159
Nozick, R, 68
Nuremberg trials, 95, 171
Nuttall, J, 39
Nyberg, D, 101
O'Neill, O, 67
Organ transplants, politics and justice (case of), 182
Overpopulation, 196-198
Pacifism, 148
Paedophilia, 127
Peck, M Scott, 94, 103, 110, 111, 114, 127
Pence, G, 60, 68
Persons/personhood, 26, 50, 132-138
  concept of, 133
  defined, 228
  and human beings, 133, 187
Philosophy, 21-23, 68
  defined, 228
  and ethics, 21-23, 230
  political, 21, 44, 52
  social, 21, 47, 52
Phronesis, 60, 76, 212
Plato, 26, 63, 97, 230
Pleasure, 110, 111, 113-114
Political ethics, 13, 42, 90, 164-168
  compromise in, 99, 167
Pollock-Byrne, JM, 86
Ponting, C, 171, 184
Pope John Paul II, 9, 48, 158
Pornography, 121-122
Positive discrimination, 163
Positive Morality, 24
Post-modernism, 7, 11, 60, 63, 93
Post-structuralism, 7, 16
Poverty, 196-198
Preston, N, 179, 224
Prima facie duty, 51
Private and public responsibility, 162
Procedural values, (see Ethic of response)
Procreation, 107, 110, 111-112, 123
Professional ethics, 8, 10, 62, 70, 79, 171, 17178, 215,
  development of, 216-219
Profits and community responsibility, (case of), 181
Promises, 48, 73, 88, 90, 103
Proportionalism, 67
Prostitution, 120-121
  and integrity, (case of), 126
Public good, 162-164, 170, 173, 174, 177, 178
  definition of, 162-164
Public interest, 162-163, 168, 171, 178
Public sector ethics, 170-173
  Act 1994, 183
  decision-making model, 80
  Principles of Public Life, 172
Punishment, theories of, 145-147
Punzo, V, 116, 117, 128
Quality of life principle, 134-140
Quinlan, KA (case of), 130
Rachels, J, 66, 140
Rape, 113, 120, 127
Rationalism, 58
  defined, 228, 230
Rationality, 20, 49, 50, 54
  and disinterestedness, 20, 44, 53
Rawls, J, 53-55, 67
  original position, 53
  principles of justice, 54
Rawlsian theory, 162
  defined, 228
Regan, T, 196, 203, 206, 207
Relativism, 44, 46, 48, 61, 63, 74, 144
  and absolutism, 34-37
  cultural, 34, 93
  defined, 229
  ethical, 34
Religion, 25-28, 46, 209, 230
Reproductive technology, 111, 145, 157
Respect for Life, principle of, 13, 75, 132, 136, 146

Respect for persons, 24, 50, 114
Responsibility, 31, 76, 83, 130, 161-185
Responsiveness, 70-74

Reuther, RR, 193
Rights, 51-55, 196, 199, 201
 (see also Contractarianism)
Role morality, 32, 164, 166, 170-173, 176
Ross, WD, 51, 67, 228
Sampford, C, 225
Sanctity of life principle, 23, 43, 135
Sandel, M, 68
Sartre, JP, 34, 230
Schools and ethics, (see Ethics education)
Scruton, R, 124
Self-deception, 94-96
 and self-respect, 95
 and race discrimination and prejudice, 95
Self-interest, 28-30, 44, 47, 116, 200
 (see also Egoism)
Sentientism, 192, 196, 201
Sex,
 conservative view of, 106-108, 123
 love and morality, 105-128
 pleasure and, 113-114
 power, 112-113
 procreation and, 1111-112, 123
 purpose of, 1111-115, 123
 responsible, 116-118
 Roman Catholic view of, 106-107
Sexual ethics, 13, 46, 105-122
Sexual harassment and discrimination, 113, 119, 123
Sexual relationships, 42
 honesty and consent in, 115-116, 123
Sexuality, 90
 and identity, 105
 and public policy, 118-122
Shakespeare, W, 109, 127
Shann, F, 154
Sidgwick, H, 41, 63
Silver, CS, 190
Singer, P, 3, 8, 16, 39, 44, 64, 67, 68, 103, 123, 135, 136, 153, 155, 157, 158, 159, 185, 195, 196, 201, 203, 206, 207, 231
Situation-ethics, 46, 57, 63, 66, 72
Slote, M, 64
Social analysis, 9, 188, 222
Social ethic of responsibility, 6, 10, 119, 171, 174
Social justice, (see Justice)
Social solidarity, 73-74, 82, 83, 86, 162, 178, 181, 194
Social transformation, 8-11, 200
Social values, 132-138
Socialism, 52
Socially-critical ethics, 215
Socrates, 2
Solomon, RC, 64, 177, 185
Speciesism, 189
Starratt, R, 214, 224
Steinbeck, B, 190, 206
Sterilisation, 197
Straughan, R, 224
Study of ethics, (see Ethics, study of)
Suicide, 131, 137, 138, 139, 145, 146, 152
Suu Kyi, AS, 3, 23
Swimme, B and Berry, T, 205
Taylor, C, 206
Teichmann, J, 153
Teleology, 43, 47, 48, 59, 66
Temple, W, 46, 66
Ten Commandments, 22, 27, 35
Theology, 19, 26, 27, 49, 60, 189, 197
Thompson, J, 200, 207
Thomson, DF, 179
Trouble with Jack, (case of), 155
Truman, H, 81-83, 88
Truth,
 and response, 100-101
 situational (selective), 97-100

Truthfulness, 90
definition of, 92
and ethics of response, 100-101
and lying, 90
Truth-telling, 21, 59, 89-104
the golden rule on, 90
integrity, 90-91, 94, 98, 100
Uhr, J, 184
United Nations Universal Declaration of Human Rights, 35, 36, 51, 218
Utilitarianism, 43-47, 52, 59, 63, 66, 67, 70, 72, 100,, 120, 122, 135, 137, 140, 141, 142, 146, 151, 192, 230
defined, 229
Universal,
moral law, 17, 36, 50, 230
principle, 23, 36
viewpoint, 20, 37, 63
Universalism, 229
and absolutism, 35, 36, 39
and communitarianism, 62-63, 64, 68
defined, 229
Value of Life principle, 90, 190
Values, 2
charter of, 215, 216
defined, 18
substantial, (see Ethic of response)
Vannoy, R, 113, 128
Vardy, P and Grosch, P, 231
Violence, 137, 138, 146, 148, 149. 165
Virtue theory, 58-62, 70, 72, 74, 100, 215
defined, 229
limitations of, 61
Walzer, M, 67, 68, 163, 167, 183
War, 1147-149
Warnock, M, 141, 142
Weber, M, 167-168, 178, 184
Weekend Australian, the 4, 5
Wesley, J, 96, 103
Western moral tradition, 23, 63
history of, 230-231
and philosophy, 13, 55, 191
White, JE, 64, 124, 128, 159, 204
White, L, 206
Williams, B, 165, 166, 183, 190, 206
Work Ethic, 214
Workplace ethics, 214, 216-219
World Health Organisation, 197
Zoocentrist views, 193, 201